# Dimensions of Intervention for Student Development

Wiley Series in Counseling and Human Development
Leo Goldman, Editor

Community Counseling: A Human Services Approach
Judith A. Lewis and Michael D. Lewis

Research Methods for Counselors:
Practical Approaches in Field Settings
Leo Goldman, Editor

Dimensions of Intervention for Student Development
Weston H. Morrill and James C. Hurst, with E. R. Oetting, and others

# Dimensions of Intervention for Student Development

**WESTON H. MORRILL**
UNIVERSITY OF UTAH

**JAMES C. HURST**
UNIVERSITY OF TEXAS AT AUSTIN

**with E. R. OETTING**
COLORADO STATE UNIVERSITY

**AND OTHERS**

A WILEY-INTERSCIENCE PUBLICATION

JOHN WILEY & SONS

New York • Chichester • Brisbane • Toronto

**Library of Congress Cataloging in Publication Data**

Main entry under title:

Dimensions of intervention for student development.

(Wiley series in counseling and human development)
"A Wiley-Interscience publication."
Includes indexes.
1. College student development programs—Addresses, essays, lectures. 2. College environment—Addresses, essays, lectures. I. Morrill, Weston H. II. Hurst, James C. III. Oetting, Eugene Richard, 1929–

LB2343.4.D55 378'.198 80-16939
ISBN 0-471-05249-3

Printed in the United States of America
10 9 8 7 6 5 4 3 2 1

# Contributors

**James H. Banning,** Vice President for Student Affairs, Colorado State University, Fort Collins, Colorado

**Margaret J. Barr,** Associate Dean of Students, University of Texas at Austin, Austin, Texas

**Kathleen R. Boggs,** Associate Director, Counseling Center, University of Utah, Salt Lake City, Utah

**Jan M. Carlson,** Director of Student Activities, Oklahoma State University, Stillwater, Oklahoma

**Ernest L. Chavez,** Psychology Department, Colorado State University, Fort Collins, Colorado

**A. Garr Cranney,** Department of Education, Brigham Young University, Provo, Utah

**David Drum,** Director of Counseling, University of Texas at Austin, Austin, Texas

**James C. Hurst,** Dean of Students and Assistant Vice President for Student Affairs, Professor, Counseling Psychology, University of Texas at Austin, Austin, Texas

**Sharon H. Justice,** Assistant Dean of Students, University of Texas at Austin, Austin, Texas

**David McClintock,** Associate Dean of Students, University of Texas at Austin, Austin, Texas

**Donna L. McKinley,** Director of Counseling, Colorado State University, Fort Collins, Colorado

**Weston H. Morrill,** Director of Counseling, Professor of Educational Psychology, and Clinical Associate Professor of Psychiatry, University of Utah, Salt Lake City, Utah

**E. R. Oetting,** Professor of Psychology, Colorado State University, Fort Collins, Colorado

**Ted Packard,** Chairman, Department of Educational Psychology, University of Utah, Salt Lake City, Utah

**Stephen C. Paul,** Psychologist, Counseling Center, University of Utah, Salt Lake City, Utah

**Shirley Bird Perry,** Assistant to the President, University of Texas at Austin, Austin, Texas

**John H. Schuh,** Director, Department of Residence Life, Indiana University, Bloomington, Indiana

**Melba J. Vasquez,** Senior Psychologist, University Counseling Center, Colorado State University, Fort Collins, Colorado

***To Jane, Suzanne, Julie Anne, Rusty, and Bill***
***Joan, Kathy, Jeff, Brad, and Jennifer***

# Foreword

Colleges and universities in the United States face crises that demand major change if these institutions are to survive, let alone grow and prosper. Among the roots of these crises are such factors as changing patterns of job opportunities, declining populations in the traditional college-age range, and increasing costs due to inflation. With all these factors, it is not surprising that youth, parents, educators, and government agencies are reconsidering the purposes of higher education, the value to be placed on it, and the wisest choices for students to make among the options available to them.

This book could hardly come at a more propitious time. Higher education is experiencing an increasing diversity of students as to age and goals, and is contemplating if not already offering an increasing diversity of curricula and special programs. The book is especially helpful in this era because it gives so much attention to the dynamic interaction between students and the college environment—the ecology of the campus—at a time when both students and environments are in flux.

More fundamentally, the book provides college student personnel workers with a new and well-developed theoretical base for their work and then examines each service area within the context of that base. Further, the book offers a model for continual assessment of needs, systematic evaluation of programs, and planned programmatic change as suggested by results of the assessment and evaluation.

Although no framework or point of view can last long in times of such rapid change, this book offers a comprehensive guide that helps us plan for today and tomorrow and that can also help produce the framework that will be our guide for the day after tomorrow. Wes Morrill, Jim Hurst, Gene Oetting, and their associates have built upon many years of creative thinking and careful study. Their contribution will help our field and higher education in general find their place during the 1980s.

LEO GOLDMAN

*Graduate School and University Center*
*The City University of New York*
*August 1980*

# Preface

One of the major challenges of the next decade for student development professionals is that of articulating clear, conceptual models for directing and stimulating practice, for delineating the role of student affairs or student development professionals in education, and for providing professional identity, direction, and training. This book acknowledges the evolution of the student affairs profession through in loco parentis to the adoption of student development and environmental development as foundations on which theory and practice are based. Its purpose is to prepare student affairs professionals to be proactive interveners for student development rather than reactive managers. This book introduces a conceptual model to provide student services professionals with an understanding of their roles in education and to provide models for carrying out those roles. This is accomplished by weaving together two highly useful models, the first to indicate the purpose of student personnel services, why we exist, our roles, and our relationship to educational institutions in which we work. This involves understanding the students entering the educational system, the educational environment, and the resulting interaction of students with that environment. Chapters on each of these topics, that is, understanding development during college years, the role of the environment as a determinant of human behavior, and understanding student–environment interaction, provide the organizing constructs and body of knowledge behind the student personnel or student development profession. The second model, then, addresses the area of practice and is most helpful in conceptualizing the targets, purposes, and methods of intervention by student personnel professionals. This award-winning model provides a means of thinking about and planning program alternatives, thus opening the intervention process to exciting decisions about how to best utilize resources with a proactive, preventive, and developmental orientation rather than just a reactive or managerial one. The overriding focus is the development of students, with the interventions designed to enhance their ability to utilize available environments for growth, and intervention in environments to make them more conducive to human development. These challenging roles bring us into partnership with the academic segment of the institutions where we work in accomplishing the goals of education. The third section of the book describes actual applications of the models as they have developed in institutions of higher education.

The book is unique in that it presents a solid foundation for understanding the theory of student development, environmental development, and the interaction between the two; builds with a precise, but succinct, model for program intervention; follows with practical examples of programs in a variety of settings; and concludes with a statement about training and future challenges.

We have been stimulated by colleagues who have contributed to this volume and are hopeful that we can share this same stimulation with colleagues in the profession as we strive to meet the challenges of the 1980s. It would be impossible to acknowledge all those people who have positively contributed to the development of the ideas this book represents. We must, however, acknowledge the impactful contributions of former mentors and colleagues such as Clyde Parker, Al Ivey, Burns Crookston, Gene Oetting, and colleagues at Colorado State, the University of Utah, and the University of Texas at Austin. A special thanks to A. Reed Morrill and Roland Lee for their reading and editorial suggestions. In addition, a special thanks to Barbara Hope, Cindy Wilson, and Suzanne Morrill for their help in the preparation of the several drafts of the manuscript.

WESTON H. MORRILL
JAMES C. HURST

*Salt Lake City, Utah*
*Austin, Texas*
*August 1980*

# Contents

# I

# Student Affairs and Student/Environmental Development

Part I presents an introduction to the body of knowledge on which the student affairs or student development profession is based. This is accomplished by discussing the evolution of the profession from the concept of in loco parentis to that of student resource development and environmental resource development. That evolution and the role of student affairs professionals are presented in Chapter 1. David Drum, in Chapter 2, presents a highly useful, seven-dimensional model for understanding student development. This chapter provides an excellent basis for bridging the gap between developmental theory and the practice of promoting and assessing development. Chapter 3, by Banning and McKinley, provides a basis for understanding the campus environment. Steven Paul then, in Chapter 4, provides a solid discussion of the interaction between the individual student and the college environment and provides a means for understanding the role of this interaction in affecting the outcomes of the educational experience.

# 1

# Student/Environmental Development as the Conceptional Foundation for Student Affairs

JAMES C. HURST AND
WESTON H. MORRILL

The purpose of this chapter is to present the historical emergence of a conceptual model that will help student development professionals articulate their role in higher education. From the beginning there has been much serious reflection and a good deal of confusion concerning the identity of professionals working in the student services areas of higher education. This lack of a well-defined identity has left student services in an ancillary position to academic endeavors. Historically, it has been difficult for many of our academic colleagues to recognize our role on campus as being much different from the auxiliary services of keeping buildings clean and grass clipped. This circumstance is the result of the inability student affairs professionals have experienced over the years to articulate their relationship with the academic mission of the institutions in which they operate. This inability certainly contributes to the profession being viewed in an ancillary role by many. As members of the profession we must assume much of the blame for that because of our inability to clearly define and describe our role and function.

## VARIABLES AFFECTING EDUCATIONAL OUTCOMES

If we are to articulate a role for student development professionals which interfaces with the academic mission of the institution, we must pay particular attention to the mission and goals of higher education. Student affairs exists for the purpose of contributing to those goals. Higher education does not exist to provide jobs for student affairs professionals. Unless we can relate to the mission and goals of higher education our future is questionable. Although the role of the student development professional in the achievement of goals and objectives may be different from that of the professor in the classroom setting, that role must be compatible with and supportive of the overall institutional goals. These goals extend beyond the mere acquisition of knowledge. Sanford, in the introduction to *Where Colleges Fail* (1967), indicated that one of the most depressing aspects of higher education is the narrow manner in which most people react to it. For many, "getting an education" means acquiring units of education—measured mainly by the number of hours spent in a classroom. Yet the goals of higher education suggest that college should influence the development of individuals in personal as well as intellectual ways.

In order to determine the role of student personnel professionals in the achievement of students' and institutional goals (both personal and intellectual), it is important to understand the variables affected by the outcomes of the educational experience. Using an adaptation of a figure describing the ACE longitudinal research design (Creager, 1968), the variables affecting the education are conceptualized as (1) the student or the input variable, (2) the educational environment, and (3) the interaction between the student and that environment; the results of these variables are the outcomes or outputs of education (Figure 1).

## THE ROLES OF STUDENT SERVICES

The roles of student services professionals in education are related to the above variables and very simply these roles are as follows:

**1** To study and understand the student, the environment, and the outcomes of their interaction in order to identify potential mismatches and needed interventions.

**2** Growing out of the first, to facilitate student resource development by providing students with the skills, attitudes, and other resources

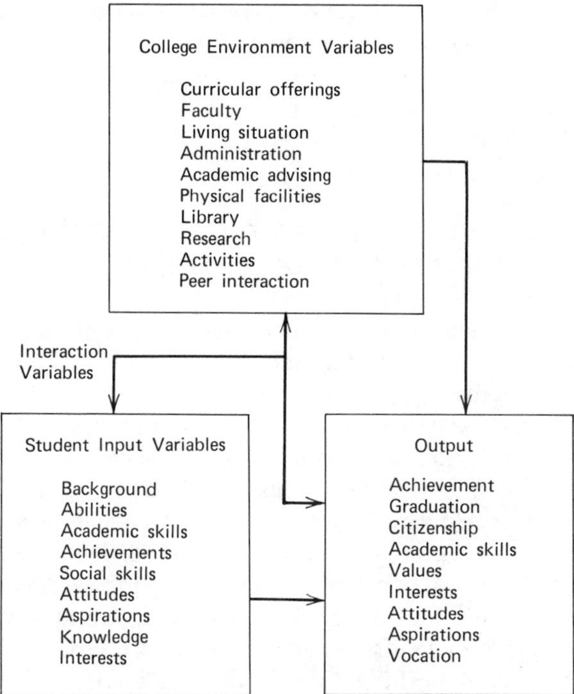


**Figure 1** Variables affecting higher education.

they need in order to take advantage of and profit from the learning environments.

3 To promote environmental resource development by restructuring, redesign, and modification interventions designed to create the optimal environment within which human development may occur.

Each of these roles needs greater elaboration. Some aspects of the university environment are clearly designed to facilitate the development of intellectual skills and the acquisition of knowledge. Prime examples are the academic classroom, the laboratory, and the library. Other aspects of the environment are more conducive to the development of personal and social resources such as student activities, residence halls, and student union buildings. Obviously one does not exclude the other, for some academic learning takes place in residence halls and student unions, and some social development occurs within classrooms and libraries. It is a matter of primary emphasis rather than exclusive domain. It is the total university environment that provides the students with the opportunity to undertake the all-important task of developing a personal identity and skills needed for successful living. A brief historical review is necessary for a full appreciation of the ACE conceptualization.

## THE EMERGENCE OF STUDENT/ENVIRONMENTAL DEVELOPMENT FROM IN LOCO PARENTIS

Student/environmental development has emerged over the past 15 years as the needs of students and characteristics of institutions have changed. For many years the concept of in loco parentis provided a rationale for the existence of student personnel work. However, it has from its very inception been on a track of obsolescence not because of what it provided, but rather because of what it did not provide. Although it provided a rationale for the existence of student personnel work, it said nothing of how to understand students in the academic environment, how to accomplish the task of helping students succeed, or how to predict and plan for the future. In loco parentis, as a rationale, had student personnel workers acting in the place of parents, but ultimately contributed nothing to their understanding of the difference between good and bad parents. It said little about what helps people to learn and mature. It said much about regulatory functions relating to student conduct but little as to why or how or to what end.

The obsolescence of in loco parentis was also inevitable because it is basically nontheoretical. Theory is necessary to understand present experience, predict future events, provide a basis for communication, and construct hypotheses from which systematic research may occur and academic disciplines develop. In the past student personnel workers worked diligently to provide for students what good parents provide. They were therefore concerned about food, shelter, finances, social interaction, advice, discipline, and care when sick. The result was the development of food services and housing through fraternities, sororities, and eventually institutionally owned housing; union buildings within which social and cultural activities could occur; financial aid services designed to facilitate the acquisition of the necessary money to continue education; counseling centers designed to provide good advice and assist with personal problems; discipline functions to deal with deviant behavior and "dean's lists" to provide recognition for good and successful behavior; and health centers for times of sickness.

In loco parentis led to the development of these services and agencies along with the basic skills that were acquired in the management of these service agencies. As student personnel professionals worked to serve a parental role, they became competent administrators and managers. The concept was incapable, however, of providing the theoretical umbrella under which management skills, administrative competence, and counseling expertise could be developed. It is no accident that human development theory emerged primarily in academic settings with minimal contributions by student personnel workers. In loco parentis spawned administrators, not conceptualizers. Practitioners tended not to take time to conceptualize. Counseling theory developed primarily out of education and psychology departments. Management and administration theory was developed in colleges of business and institutes of higher education. The conceptual base that was to replace in loco parentis was destined to emerge primarily out of academic endeavors, not from within the student personnel field as such. Human development theorists such as Piaget (1963, 1968, 1969), Peck and Havinghurst (1960), Erikson (1959), Chickering (1969), and Loevinger (1976) provided the basic ingredients for a transition from in loco parentis to student development. All that was needed was professionals involved in student personnel work insightful enough to recognize the need and provide the actual transition.

In summary, in loco parentis has left a useful legacy in the specific services and agencies developed under its rationale. It also provided the impetus for the identification of administration, counseling, and management as generic skills related to carrying out programmatic efforts. It became obsolete as the demands on student personnel workers became more complex and required a more substantial foundation on which to build new services, predict the future, and evaluate what was being done. By the mid 1960s, in loco parentis was unable to meet all the demands of a new generation of students who were confronted with the complicated issues of their time. The demands of the 1960s and 1970s placed student personnel work on notice that unless it became capable of more substantial contributions to the changing process of higher education it would be deemphasized or even eliminated.

## THE EMERGENCE OF STUDENT RESOURCE DEVELOPMENT

In 1967 Oetting proposed a working definition of student development that has continued to be useful. Oetting considered the differences between the active and passive learner and their individual characteristics. He postulated that more mature learners interact with their learning environment as contrasted to passively absorbing what is offered. Oetting's definition of student development emphasized the need to help students acquire the skills, attitudes, and knowledge necessary to interact constructively with the educational environment and to take full advantage of what is offered. In essence, he saw students as having great resources not only to learn from but also to contribute to the teaching/learning circumstance. He strongly encouraged the development of these resources. Subsequently, other writers have designated resource development as including intellectual, interpersonal, moral/ethical, societal/citizenship, and physical development. Although there is some overlap between student resource development and traditional academic activities, student development is unique in that it is the only group of activities in higher education specifically designed to provide students with the skills and knowledge they need to take full advantage of the environment in which they are immersed. For example, students must have at least a minimal level of both reading and study skills if they are to take full advantage of the well-equipped libraries characteristic of most college campuses. Also, if students do not have minimal interpersonal skills the enriching experience of interacting constructively with hundreds of other students will not occur. Further, the moral/ethical dilemmas faced by students in higher education such as honesty or cheating, sexual intimacy, and priority use of parents' hard-earned money provide excellent "laboratory" experience in which students can learn valuable lessons for later life if attended to intentionally.

A major strength of student resource development is that it is complementary and additive to the concepts of in loco parentis. It is not a replacement for either the structure or function of the administrative arrangement that developed under in loco parentis. It provides a new rationale for continuing most of the same services. Health education and recreation programs grew up to complement the health care of health centers. Residence education programs grew to complement the management operations in housing. Student unions placed increased emphasis on cultural and social development, and financial aid offices considered the necessity of teaching students how to better manage the money that was being distributed. In addition to remedial therapy, counseling centers began to emphasize more preventive and developmental programs designed to teach students the prerequisite skills for maximum utilization of their environment. The theory underlying student affairs work also took on new meaning. Human development, and especially the critical developmental tasks and stages of late adolescence and early adulthood, received new attention. As a result, increased emphasis was given to intervention strategies that deal with larger groups of students as opposed to one-to-one counseling. Program development became an accepted and valued skill for student personnel workers. Student resource development then emerged and complemented all that had occurred under the in loco parentis rationale.

## THE EMERGENCE OF ENVIRONMENTAL RESOURCE DEVELOPMENT

The American Council on Education conceptualization (Creager, 1968) referred to in Figure 1 specified three primary variables in the higher education process that student affairs professionals might best attend to. This model was particularly significant in pointing out the third basic component of a comprehensive foundation for student affairs. That component is the educational environment. The in loco parentis rationale emphasized the student and his/her adaptation to the educational process. Student resource development expanded upon that by preparing the student to be an active agent in interacting with the educational process, but still did not attend directly to the other primary variable in the educational process, the environment. Fortunately, a rather extensive body of literature already existed concerning the impact of the environment on individuals. In the 1930s Murray (1938) talked about environmental press and Lewin (1935, 1951) talked of field theory and the various forces in the environment that have an impact on individuals. In fact, almost every theory of human development acknowledges the importance of the environment in shaping human behavior, attitude, and knowledge. In the mid 1960s, a concerted effort was made to relate this body of information directly to the college environment. Pace (1958, 1974), Stern (1970), Brofenbrenner (1976), Barker (1978), and Moos (1976) are among those who have more recently written about the characteristics of environmental impact on students. The environment, as a part of this conceptualization, is comprehensive in including physical, social, cultural, academic, and administrative components. Other writers have dealt with other abstract approaches to describing the environment. One particularly productive example is that of Blocker (1978), who designated opportunity subsystems, support subsystems, and reward sybsystems in educational environments that play a role in shaping the educational experience.

A major advantage of the concept of environmental resource development was that it complemented both student resource development and the management and administration emphasis of the in loco parentis rationale. With this addition, student affairs work included all the variables that are critical to enhancing the educative process. It also introduced some additional knowledge and skill content areas to student affairs. Investigative skills, including data generation, program evaluation, and deriving and testing hypotheses, took on a new importance as the need for descriptive information regarding both students and their environment was recognized. Interventions that included consultation and administrative intervention were also emphasized in this addition to the foundation of student affairs work.

## A COMPREHENSIVE FOUNDATION FOR STUDENT AFFAIRS WORK

Figure 2 provides a summarization of the movement from the initiation of student personnel work with the rationale of in loco parentis and its emphasis on management and administration. The emergence of student resource development complemented what had already come forth under management and administration and was itself complemented and balanced by the emergence of environmental resource development. These three components provide the conceptualization within which the modern student affairs professional may attend completely and comprehensively to the primary variables of the education process.

One more step in the evolution of the conceptualization must be noted. A foundation of knowledge and skills is essential to any bona fide discipline. This foundation must include an emphasis on theory as well as practical application in order to be seriously considered by student affairs professionals and also by academic colleagues in higher education.

Figure 2 identifies the three components of the foundation of knowledge and skills. The first is investigative. Skill and knowledge in this area are necessary to provide an adequate data base from which to predict the needs and describe the characteristics of a particular institution and its students. In a prediction more than a decade ago about student personnel professionals in 1980, Sanford (1968, p. 182) indicated that ". . . by 1980, counselors, deans, and other specialists in student personnel will have discovered that one of the best things to do about students singly or in mass is to study them; accordingly, these professionals will be producers as well as consumers of knowledge about students." It is clear that we need much more knowledge about the complex relationships between students' characteristics, their development patterns, and the varied learning environments of educational institutions. Thus, as Sanford indicated, we must be both consumers

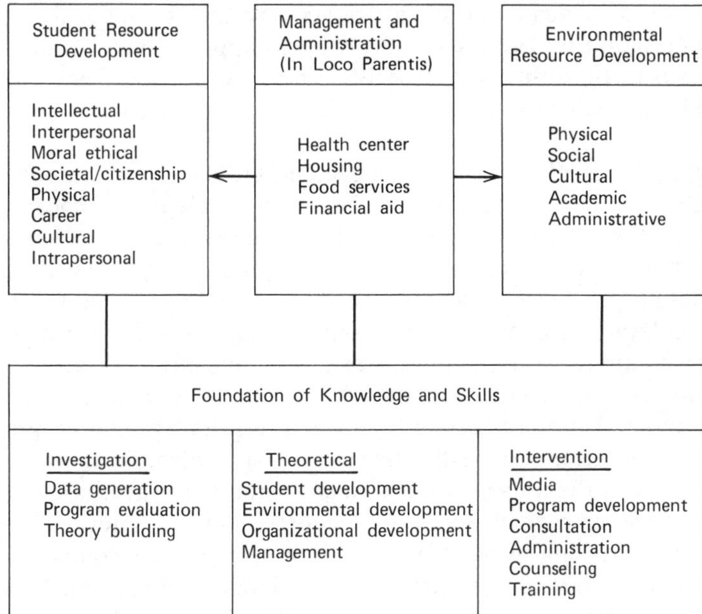


**Figure 2** A conceptual foundation for student affairs [from Hurst 1980]

and producers of knowledge about the development of students, about environments and their impact, and about the interactions between various environments. As producers of knowledge, our understanding can be based on both formalized evaluations and ecomapping studies or on an ongoing assimilation of data through constant interaction with students.

Investigative skill also includes program evaluation. This reflects a commitment to offer only those programs that can demonstrate empirically their value and effectiveness. The theory building aspect of the investigative skills is based on an understanding of the importance of deriving testable hypotheses from human development theory, environmental development theory, and management theory. Only in this way can a body of knowledge unique to student affairs work be developed that will provide for the continual growth of the foundation of the profession.

The second component of the foundation of knowledge and skills is theoretical. As noted previously, the three basic areas of theoretical development are the student, the environment, and management. Although at present most of the material written concerning this theory has occurred in academic departments, increasing emphasis is being placed on adapting the theory to practical applications within student affairs work. In addition, the derivation of hypotheses from theory as they relate specifically to student affairs work is of continuing importance.

Finally, a foundation of knowledge and skills in interventions is necessary to complete the foundation. Program development, consultation, administration, training, media, and counseling are all procedures by which interventions take place. This is the realm of the practitioner. All intervention processes, however, are ideally based on data and theory. The foundation of knowledge and skills described in Figure 2 provides the curriculum for training programs in students affairs. It also provides the framework for continuing staff development. At present it does not appear to be common practice for student affairs training programs to require preparation in investigative skills. There also seems to be a lack of emphasis on theory as it relates to environmental variables and management. Important advances are occurring in the intervention area with more training programs attending not just to counseling and administration but also to program development and consultation as essential intervention strategies for the well-trained student affairs professional (Morrill, Oetting, and Hurst, 1974).

The foundation of skills and knowledge provides a basis for the evaluation of training programs. It also provides a diagnostic measure by which the thoroughness of any particular training program can be assessed. Finally, the foundation provides the basis on which programs designed to train student affairs professionals might be accredited. Until the profession is fully aware of the specific knowledge and skills that are needed for a fully functioning professional, and until it is able to accredit training programs for their effectiveness in providing students with these skills and knowledge, it is destined always to be a second-class citizen in academia.

## REFERENCES

Barker, R. G. *Habitats, Environments, and Human Behavior.* San Francisco: Jossey-Bass, 1978.

Blocker, D. H. Campus learning environments and the ecology of student development. *Campus Ecology: A Perspective for Student Affairs.* NASPA Monograph, Cincinnati, Ohio: National Association of Student Personnel Administrators, 1978.

Brofenbrenner, U. The experimental ecology of education. *Teachers College Record,* 1976, **78**, 157–204.

Chickering, A. W. *Education and Identity.* San Francisco: Jossey-Bass, 1969.

Creager, J. A. Use of research results in matching students and colleges. *Journal of College Student Personnel,* 1968, **9**, 312–319.

Erikson, E. H. *Identity and the Life Cycle.* New York: International Universities Press, 1959.

Hurst, J. C. The emergence of student/environmental development as the conceptual foundation for student affairs and some implications for large universities. *Current Issues in Student Development.* American College Personnel Association Monograph, 1980.

Lewin, K. *Dynamic Theory of Personality.* New York: McGraw-Hill, 1935.

Lewin, K. *Field Theory in Social Science.* New York: Harper and Row, 1955.

Loevinger, J. *Ego Development.* San Francisco: Jossey-Bass, 1976.

Moos, R. H. *The Human Context: Environmental Determinants of Behavior.* New York: John Wiley & Sons, 1976.

Morrill, W. H., E. R. Oetting, and J. C. Hurst Dimensions of counselor functioning. *The Personnel and Guidance Journal,* 1974, **52** (6). 354–359.

Morrill, W. H. and J. C. Hurst A preventative and developmental role for the college counselor. *The Counseling Psychologist,* 1971, **2** (4), 90–95.

Murray, H. A. *Explorations in Personality.* New York: Oxford University Press, 1938.

Oetting, E. R. A developmental definition of counseling psychologyy. *Journal of Counseling Psychology,* 1967, **14**, 382–385.

Pace, C. R. *The Demise of Diversity: A Comparative Profile of Eight Types of Institutions.* New York: McGraw-Hill, 1974.

Pace, C. R. and G. G. Stern An approach to the measurement of psychological characteristics of college environments. *Journal of Educational Psychology,* 1958, **49**, 269–277.

Peck, R. F. and R. J. Havinghurst *The Psychology of Character.* New York: John Wiley & Sons, 1960.

Piaget, J. *The Psychology of Intelligence.* Totowa, N. J.: Littlefield-Adams, 1963.

Piaget, J. *Six Psychological Studies.* New York: Vintage Press, 1968.

Piaget, J. and B. Inhelder *The Psychology of the Child.* New York: Basic Books, 1969.

Sanford, N. *Where Colleges fail.* San Francisco: Josey-Bass, Inc., 1967.

Sanford, N. The college student of 1980. In A.C. Eurich (Ed.), *Campus 1980: The shape of the future in American higher education.* New York: Delacorte Press, 1968.

Stern, G. G. *People in Context: Measuring Person–Environment Congruence in Education and Industry.* New York: John Wiley & Sons, 1970.

# 2
# Understanding Student Development

DAVID DRUM

The focus of this chapter is development during the college years. It seems important to understand student development in order to find more appropriate ways to assist and support students' growth and to better understand the forces swirling within the individual which affect his/her behavior and judgments. Since the student is the input variable in the educational enterprise, gaining a perspective on the principles governing development can be helpful if growth is to be maximally facilitated.

Development is not dormant during late adolescence and early adulthood. The college years are times of developmental expansiveness, and while attempting to order the diversity and complexity encountered in college life, students can be seen (1) exploring new ways of thinking; (2) engaging in novel activities, (3) shifting attitudes, values, and beliefs, (4) employing new standards of conscience, (5) forming a changed sense of self, (6) setting career directions, (7) becoming more tolerant of individual differences, and (8) making other types of adaptations. Although it appears that dimensions within which such changes could be studied are many, they can be grouped into three major categories of change: (1) cognitive development (e.g., changes in style of thinking, creative expression, and aesthetic sensitivity); (2) development of a self system (e.g., intrapsychic changes in moral reasoning, values, identity, and ego); and (3) social development (e.g., changes in interpersonal relationships and cultural beliefs).

This chapter begins with a review of the various theories of human development that have application to college student development and offers a system for categorizing them into four types: behavioral, structural/adaptive, psychosocial/psychoanalytic, and descriptive. Since theories of development within the structural/adaptive category are currently having the most impact on student affairs work they are highlighted throughout the chapter. Because of the sheer number of human development and student development theories applicable to work with college students, many of these theories receive only brief review. Summaries and comprehensive reviews are readily available elsewhere, for example, in the work by Knefelkamp, Widick, and Parker (1978), as well as in the original writings of the theorists.

Next, a brief historical perspective outlines the gradual shift over the past few years toward more theory-based practice and programming in student affairs work. Despite the fact that student affairs workers long have devised and implemented programs that are developmental in nature, it has been only within the past few years that any really systematic effort has been made to link interventions to specific principles of human or student development.

The final portion of this chapter attempts to increase the reader's understanding of the developmental changes and refinements many students experience during the college years, by outlining and describing the design of a seven-dimensional model of student development. This model and the descriptions of each scale were developed by the Student Development Task Force (SDTF) of the Division of Student Affairs* at the University of Rhode Island. The model, entitled "Some Modes and Dimensions of Student Development," is built on principles of several major developmental theories. The goal in designing such a model was to connect theory and practice in as comprehensive a manner as possible so that changes on one dimension of development could be studied in relation to movement in other developmental areas. In short, the purpose of the model is to provide some context for the wide range of developmental changes that often characterize the college years.

## DEVELOPMENT AND THE LIFE-SPAN

Almost all developmental theorists seem to point to a specific, although often different, part of the life-span as the most important to overall

---

*The participants in the Student Development Task Force who contributed to the design of this model and description of the seven-dimensions are David Drum (chairman), Harry Amaral, Douglas Daher, Russel Gilmore, Richard Katzoff, Ed O'Connell, Hazel Temple, and Ronald Weisinger. In addition, J. Eugene Knott and James O. Prochasha were contributors during the early stages of formulation of the model.

development. Historically, the critical developmental periods have been viewed as occurring in childhood. Therefore, the first decade of life has been singled out for microscopic review by many theorists. During the past quarter-century much interest has been directed toward formulating the principles of growth and development of the adolescent and adult years. This new focus of activity has led to a number of theories having special application to the college-age population. This emphasis has coincided with accountability pressures which are stimulating people to determine what types of development occur during the college years and, more specifically, what accentuates or retards desirable developmental changes.

The writings of several theorists, including Chickering (1969), Erikson (1959, 1963), Havinghurst (1952), D. Heath (1968, 1977), R. Heath (1968, 1977), Kohlberg (1969), Loevinger (1976), Perry (1970), Sanford (1962), and, more recently, Gould (1972), Levinson et al. (1978), and Sheehy (1974), provide insights into the needs of college students. Indeed, the work of the latter is becoming more important to college administrators and faculty in their increasing efforts to understand the needs of older-than-average students (over 22 years) and entice them to the campus.

## THEORIES OF HUMAN DEVELOPMENT

The desire to develop a comprehensive, well-integrated theory of human development (physical, cognitive, psychological, social) has been a driving force for many writers, researchers, and theorists for the better part of the twentieth century. They have constructed both comprehensive and single-dimensional systems which describe development in such terms as specific tasks, stimulus–response bonds, instinctual drives, maturation, physical growth, cognitive structures, life themes, and changes in the self or ego. Major theorists such as Erikson (1959, 1968), Freud (1938), Kohlberg (1969), Loevinger (1976). Piaget (1950, 1964) and Skinner (1953, 1963) and others have stimulated substantial thought about factors, s–r bonds, forces, tasks, and needs that might be both common and central to the process of human development.

The important goals of most developmental theorists continue to be the deepest possible understanding of the process and outcome of healthy development, and the identification of the basic principles and mechanisms governing growth and change throughout the life-span. When the wide range of developmental theories proposed during this century is reviewed, four categories emerge. Each category contains the works of several theorists who share certain fundamental beliefs about development, that is, the process by which people undergo change. The four categories are (1) behavioral, (2) structural/adaptive, (3) psychosocial/psychoanalytical, and (4) descriptive.

## Behavioral Theories of Development

Behavioral-based theories of development are built primarily on the principles of stimulus–response learning theory, wherein the individual being studied is viewed primarily as reactive rather than proactive in dealing with the world. Development or change is seen as being quantitative rather than qualitative. Therefore, theorists working from the behavioral viewpoint search for the antecedents of a specific action and study the consequences of a given behavior. From these data, they deduce the laws or principles governing development.

The behavioral perspective on development has been variously labeled reductionistic, mechanistic, environmental, or atomistic. The labels reflect attempts by these theorists to isolate the basic principles and laws governing all human behavior. Unlike the structural/adaptive and descriptive theorists, the behaviorists have attempted to identify developmental principles that apply to the entire life-span. They are not just child- or adult-centered in their formulations (Skinner, 1953).

## Structural Adaptive Theories of Development

A second major theoretical view of the developmental process can be labeled structural/adaptive. According to this perspective, the individual (organism) is considered to play a significant role in structuring, selecting, and organizing stimulus perception and in formulating adaptive responses to perceived demands. These theorists hypothesize that in the process of living each individual faces innumerable challenges which require increasingly more complex coping skills and adaptive capacity. Each new challenge or task successfully handled propels the individual to incorporate more complex or qualitatively different modes of adaptation or problem solving. During the life-span, the individual is viewed as (1) developing through stages or undergoing transformations which alter or influence his/her way of perceiving and formulating responses or (2) confronting specific developmental tasks which require new or more complex modes of adaptation.

Developmental theories placed in this category differ from behavioral and descriptive theories in that they are based on a highly proactive view of the individual. Developmental change is seen as being primarily qualitative, although some attention is given to quantitative changes. Therefore, structural/adaptive theorists postulate change in terms of resolution of conflicts, achievement of specific tasks, emergence of new modes of problem solving or reasoning, or attainment of a particular stage in an ordered sequence of stages. Words such as transformation, adaptation, stage, and hierarchy imply some form of structural change in the way an individual perceives, integrates, and responds to the environment. A major goal of structural/adaptive theorists is to identify the dimensions of adaptation and formulate hypothetical constructs accurately describing structural changes which occur within the perceptual/value system of the individual.

The structural/adaptive perspective has been variously labeled organismic, cognitive, and moral, for example, reflecting both the rather diverse foci and lack of comprehensiveness of theories within this category. Early structural/adaptive theorists tended to be heavily child-centered in focus, whereas more recent theorists have increased the span of study to include the adolescent and adult years.

The structural/adaptive category embraces a vast diversity of viewpoints concerning what principles or forces govern human development. These views can be divided into those primarily focused on cognitive development and those centered on development of a self system. This differentiation of emphasis is provided to draw attention to two clusters of thinking within the structural/adaptive area rather than to create the impression that these theories are highly independent of each other. In fact, all the theories in this category have many common properties and place significant reliance on the concepts of adaptation and structural changes within the individual as the cornerstones of development.

Structural/adaptive theorists who are primarily cognitive in orientation look at how the mind changes in its style and complexity and its capacity to integrate and process knowledge and information. In short, they elucidate the principles, structures, and sequence of mental development that purportedly influence an individual's perception of stimuli, integration of various inputs, and response to events. Harvey, Hunt, and Schroder (1961), Perry (1970), and Piaget (1950, 1964) are representative of cognitive theorists.

Self-system theorists describe development in terms of the emergence of the self as the frame of reference for dealing with the world. From birth through the life-span different aspects of the self are hypothesized to emerge and to influence how the individual interprets events and translates stimuli. Self-system theorists formulate principles or stages through which the individual progresses as he or she develops a moral belief system, a sense of identity, or some intrapsychic structure through which environmental stimuli are filtered and given a personal perspective. New and higher levels of the self are viewed as having been spawned and incubated during the previous stage. Therefore, self-system theorists usually posit an ordered hierarchy of stages within the developmental process in which effective functioning in the previous stage is a prerequiste to movement to the next. Chickering (1969), Kohlberg (1969), and Loevinger (1976) are representative of major self-system theorists.

## Psychosocial/Psychoanalytic Theories of Development

The psychosocial/psychoanalytic theorists view development as occurring in stages, with each hypothesized stage having discrete psychological characteristics and requirements. Every stage is considered to have unique instinctual qualities or basic conflicts that initiate the need to resolve particular developmental tasks or issues and provide the impetus for growth and development.

Psychosocial/psychoanalytic theorists posit that development is enhanced by successful resolution of conflicts and crises. In the psychoanalytic view, conflict is hypothesized to occur when the unbound expression of an individual's basic instincts is tempered by the demands of social realities. Psychosocial theory, however, indicates that development results from changes in focus of instinctual drives, according to some internal time schedule, along with the emergence of environmental challenges that demand resolution. Since both the psychosocial and psychoanalytic theorists hypothesize that instinctual strivings strongly influence development, they focus on the early years of life as being the most important developmentally. Consequently, they assign a less proactive role to the individual than do structural/adaptive theorists. In addition, maturation is a key concept. Instinctual drives and certain developmental tasks are believed to be encoded within the individual according to an approximate timetable. Freud (1938) and Erikson (1963, 1968) are two major psychosocial/psychoanalytic theorists.

## Descriptive Theories of Development

The fourth major category of developmental theory is labeled descriptive. Theorists in this category classify and describe development according to the key issues or themes that dominate a particular segment of life-span. They work toward identifying important life themes common for those in a certain age range. They also tend to focus on people who have reached adult status. Most descriptive development theories do not posit that successful resolution of a previous stage is required in order to handle the problems encountered in the next stage of life, nor do they imply that succeeding stages of development require more complex behavior. In fact, these theorists use words such as "period" or "phase" rather than "stage" to describe a certain time frame of development. They attempt to match specific age ranges with given life themes or issues, such as "becoming independent from parents." According to this perspective, a person's development is considered to be progressing normally if he/she confronts certain themes within the expected time frame, given the average time occurrence in the population at large.

In comparison to other theoretical perspectives, the descriptive theories of development do not propose that a person's way of perceiving changes with successful resolution of the previous period. Each new developmental theme is simply described in terms of the particular issue to be faced during that period of time. This is a major distinction between the descriptive and the structural/adaptive theorists. In addition, descriptive theorists describe life in terms of coping rather than adapting. Therefore, their theories seem more content-oriented and the structural adaptive theories seem more process-oriented. Descriptive theorists also differ from both the behavioral and structural/adaptive theorists in that they do not focus on formulation of basic mechanical laws or principles of development. Gould (1972), Levinson (1978), and Sheehy (1974) are considered descriptive developmental theorists.

## Application of Human Development Theory to Student Development

Student development practices have their roots in all four categories of human development theories. Historically, the first applications of human development principles to student affairs work were based on behavioral theories. Although early-day student affairs administrators did not consciously apply behavioral principles of development, their heavy reliance on reinforcement and punishment as ways to shape appropriate development is clearly evident. At that time, personal and social behaviors were more prescribed within the collegiate environment, and very little divergence from these expectations was tolerated. Clearly, developmental principles were being applied in an unconscious, yet systematic, manner. Emphasis was more on the content of development (e.g., specific beliefs, styles of dress, forms of response) than on concerns about the developmental process (e.g., belief system, identity development, aesthetic awareness).

Over time, student affairs workers began to make the developmental process a more conscious focus of their thinking, and a gradual shift away from the catechetical approach to character development occurred. Discussions and writings about student development began to focus on some of the unique tasks and challenges that students face during the college years. Important changes were hypothesized with regard to personal and social, as well as cognitive, development.

As a result of the growing awareness of the rapid, diverse, and complex nature of college student development, there emerged a more serious search for a theoretical framework that could provide a better understanding of the changes that occur during this time frame. The awareness that so much was happening developmentally in the affective as well as the cognitive realm spurred student affairs workers to (1) search for a theory of human development that would promote more accurate understanding of college students and (2) design a developmental theory unique to the college years.

Both human development and student development theory have had useful and widespread influence on the programs and services being offered within student affairs, although their impact has been relatively recent. Currently several human development theories are being applied and researched within the college setting, for example, by Erikson (1963, 1968), Kohlberg (1969), and Loevinger (1976). In addition, a larger number of student development theories proposed in recent years are also being applied, for example, by Chickering (1969), D. Heath (1968, 1977), R. Heath (1964, 1973), and Perry (1970).

## MOVING FROM PRACTICE TO THEORY AND BACK TO PRACTICE

Student affairs practitioners face a somewhat unusual situation in that many programs considered to be developmental in nature preceded the emergence of a comprehensive theory that could provide a context for those efforts. As a result, much current programming is either atheoretical or based on assumptions from a variety of theories which are not linked together in a systematic fashion. Early efforts at student development programming seem to have been dominated by pragmatic considerations rather than developmental concepts. A major focus was placed on the content or end product of development rather than the developmental process. In essence, changes that were encouraged in students were not integrated with a larger developmental context. Therefore, the value, validity, and appropriateness of such programs or interventions were difficult to judge and support.

The challenge currently facing student affairs workers is how to move from programming to theory (for context) and then back to programming while operating under the current financial constraints and day-to-day realities of administration. Nevertheless, without taking steps to establish a solid theoretical base that can provide a perspective to intervention efforts, student affairs workers will be hard pressed to answer such questions as: How do you know what you are doing is worthwhile to students? What are the long-term developmental benefits? These are primarily questions of "context." Although the people asking such questions realize that the student development years are only a fraction of the frames of a larger life-span movie, they are asking for those frames to be magnified for closer inspection.

## Building a Working Definition of Student Development

The task of blending theory and interventions is made genuinely difficult because many theorists do not specifically define development in their writings. The reader of a particular developmental theory is often expected to extract a formal definition of development from the principles or assumptions inherent in a given theory. Therefore, practitioners trying to employ and research a specific theory often must formulate their own definitions which probably lead to many differences in interpretation of the particular theory.

In contrast, some practitioners provide definitions of student development that are not grounded in specific developmental theory. For example, Tomorrow's Higher Education Project defined student development as "the application of human development concepts in postsecondary settings so that everyone involved can master increasingly complex developmental tasks, achieve self-direction, and become interdependent. . ." (Miller and Prince, 1976, p. 3). This definition is essentially atheoretical and allows the practitioner to select from among all human development theories those concepts he/she will utilize. With this type of definition, the reader is confronted with the problem of selecting developmental concepts and principles that are based on compatible assumptions about the growth and change process. This task is not as simple as it may seem, since significant conceptual differences exist among behavioral, structural/adaptive, psychosocial/psychoanalytic, and descriptive theorists. Furthermore, within the structural/adaptive category, substantial conceptual differences exist among the task, invariant hierarchical, and maturity theorists.

In an effort to eliminate the concern noted above, a definition of student development was created by Drum (1977) and served as the basis for the construction of the model entitled "Student Development: Some Modes and Dimensions." The definition states (Drum, 1977):

> Student development is a process in which an individual undergoes a number of changes toward more complex behavior, that result from mastering the increasingly demanding challenges of life. These changes toward more complex behavior often culminate in the individual transforming to a higher developmental position which results in his/her viewing people, events, and things in fundamentally different ways.

"Changes" in this definition refer to the smaller units of development (building blocks). These units form the supportive structures for larger, more radical transformations to more advanced developmental stages. Operationally defined, "changes" are considered to be (1) shifts in the content of what one knows, (2) increases or decreases in attributes, values, or beliefs, and (3) increases in response complexity or stimulus discrimination. The "changes" are quantitative in nature; they are both necessary and desirable precursors to the more qualitative developmental transformations to new stages.

For example, Perry's (1970) theory of intellectual and ethical development during the college years posits a nine-stage change process through which the person undergoes three transformations. The first two stages represent changes within a "dualistic" frame of reference. They are necessary steps for achieving the transformation to what he labels "multiplistic" thinking, which is exhibited in stages three and four. When the student enters stage three, he/she is a fundamentally different person who views people, things, and events from a new, transformed vantage point. This single transformation from dualistic reasoning to multiplistic thinking was the result of the accumulation of a wide range of less dramatic changes, which probably were the result of participation in various interventions such as academic studies, student activities, dorm programs, peer encounters, and/or an assortment of other incidental life events.

Given this two-phase developmental process of change and transformation, it seems particularly important to develop multiple modes of intervention and to utilize a wide range of change-oriented options in dealing with college students. The more building blocks used in constructing a foundation, the sturdier and more supportive the platform for later transformation to higher stages of development. In order for students to complete these more dramatic and verifiable transformations they must first experience growth and development on seemingly minor, yet important, "change" dimensions.

### Establishing a Theory-Based Student Development Model

Since the college years are a time of developmental expansiveness, staying within the boundaries of a given theory has proved to be too restrictive for most practitioners. Therefore, a model of student development was needed so that the seemingly diverse and apparently unrelated goals of various theoretical perspectives could be integrated into an overall developmental approach. The Student Development Task Force, mentioned earlier in this chapter, designed such a multidimensional model which is comprehensive yet open to including new dimensions and changing existing scales as the need arises.

## THE SEVEN-DIMENSIONAL MODEL OF STUDENT DEVELOPMENT

The model displayed in Table 1 identifies seven key dimensions of development stimulated during the college years. All seven scales identify three developmental positions, with the most basic level located on the left side, the next highest in the middle, and the highest level of development on the right side of the scale. Movement from the most basic to expansive and from expansive to refined positions on the scales represents transformations. Each transformation is the result of a large number of factors, interventions, and the proper blend of challenge and support. Although each dimension is accompanied by a description of the expected form and direction of change, no scale points are considered sacred. Each dimension should be viewed as being elastic. Therefore, as more data are accumulated, the points on each scale will become better differentiated. As this occurs, it will most likely be necessary to include more than the current three positions. Furthermore, each scale is a magnified look at the developmental process of the college years. Important development on each scale occurs prior to college and significant development lies beyond college on each scale. It is expected, and has been verified by initial findings, that students enter college at various places on the scales, with some students at the most basic stage of development on one or more scales.

This model is designed to profile major stage transformations on seven developmental dimensions. These seven dimensions are intended to chart important developments in three major life systems: (1) cognitive development (changes in how students think, solve problems, and seek and evaluate knowledge); (2) development of the self (changes in how students relate to questions of "essence" and responsibility, as well

**Table 1 Student development—some modes and dimensions**

| Areas of Development | Levels of Development | | |
|---|---|---|---|
| | Basic | Expansive | Refined |
| **Cognitive structures** | Simplistic | Relativistic | Reflective |
| **Aesthetic development** | Instilled preferences | Broadened appreciation | Enhanced sensitivity |
| **Identity formation** | Conforming | Experimental | Intentional |
| **Physical self** | Unintentional practices | Selective management | Personal responsibility |
| **Moral reasoning** | Externalized locus | Internalized locus | Integrated |
| **Interpersonal relatedness** | Self-centered | Role-dominated | Intimate |
| **Social perspective** | Ethnocentric | Culturally relativistic | Anthropocentric systems |

as how a sense of personal identity emerges); and (3) social development (changes in how students relate to friends and acquaintances, as well as to others such as ethnic groups and foreign cultures).

The seven dimensions of development are not assumed to be entirely independent. In fact, since this model was constructed largely on principles and concepts from a wide range of structural/adaptive developmental theories, it is hypothesized that there will be an interaction effect among several scales, wherein developmental growth on one scale might substantially influence movement on another. Does change in one system or dimension automatically result in change in another? The model is designed to help sharpen the ability to ask critical questions of student development theories.

The model is built upon several central developmental assumptions, many of which are key beliefs of other human and student development theorists:

*Assumption 1.* Human development is characterized by growth toward more complexity, internal integration, and finer discrimination. Development proceeds most favorably when sufficient demands, challenges, and threats are perceived by the individual, and when fear of being overwhelmed by them is minimized by both external support and inner coherence.

*Assumption 2.* As development proceeds there is less tendency to anchor beliefs, values, and judgments external to the self and more to utilize internalized personal beliefs in negotiating life. In short, as developmental level increases, less emphasis is placed on the form of a response and more attention is focused on the substance of one's beliefs or actions.

*Assumption 3.* Developmental change is a continuous process. Student development seems to be characterized by a gradual blending of one stage into the next, with small units of growth and change fusing to provide the supportive base for transformation to a higher stage.

*Assumption 4.* Even though developmental change is a continuous process, it is not uniformly one-dimensional. Developmental advancements, as well as regressions and stabilizations, are important factors in the change process. It appears that following the attainment of a higher stage of development, a period of stabilization and integration occurs as the individual develops more coherence within the stage.

*Assumption 5.* Quantitative changes, such as (1) shifts in the valence of an existing value or quality, (2) addition of a new response mode, (3) utilization of more data in decision making, (4) development of slightly different tastes and preferences, are the important building blocks upon which the more qualitative (stage) changes are built. Therefore, movement from one stage to another is likely to be based on a host of more quantitative shifts in beliefs, values, attitudes, and so on, which occur as a person attempts to adapt to the increasingly complex demands of living.

**Cognitive Structures Dimension**

Simplistic — Relativistic — Reflective

Cognitive development has been considered to be the major goal of higher education. Research on cognitive development supports the notion that the late adolescent and early adulthood periods are times when substantial refinements in thinking structures can occur. Through the early work of Harvey, Hunt and Schroder (1961), Perry (1970), and Piaget (1950), much of the "content" and "process" of cognitive development has been explored.

This scale attempts to account for the transformations that take place in terms of how an individual utilizes cognitive mechanism to process and interpret information, ideas, concepts, and knowledge. The development of this scale has been heavily influenced by the theoretical formulation of Perry (1970) and, to a lesser extent, the broader theories of Chickering (1969) and D. Heath (1977). In general, cognitive theorists postulate that cognitive development during the college years is characterized by increased complexity of thought in problem solving, reduction in utilization of biased data, finer differentiation and integration of conflicting stimuli, and better ability to distill, analyze, and synthesize data.

It is expected that students enter college at different places on this scale and progress at varying rates of acceleration, and that most students will make important advancement on this dimension. The academic, social, and problem-solving dilemmas that students encounter in college life force them to adopt new modes of thinking in order to deal with the diversity and complexities encountered. The challenges resident in the university environment are felt to play an important role in breaking an individual's homeostatic balance and propelling him/her toward more refined modes of thinking.

During the college years there are observable changes in how students cognitively process a variety of social, intellectual, and interpersonal events. For example, in the time period between the freshman and senior years, changes can often be observed in how students study for examinations. Whereas the amount of emphasis placed on learning and repeating the "truth" tends to decrease, the awareness of the need to be able to view something from several perspectives and to select a personally preferred interpretation tends to increase a student's progress toward graduation.

The *simplistic* position is considered to be the most basic cognitive style on the cognitive development scale. A student at this position views knowledge as absolute, uses available data poorly, and utilizes fewer variables in problem solving. This position is characterized by the dualism Perry (1970) describes, in which concepts and ideas are viewed as either right or wrong, good or bad, and so on. In addition, individuals who are characterized by this style of thinking are not easily able to tolerate people whose perspective on things is substantially different from their own.

The *relativistic* position is considered to be a more expansive phase of development in which the individual has adopted a more open and flexible style of relating to knowledge, ideas, and concepts. In the relativistic mode of thinking, many perspectives of an event or concept are considered valid, and holding steadfast to a specific interpretation becomes more difficult. Concepts and ideas are viewed as highly differentiated and not integrable, and therefore multiple perspectives prevail.

The *reflective* position is considered to be the highest form of development along this dimension. A person who shows reflective thought is capable of utilizing multiple perspectives in reflecting upon ideas or concepts and in synthesizing solutions to problems. Reflective thinking requires the ability to synthesize and manage disparate data and to take a personal stance with regard to those data.

### Aesthetic Dimension

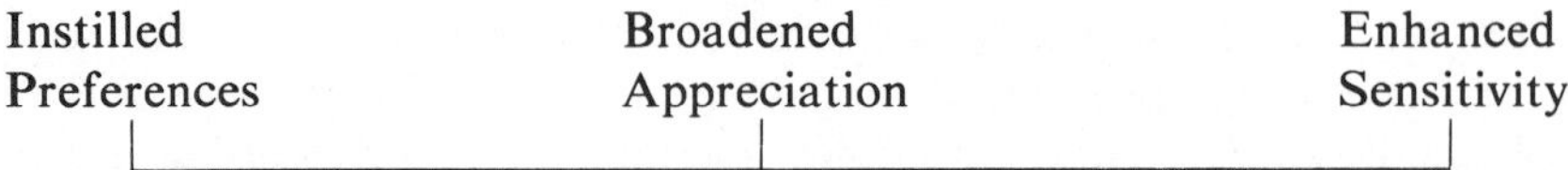


Aesthetic development has always been considered to be an important outcome of the college experience. College catalogs, academic administrators, faculty, and student affairs workers often state that important strides are made by students toward acquiring a more refined aesthetic appreciation during the college years. Student affairs personnel often provide a diverse array of programs, such as films, presentations, cultural events, and concerts, in an attempt both to provide entertainment and to spur aesthetic development.

Even though existing theories of student development do not deal specifically with aesthetic development, it is considered to be an important dimension of the model because of the importance attached to encouraging growth in this area. Although direct application of student development theory is not possible on this dimension, it is possible to infer that changes will be influenced by growth on the cognitive structures and identity formation scales.

Students enter at varying points along this scale; however, the desired progress of aesthetic development during a college career would be from *instilled preferences* at the start of college to *broadened appreciation*, and eventually toward acquiring an enhanced sensitivity to various forms of aesthetic beauty. Ideally, as students progress along the aesthetic dimension, they expand their cultural tastes from those of parents and friends (e.g., rock music and Hollywood films) by experimenting and trying out such things as modern dance, sculpture, and rodeo, and through this process develop the sensitivity and skill to experience beauty in a variety of forms and settings.

The *instilled preferences* position is considered to be the most basic aesthetic form of development. At this position, the students' tastes and judgments have been adopted from preferences held by their peer group, parents, and important others. They tend to find it difficult to explain or analyze why these preferences are held.

The *broadened appreciation* position is considered to be a more expansive phase of aesthetic development. In this phase, the students' aesthetic judgments and preferences are built less on imitation of others' tastes and more on the basis of personal experimentation in which they have sampled new cultural stimuli with both positive and negative reactions. Adoption of new preferences may be based on exposure to new or different forms of aesthetic expression and skills involved in various works of art and drama.

*Enhanced sensitivity* refers to an individual's increased desire to seek out and respond to a personalized image of beauty. Development of a specific set of aesthetic preferences is not viewed as being as important as building an appreciation for the intricacy and beauty present in a wide range of life events. A person who reaches the stage of enhanced sensitivity is not necessarily someone who has learned to like certain approved, classic works of art or drama. Heshe is someone capable of being sensitive to beauty regardless of its source and articulating the personal meaning or value derived.

## Identity Formation Dimension

Conforming — Experimental — Intentional

Identity confusion is often assumed to be a typical part of the late adolescent scene. Anyone working in the college setting can attest to the struggles students experience as they attempt to form a coherent self-image and provide meaningful stability to their daily life. Most theories of student development either directly or indirectly deal with the question of identity development. Most notable are those of Erikson (1959, 1968), Loevinger (1976), and Marcia (1966). Their ideas, along with the writing of Chickering (1969), Heath (1968, 1977), and Kohlberg (1969) provide guidelines for selection of the major transformations students often experience in the process of forging a personal identity.

This scale charts the transformations that take place as the individual employs a sense of self in negotiating everyday events and challenges. Clearly, most college environments present students with substantial diversity and require significantly more complex modes of responding than was previously necessary to satisfactorily accomplish daily responsibilities and/or handle crises. It does not seem to be a question of whether the college environment can present enough challenges to the student to provide stimulation toward achieving a sense of personal identity, but rather if it can offer the challenges within a supportive context. With students entering college at varying stages of identity formation, it is likely that the college environment will present a good blend of challenge and support for some students while seeming so threatening or overwhelming to others that they will retreat or avoid dealing with issues of identity.

The *conforming* position is considered to be the most basic identity formation position on the scale. According to this model, the *conforming* person defines his/her identity in terms of how successful he/she is at living withing the constraints of certain rules or externally verifiable criteria. The student tends to presume an absolute quality to his/her criteria and is apt either to display rigid behavior in attempting to conform to such criteria or to be in some turmoil about the mismatch between his/her behavior and the criteria. Students at this point may express feelings of being trapped by the limited options that their criteria allow and indicate great concern for how others evaluate them. They tend to be motivated by extrinsic rewards or punishment and may be suspicious and/or envious of others' nonconforming behavior. The identity question people at this position ask is, "Who am I supposed to be?," not, "Who am I?"

The *experimental* position represents a significant, qualitative departure from the conforming point on the scale. A student at the *experimental* position is less prone to rigidity or guilt, and is beginning to face the dilemmas of identity ambiguity. Such dilemmas might include (1) a lack of confidence about any system of self-referral, (2) inconsistency, (3) possibly some discouragement, and (4) a variety of coping devices which attempt to neutralize or counter growing doubts. The student's emerging self-image has many dimensions and is readily affected by the successes and failures of his/her experimental behavior. In addition, self-evaluation does not depend solely on external feedback, but on a growing understanding of what is personally satisfying. The identity question people ask at this position is, "Who do I happen to be?" Considerable ambivalence develops about what criteria could be employed to adequately embrace one's self-concept.

The *intentional* position is considered to be the highest position on this scale and represents the emergence of a personal definition of the self which is based on resolution of the identity questions, "Who am I?" and "Who can I become?" The resolution of these questions provides a sense of context and stability to the self. A person who has reached the intentional level of identity development has forged a more unified self-view than the experimental person and bases this new self on internal beliefs rather than societal expectations. The intentional person has confidence in his/her identity and the process through which that identity is built. Such enlightened confidence not only allows useful reflection about one's present state, but enhances clearer judgment of potentials for oneself. Reflections about the self are experienced less as intrusions that interrupt completion of daily tasks and functions, and more as a supportive process necessary for further refinements of identity.

**Physical Health Dimension**

| Unintentional Practices | Selective Management | Personal Responsibility |
| --- | --- | --- |

Physical health has been thought by many educators to be critically important to intellectual and affective development. Colleges have made provision for participation in physical education courses, encouraged involvement in intramural and varsity sports activities, supported efforts at increasing the awareness of the effects of drugs and alcohol, promoted awareness of the effects of stress on health, and in many other ways attempted to create a sense of respect and responsibility for physical health.

The college environment provides substantial opportunity for students to develop and increase an awareness of the importance of personal management of physical health. During the college years, observable changes often occur in (1) eating habits, (2) drug use and abuse, (3) exercise patterns, (4) sexual activity, and (5) relaxation and leisure activities. For example, an individual may eat only what is provided by the family until entrance into college. Upon entry there are few external restrictions concerning the source, type, and time of eating. Fad diets, binge eating, and poor nutrition, as well as concerns about body image, are factors that can lead to the development of a more internalized and personal sense of responsibility for physical needs.

This scale attempts to detect the changes and transformations that take place as the individual gradually acquires a more intentional involvement in the development of physically healthy patterns of living. The typical progress of development on the physical health scale tends to be from unintentional practices to selective management during the early college experience, and, in some cases, to personal responsibility. This does not imply an expectation that healthful behavior will be necessarily achieved. Rather, it hypothesizes that awareness and appreciation of the consequences of one's choice of behavior will increase.

The *unintentional practices* position is considered to be the most basic point on the physical health scale. A student at this position has largely incorporated the ideas of a few select others, particularly parents, about how to lead a healthy life. This position is characterized by behavior in terms of physical health as highly influenced by what others dictate. For individuals at this position on the scale few, if any, criteria for "wellness" guide their health practices.

The *selective management* position is considered to be the point at which an increased sense of internal management of healthful behaviors leads to a period of experimental activity in which the student tries new behaviors (which may be stimulated by real or imagined peer pressure) and loosens his/her reliance on habits incorporated from parents. Management of physical health is considered to be somewhat compartmentalized and selective, with increased recognition of the consequences of certain physical behavior limited to a fairly narrow range of physical health practices.

The *personal responsibility* position is considered to be reflective of the highest form of development on this scale. A person who evidences personal responsibility shows awareness and an understanding of the consequences of physically abusive practices, and is able to judge the short- and long-term effects, both positive and negative, of his/her actions. Such an individual assumes a sense of personal responsibility for healthful or nonhealthful behaviors.

### Moral Reasoning Dimension

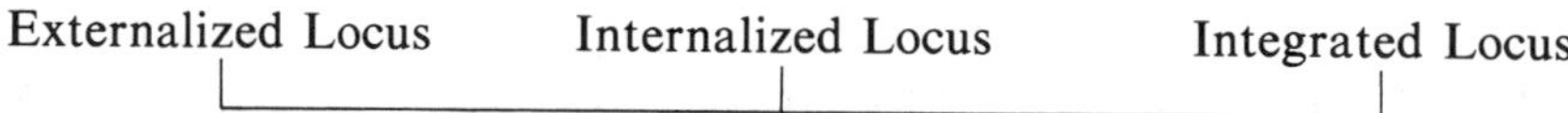


The college years are characterized as a time in which an individual is confronted with numerous moral dilemmas, ranging from those induced by academic demands to those posed by the social environment. The diversity inherent in the college environment provides a fertile ground for grappling with personal values, ethics, and beliefs. Often important shifts in moral reasoning occur during ths time (Kohlberg, 1969; Turiel, 1977).

This scale attempts to detect changes in moral reasoning that take place during the college years. The design of this scale has been influenced by the theoretical system developed by Kohlberg (1969) and by ideas expressed by D. Heath (1977) concerning the mature individual. In general, Kohlberg developed a six-stage, three-level theory to describe changes in moral reasoning. In this theory he indicated that (1) the stages are universal, (2) development through the stages is invariant, and (3) changes in moral reasoning level continue into adulthood.

It is expected that students (1) vary with regard to level of development of moral reasoning when they enter college, (2) progress at uneven rates, and (3) make significant advancements in this dimension. The content of various academic courses, living experiences of dormitory residency, the diversity of programs, and variety of life-styles will all help to encourage students to challenge their current belief system. Development on this scale is posited to move from the employment of exclusively externalized factors in moral reasoning to an almost exclusive utilization of internalized, self-centered considerations and, finally, to a mature reasoning process that accounts for and integrates both valid internal and external criteria.

The *externalized locus* position is considered to be the most basic style of moral reasoning on the scale. A student at this position employs almost exclusively external criteria and standards in making moral judgments. Decisions involving moral reasoning reflect a preoccupation with conformity, parental standards, societal trends, peer status, and loyalty. Within a person's childhood and adolescent milieu there often is a set of significant people who provide information defining right or wrong. This information is provided either through explicit instruction or implicit example. The person whose development is described by the externalized locus position is basing his/her moral reasoning or decisions on full acceptance of these instructions or examples.

The *internalized locus* position is considered to be a more expansive phase of moral development in which the individual has (1) shed reliance on external criteria in making moral decisions, (2) accepted the belief that moral decisions are "relative" in nature, (3) disowned previous standards of valuing and judging, and (4) employed the principle "I am the judge of what's best." The new criteria for moral reasoning are more personal and unsteady, and they involve substantial rejection of externalized authorities.

The *integrated locus* position is considered to be the highest form of development along the dimension. A person who has reached this stage of development is able to integrate personal experiences and opinions with external factors and to formulate an adaptable moral stance. This locus implies the development of an integrated set of beliefs that are based on a critical analysis of both internal and external factors.

**Interpersonal Relatedness Dimension**

Self-Centered Role-Dominated Intimate

Student development theorists often indicate that the late adolescence and young adulthood years are times when significant shifts occur in the ability to form meaningful interpersonal relationships. Chickering (1969) suggests that an important area of development for college students is the "freeing of interpersonal relationships" in which an increasing tolerance of individual differences leads to the possibility of more intimate forms of sharing and relating. D. Heath (1977) points out that the college years are a time when important strides are often made in developing more mature interpersonal relationships.

This scale attempts to account for transformations which take place in how college students interact with others (friends and acquaintances). The interpersonal relatedness scale describes the anticipated changes in the style of relating that students tend to experience as a result of frequent and sometimes intensive interactions with others. Specifically, the scale is designed so that changes in ability to enter relationships can be plotted as the student moves from a self-centered focus on his/her own needs to an awareness of the needs of others and, eventually, to a trusting, free, and open manner of interacting and relating.

Students enter college at different points on this scale, progress at widely differing rates, and often complete college before arriving at the highest developmental position on the scale. It is expected that the college years are marked by a movement from a egocentric, rather unconscious form of interacting with others, in which unknown aspects of the self guide relationships, toward a position dominated by increasing awareness of self, the avoidance of disapproval, and the seeking of confirmation by others. Finally, some students begin to develop relationships characterized by openness, trust, and mutual sharing without betrayal of principles central to the self in order to satisfy needs.

The *self-centered* position is considered to be the most basic interpersonal position on the scale. Students at this developmental position are characterized by egocentric focus on their own needs and interests, and their actions are usually structured to satisfy them. At this position there is very little awareness of the needs that motivate and compel various behaviors. This often leads to relationships with low trust levels and superficial openness.

The *role-dominated* position is characterized by an increased uncertainty about how one must behave in order to be viably connected with other people. Relationships at this stage of development are more concerned with "form" than "substance." The notion of permission and restriction (give-and-take or reciprocity) in interactions is recognized. Although interactions are still somewhat calculated experiences designed to meet basic internal needs for self-confirmation, the individual also attempts to fulfill what he/she believes to be valid external expectations.

The *intimate* position is considered to be the highest form of interpersonal development. It is reached when the student comes to appreciate the intrinsic value of reciprocity in relationships. A sense of commitment, autonomy, freedom, trust, openness, and self-awareness characterizes relationships. Mutual satisfaction is viewed as a likely outcome by people who share openly, nondefensively, freely, and warmly in interpersonal relationships.

**Social Perspective Dimension**

Ethnocentric Cultural Relativism Anthropocentric

College life seems to provide a supportive yet challenging environment in which an individual's cultural and social world view undergo modification. Through the curriculum, residential life experiences, and incidental learning situations, university communities tend to provide a basis for expansion and qualitative changes in social perspective. As colleges have become less homogeneous over the past two decades (more coeducational institutions, more cultural diversity and representation, broader ranges of learning styles, expanded curricular offerings, etc.), there is greater opportunity for reflecting on the adequacy and appropriateness of one's cultural perspective. Given a supportive atmosphere and opportunity for synthesis of new learnings, such challenges to one's equilibrium often lead to growth and development.

The social perspective scale attempts to detect shifts in how the student perceives, conceptualizes, and deals with a diverse, multiethnic world. It focuses on the extent to which a student's world view is embedded in his cultural origins. The individual may become fossilized in total identity with his/her ethnic models, or may develop the perspective to recognize that his/her cultural base, though valued, is not inherently better than any other person's cultural base.

On this scale, development is hypothesized to progress from ethnocentric through culturally relativistic to anthropocentric, as the individual's point of reference gains perspective through exposure, education, and input from all the other conceptual systems in the model. In the college setting, the development from ethnocentricity toward higher forms of social perspective is displayed as a willingness to participate in an appreciative way in other cultures and to socially accept and value people whose ethnic identity is dramatically different. In college, the culturally induced preconceptions are hypothesized to diminish because of the exposure to the more diversified environment. The first transformation is a willingness to discount preconceptions. The next step is an understanding that there are cultural differences, and that the differences are not just something to be tolerated, but actually appreciated and sought.

The *ethnocentric* position is considered to be the most basic point on the scale of social perspective. A student at this position believes his/her culture should be valued above all others, but has no rationale for that belief other than ancestral identifications and familiarity with that culture. The bias is learned from past experiences and is accepted without any real reflection. This also implies that people of all other cultures are inferior. The student has usually received strong reinforcement of his/her ethnocentricity from family, friends, and community and therefore has difficulty adopting another perspective or way of considering the actions, tastes, and preferences of others from different ethnic backgrounds.

The *culturally relativistic* position is considered to represent a transformation to a more empathic, enlightened perspective due to exposure to other cultures. When such exposure is guided and supported by the environment, the student can develop an experimental, investigative point of view and an increased tolerance of what has previously been alien cultures. At this position on the scale, a student is still embedded in his/her culture of origin. However, the student is able to learn about other cultures and is beginning to understand the whole concept of culture and its contributions to his/her personal identity. An increased tolerance for diversity and a decreased number of prejudices are characteristic of this level.

The *anthropocentric* position is considered to be the highest level of development along this dimension. At this position, the student recognizes that any culture is merely a relatively localized expression of those elements that are identified as human. In addition, he/she realizes that although people's languages, religions, customs, dress, and holidays differ from one culture to another, the most significant fact is that all people evidence a need for communication, spirituality, uniqueness, and celebration.

## SUMMARY

Indeed the student is the input variable in the education enterprise and college personnel are seeking to better understand the growth students experience. The desire to have more complete awareness of the developmental changes students make resulted in an upsurge of interest in developmental findings. Specifically, a search for relevant theories that could provide context for the myriad of developmental changes that occur in late adolescence and early adulthood was initiated.

This chapter examines some of the issues and problems involved in establishing linkages between developmental principles and educational interventions. One major problem confronting educators seeking to explain or catalyze developmental changes is the sheer number and diversity of developmental theories. To help reduce some of the confusion generated by the large number of theories, a four-part system for categorizing them is presented. A second serious problem is encountered when educators attempt to locate a clear, concise definition of development. Surprisingly, few theorists present a terse, thorough definition of either the outcomes of development or the process by which growth occurs. Although it is true that one can construct such definitions by distilling the central developmental principles of a given theorist, it would be helpful if each theorist clearly spelled out the process and outcomes of developmental change. Another major difficulty for educators desiring to understand the magnitude of growth during the college years is the rather limited focus of many developmental theorists. Theorists tend to limit their attention to inspection of the change process of a given aspect of development. Thus there are theorists whose total focus is explaining how either cognitive, ego, moral, physical, social, interpersonal, or some other dimension of growth occurs. Few theorists attempt to explain development from an organismic perspective which would allow readers to understand how various dimensions of development interact.

The final section of this chapter describes a seven-dimensional model entitled "Student Development—Some Models and Dimensions." This model is constructed from the theoretical propositions and findings of a host of prominent developmental theorists. The basic developmental assumptions are identified, a definition of development is presented, and each of the seven dimensions of the model is explained. The seven dimensions are arranged within the format of a model so that change within a particular area can be studied relative to change in other areas. The model is experimental and is being tested through Project Synergy, an intentional development program for underclassmen at the University of Rhode Island. Clearly, it is just *a* model and not an attempt to find *the* model of student development.

This chapter should serve to point out that there is a lot of interesting and exciting theorizing and research being conducted in the area of student development. Though much has been done we are still only at the beginning of understanding and explaining both the process of growth and the interaction among the various dimensions of development.

## REFERENCES


Chickering, A. *Education and Identity*. San Francisco: Jossey-Bass, 1969.

Drum, D. J. Dimension of student development. Keynote address, *Student Development Conference*, University of Connecticut, Storrs, Conn., February 1977.

Erikson, E. *Identity and the Life Cycle*. Psychological Issues Monograph. New York: International Universities Press, 1959.

Erikson, E. *Childhood and Society* (2nd ed.). New York: W. W. Norton, 1963.

Erikson, E. H. *Identity: Youth and Crisis*. New York: W. W. Norton, 1968.

Freud, S. The Psychopathology of everyday life. In A. A. Brill (Transl. and Ed.), *The Basic Writings of Sigmund Freud*. New York: Modern Library, 1938.

Gould, R. The phases of adult life: a study in developmental psychology. *American Journal of Psychiatry*, 1972, **129**, 521–531.

Harvey, D. J., D. E. Hunt, and H. M. Schroder, *Conceptual Systems and Personality Organization*. New York: John Wiley & Sons, 1961.

Havighurst, R. J. *Developmental Tasks and Education*. New York: Longman's, 1952.

Heath, D. *Growing up in College*. San Francisco: Jossey-Bass, 1968,

Heath, D. *Maturity and Competence: A Transcultural View*. New York: Gardner Press, 1977.

Heath, R. *The Reasonable Adventurer*. Pittsburgh: University of Pittsburgh Press, 1964.

Heath, R. Form, flow and full-being. *The Counseling Psychologist*, 1973, **4**, 56–63.

Knefelkamp, L., C. Widick, and C. A. Parker *Applying New Developmental Findings*. San Francisco: Jossey-Bass, 1978.

Kohlberg, L. *Stage and Sequence: the Cognitive–Developmental Approach to Socialization Theory and Research*. Chicago: Rand McNally, 1969.

Levinson, D. et al. *The Seasons of a Man's Life*. New York: Alfred A. Knopf, 1978.

Loevinger, J. *Ego Development: Conceptions and Theories*. San Francisco: Jossey-Bass, 1976.

Marcia, J. Development and validation of ego-identity status. *Journal of Personality and Social Psychology*, 1966, **3**, 551–559.

Miller, T. K. and J. S. Prince *The Future of Student Affairs*. San Francisco: Jossey-Bass, 1976.

Perry. W., Jr. *Forms of Intellectual and Ethical Development in the College Years*. New York: Holt, Reinhart and Winston, 1970.

Piaget, J. *The Psychology of Intelligence*. New York: Harcourt, 1950.

Piaget, J. *Judgment and Reasoning in the Child*. Paterson, N.J.: Littlefield Adams, 1964.

Sanford, N. *The American College*. New York: John Wiley & Sons, 1962.

Sheehy, G. *Passages*. New York: E. P. Dutton, 1974.

Skinner, B. F. *Science and Human Behavior*. New York: Macmillan, 1953.

Skinner, B. F. Behaviorism at fifty. *Science*, 1963, **140**, 951–958.

Turiel, E. Conflict and transition in adolescent moral development. *Child Development*, 1974, **45** (1), 14.

Turiel, E. Conflict and transition in adolescent moral development, II: the resolution of disequilibrium through structured reorganization. *Child Development*, 1977, **48**, 634–637.

# 3
# Conceptions of the Campus Environment

JAMES H. BANNING AND
DONNA L. McKINLEY

The environment is a potent determinant of human behavior. Few will take issue with this declaration. Despite the strong support for this position and the overwhelming evidence from our everyday personal experiences, it has been only recently that attention has been given to the importance of the campus environment in promoting the development of college students. Understanding this emerging interest in the campus environment can be enhanced by tracing the history of this new interest, by seeking ways to conceptualize the campus environment, and by exploring an application of a specific conceptual system to the everyday working environment of the student development professional.

## THE CAMPUS ENVIRONMENT AND STUDENT DEVELOPMENT

It has been only recently that attention has been paid to the importance of the campus environment in promoting development of college students. Banning and Kaiser (1974) suggest possible explanations for this lack of attention. These authors suggest that the traditional perspectives that guided the work of student services included an overemphasis on individual students and their intrapersonal and interpersonal development. As a result of this emphasis, little attention was given to the environment.

The influence of the concept of in loco parentis on the field of student personnel has contributed in part to the lack of attention to the campus environment. Banning (1975) noted that parents seldom look upon their children as being part of a community or an ecology, but are more likely to see them as individuals.

An additional factor contributing to the focus on the individual student has been the reliance of student affairs personnel on counseling psychology. Until recently the counseling psychologist was primarily interested only in the individual. Parker (1974) reports that in 1957 the editor of the *Journal of Counseling Psychology* rejected an article on group counseling because counseling at that time was being defined only as a two-person process, not as a group process.

In addition, an important part of the counseling influence was the notion of viewing students as clients. Seeing students as clients became basic to many of the programs in student services. In several of the traditional student services departments students are actually referred to as clients. Certainly this view is benevolent, and such a perspective is not inherently evil; in fact, much good can come from it for the student. One should, however, be aware of some associated tendencies that can result from this viewpoint. For example, when students are viewed as clients, it becomes easier to see them as ill or deficient in some manner. This focus turns our attention away from the environment and the transactional relationship between the student *and* his/her environment. When students are seen as clients, rarely are environments seen as ill and in need of treatment. When students are viewed as clients, our approach becomes passive and students come to our attention only when a problem develops and becomes symptomatic. At such time our attention is again turned away from understanding the causative role of the environment.

Despite the emphasis on promoting student development by direct intervention with the individual, the concern for the role of the environment historically has not been totally neglected. Pace and Stern (1958) developed the College Characteristic Index as a tool to study campus environments. Also of note are the writings of Astin and Holland (1961) and Astin (1965, 1968). Of particular importance in the history of the study of the college environment is the work of Feldman and Newcomb (1969). These authors point out the impact that campus environments can have on student development.

Recently a number of people have focused on the environment as a potent force in student development. Morrill, Oetting, and Hurst (1974) presented the notion of counseling dimensions that included full recognition of the environment as a target for intervention. Banning and Kaiser (1974) provided a systematic way through the "ecosystem model" to look at student development from an ecology perspective. The management of the environment to promote student development is suggested as a role for student affairs workers by Miller and Prince (1976). Campus ecology as a perspective for student affairs and its management as the purpose of student affairs is suggested by Banning (1978, 1980). Throughout their publication on student services, Delworth and Hansen (1980) give strong support to the importance of the environment. Parker (1978), in his work on encouraging development in college students, indicates one of the continuing issues in developmental psychology is the role the environment plays in development. Within his work this issue is addressed by Delworth and Piel (1978), who stress the need for taking an interactive perspective toward the student and the environment.

Despite the recent progress that has occurred both in terms of the interest in the environment and the number of publications focusing on this concern, a major roadblock to further advancement lies in the difficulty of conceptualizing the environment. Ways are needed to conceptualize the campus environment so that both the theorist and the practitioner can understand and use the potential for student development that lies within the environment.

## WAYS TO CONCEPTUALIZE THE CAMPUS ENVIRONMENT

The campus environment has been defined as consisting of all the stimuli that impinge upon the student's sensory modalities, and includes physical, chemical, biologic, and social stimuli (WICHE, 1973). This definition is helpful in that it underlines the encompassing nature of the concept of environment, but it does not provide a framework from which to build a conceptualization of the campus environment. Unlike our approach to the student as a personality, we have not yet developed concepts such as attitudes, values, traits, and theoretical conceptions that weave these elements into student development theory. Sells (1966) speaks to this issue as a taxonomy problem. We do not have an established taxonomy for the environment in general; certainly one does not exist for the campus environment. There are, however, a number of approaches or conceptualizations of environments that have applicability to the campus environment. In particular the work of Moos and Insel (1974) can easily be applied to the campus setting.

Moos (1974) has pioneered much of the activity in attempting to develop a classification of human environments. He suggests that the study could be organized around six dimensions: (1) the ecological dimensions of geographic and meteorological variables along with the architectural and physical design variables; (2) behavior settings; (3) dimensions of organizational structure; (4) personal and behavioral characteristics of the milieu inhabitants; (5) psychosocial characteristics and organizational climate; and (6) functional or reinforcement analyses of environments. The application of these dimensions to the campus environment would be one way to conceptualize the campus environment.

Moos's ecological dimensions include meteorological, geographic, and physical design variables. Evidence of the importance of weather and climate has long been a part of the knowledge accumulated by student affairs personnel. For example, when the opening of school was pushed forward to mid-August the college campuses in the humid Midwest and Southwest saw thousands of students pour out of non-air-conditioned dorms to find relief from the heat. Once they had gathered in large numbers and under the influence of the irritation from the heat, all kinds of prankish behavior occurred. Similar behavior is seen again at the time of the first warm spring day following a harsh winter.

Weather has always been an intervention tool for student affairs personnel, or at least a "wished-for" tool. During the demonstrations of the late 1960s and early 1970s and also today when large masses of students gather to protest, rain is usually wished for in the hope that the momentum of the crowd will be dampened. Though far more will admit to weather conditions being a causative factor than will admit to the desirability of uncertain weather as an intervention methodology, few in the student affairs field can deny having had the "let's hope for rain" experience. The common experience of the relationship between behavior and weather is confirmed by Moos (1974), who reports research studies that show a strong positive relationship between mean daily temperature and gross national product per capita across several nations. He also notes the Berke and Wilson (1951) study, as support for the often-observed relationship between heat and general rebellions, poor personal performance, poor health, increased admissions to mental hospitals, and increased suicide rates. Indeed, the meteorological variables of our environment are potent influences on our behavior and on student behavior on campus.

The potency of geographic variables associated with the environment are likewise easily observable. Even our speech patterns and styles reflect the geographic region of our developing years. Many other personal behavioral traits reflect the geography of our heritage, such as clothing styles and food preferences. The influence of geography can also be observed on our campuses. Residence halls develop certain images, and identifiable behavioral patterns emerge based on geography. Often the least desirable residence hall is the one most distant from the center of campus. As a result it is often the last to be occupied and usually then by the latecomers, who may, in fact, be less committed to coming to campus. This interactive effect often leads these geographically less desirable halls to produce greater turnover rates, higher damage and maintenance costs, and lower academic performances of the residents. The observation that the geography of the academic buildings, in terms of their location and distance from each other, will determine a student's course of study is commonplace. In fact, on some campuses the geography absolutely prevents certain combinations of classes. The geography of the environment, indeed, does influence our behavior and can be observed as being a critical influence in student behavior on campus.

The physical variables in our environment, like the meteorological and geographic, are extremely potent factors. Again, our common experiences support this assertion. We all have felt the influence of the buildings and rooms we work in, the houses we live in, and other physical design features of our habitats. The architectural and physical design features of our environment have been subjected to considerable research; this is particularly true of the residence halls on our campuses. Heilweil (1973) points out that much of the lack of privacy and opportunities for solitude are major reasons for student dissatisfaction. The relationship between different types of housing on student development and specific problem areas for students is suggested by the work of Sauber (1972). Schroeder and Freesh (1977) point out the importance of physical space and territoriality in promoting student development. Numerous other research studies could be cited, but the potency of the physical environment is well established.

The concept of behavior setting is likewise applicable to the campus environment. Through his observational study of natural environments Barker (1968) developed the concept of behavior setting to denote settings that exist in environments that select and shape the behavior of individuals who inhabit them. Murrell (1973), in his summary of Barker's findings, indicates a behavior setting has behavioral prescriptions associated with it from a number of possible sources, including history, expectations, formal rules, norms, and the constraints of physical structure. These behavioral prescriptions influence the behavior of persons who inhabit the setting and are independent of the personality of the inhabitant. The behavior in the setting persists even when the inhabitants are different. Barker studied many settings, including drugstores, churches, clubs, and schools. Out of these studies came the finding that there is an optimal number of individuals per particular setting. If the setting is overpopulated, the individuals tend to be less active in general and involved in fewer activities. Individuals in the underpopulated settings appeared to be more satisfied, to be more likely to participate voluntarily, and to find the experience more meaningful.

The application of the behavior setting to the campus environment is quite apparent. Behavior settings do exist on campus. Classrooms, dormitory rooms, student government meetings, student activities, and traffic patterns are but a few examples. These settings can vary in terms of how they produce and enhance behavioral characteristics of student development. For example, many campuses, out of tradition and perhaps the lack of alternative programming, suffer each spring through events known as "Springfest" or "College Daze." These are behavior settings, and the same general rowdiness and alcohol abuse appear each year despite an ever-changing student body. Little activity within these settings can be seen as pushing student behavior along developmental directions such as those suggested by Chickering (1969). On the other hand, the setting of student government has high potential as an aid to student development.

A further application of Barker's work to the campus environment relates to the notion of over- and underpopulated settings. The translation of this finding to the campus environment was noted by Feldman and Newcomb (1969) when they built on Barker and Gump's (1964) concept of redundancy. Redundancy occurs when the number of persons for a given activity or setting is greater than the opportunities for active participation and satisfying experiences. Feldman and Newcomb (1969, p. 147) give the following illustrations:

> . . . like when the best man joins the honeymooners. When persons are superfluous because of excessive numbers redundancy exists; if three runners end up on second base, two are redundant. Redundancy is one person driving from behind the wheel and another from the back seat, three persons to change the tire. . . . It's ten hunters per acre in Vermont, one thousand per golf course in the suburbs, ten thousand per Central Park in the city,

The authors go on to raise questions about redundancy and institutional size and hypothesize that as redundancy increases, progress along several of the student development vectors decreases.

Student personnel professionals have also recognized the problem of redundancy. For example, on many campuses the number of leadership roles is quite limited, and the task of the professional becomes that of creating additional opportunities. Often the clearest advantage in having a large Greek system on campus is that it creates many opportunities for leadership and reduces the problem of redundancy. The concept of behavior setting and the research methodology and findings associated with it have high applicability to the campus setting.

Moos's (1974) dimension of organizational structure referring to such variables as size, staffing ratios, average salary levels, and organizational control structure is also applicable to the campus environment.

March's (1975) discussion of growth and nongrowth environments and the impact of these conditions on organizational structure has particular relevance to the campus environment. He points out that firms in a growth industry, bureaucracies in a growth government, and universities in an expansion period all have similar characteristics that affect the organizational structure. The organizations during a growth period are seen as young, and people move up the organizational structure rather quickly. With the abundant resources that accompany a growth period little conflict is expected between intraorganizational structures over budget matters. Funds also are readily available to hire specialists. These features combine to make for a confident organization with high morale. Within the campus setting these conditions were most evident during the early and mid-1960s. Even student affairs experienced expansion and specialization. To the degree that such expansions lead to increased programming, student development can be seen as being affected by organizational structure and economic prosperity.

With the slowing of growth and the onset of the actual decline of resources, the foregoing characteristics began to shift in opposite directions. The organizational structure has few openings, and people are less likely to be promoted within the structure. The organization ages.

Lack of resources brings on conflicts between departmental structures. More generalized roles for the personnel result; consequently, confidence is lost and morale goes down. Low morale of student affairs personnel may lead to a similar condition in the students they serve. Even if inappropriate, such infectional spread of low morale is difficult to control. Again in a very real way economic and organizational conditions can directly affect the development of students.

Another example of this dimension can often be found in student government structure. As the student government structure becomes more organized and centralized, its impact may be greater on the institution. However, often the centralization can lead to greater use of the executive branch's ability to appoint students to positions, and less representation through the elective process occurs. The nature and form of student government certainly has a direct effect on campus issues, activities that receive funding support, and general relationships to faculty and administrators. Again, these environmental conditions have an impact on student behavior.

Environments can also be defined by the personal and behavioral characteristics of the inhabitants of the environment (Moos, 1974). The potency of this characteristic is quite obvious. At times we note that the group around us is different in age or ethnic background, and we become uncomfortable. Some "social climates" do not seem to fit, and we feel a need to search out more compatible environments. In some cases we attempt to make the adjustment ourselves in order to fit in better with existing environments. Much of our day-to-day behavior is influenced and determined by our social environment.

Examples of the campus's social environmental influence on students are numerous, but one dramatic illustration is provided in the study by Brown (1968), in which floor assignments in the residence hall were made on the basis of academic major. Students whose majors were not the same as those of the majority of the floor students were found inclined to change toward the majority major. The social interaction proved to be a potent factor in the student's feelings about their goals. Another example is the impact that coed dorms have on residents' behavior; namely, that coed dorms have more activities and programs, have more contact with faculty, have more interactions with the opposite sex, and seem to be more satisfied with their residence experiences than are their counterparts in single sex dorms. Again, the social make-up of the inhabitants of the environment influences behavior.

The psychosocial characteristics and organizational climate of different environments are also considered by Moos (1974) to be an important conceptual dimension in the classification of environments. Again the applicability to the campus setting is quite evident. For example, in discussing conditions for impacting on the development of students, Chickering (1969) points out the importance of organizational variables such as organizational climate (clarity and consistency of objectives). He hypothesizes that impact increases as institutional objectives are formulated clearly and taken seriously and as the diverse elements of the campus and its programs are consistent with the overall institutional objectives. The previous discussion of growth and nongrowth conditions also set up and influence organizational climate in terms of the level of morale. Chickering (1969) also suggests that if the organizational climate as it relates to student–faculty interaction is healthy, then the development of intellectual competence, sense of competence, autonomy, and purpose are fostered.

The work of Pervin (1968) suggests campus environments can be defined by the psychosocial characteristics attributed to it through the perceptions of its inhabitants. According to the degree to which these perceptions of the environment match or fit the perceptions the individual has of him/herself, the individual student will tend to have higher performance and more satisfaction. As the discrepancy between student and environment increases, lower performance and less satisfaction is predicted. The notion of a psychosocial fit between environment and person is also important to other interactionist theorists (Holland, 1966; Stern, 1970; Clark and Trow, 1966; and Blocher, 1974.)

Moos's (1974) final dimension which has applicability to the campus setting is the functional or reinforcement analysis of environments. This dimension is based on the social learning premise that one's behavior is primarily due to the reinforcement consequences associated with the behavior. As stated by Moos (1974, p 20), "people learn what to do in different settings through usual learning processes, i.e., classical conditioning, instrumental conditioning or trial and error learning, and observational learning or modeling." In relation to the campus environment, the question becomes: What are the reinforcement contingencies for student behaviors? Does the institution reward behavior that is in concert with student development? For example, many times within the classroom setting questioning the instructor's position is not rewarded. The reward system is too often set up to benefit the nonchallenging and nonassertive student. Students often report reward structures that communicate, "Be on time, be quiet, and parrot back," Certainly a reward structure that supports behavior of this nature is not in concert with educational/student development goals.

Campus drinking behavior provides another example where utilizing the reinforcement analysis leads to curious findings. On many campuses where the drinking age is set as 21 by the state, there are no provisions for the use of alcohol on campus. Drinking alcoholic beverages is prohibited in student unions, residence halls, and at university functions. Given this policy and the difficulty of enforcing it for large groups, the following reinforcement pattern is set up. If a student wishes to use alcohol in a responsible social manner, that is, having alcohol with a meal in the student center or residence hall, the campus police will be called and the student will be faced with a discipline situation. If, on the other hand, the student chooses to drink in an irresponsible manner, that is, becoming drunk at a football game or outdoor concert, that behavior is not punished and is tolerated. What becomes obvious by this example is that we can and often do set up environments on campus whereby we reward irresponsible behavior and punish responsible behavior. When such patterns emerge as the institution's reinforcement pattern, then there is a good reason to expect the undesirable behavior we often see on the college campus.

Other examples could be used as illustrations. There are many, but the obvious conclusion is that the functional or reinforcement analysis of campus environments is extremely useful in determining the casual patterns of student behavior as well as serving as an important consideration in program development to encourage student development.

A number of other writers have also suggested ways to conceptualize environments. Rappaport (1977), writing from the perspective of community psychology, discusses the need for conceptions of environments and systems. He poses the ecological paradigm as a conceptual alternative to the traditional person-focused conceptions. He states that our efforts must begin with an observation of environments rather than of persons, and those observations may be of the physical environment or of indivual perceptions of the environment or of the system properties of environments that are outside the person variable. From this framework, Rappaport, building on the work of Moos (1974), suggests eight approaches: (1) identification of reinforcement contingencies in the environment; (2) viewing the environment as a function of aggregate person characteristics; (3) an organizational psychology approach focusing on strategies and tactics of environmental intervention; (4) an environmental assessment approach which involves the measurement of the geographic, physical, and architectural environment; (5) behavior setting approach building on the work of Barker (1968); (6) measurement of the organizational climate variable through the perceptions of participants and observers; (7) a general systems approach focusing on the systematic properties of the environment; and (8) a social ecology approach. Again, the applicability of these approaches to the campus environment is quite evident.

Walsh (1978) also suggests several approaches to the person–environment interaction that are particularly applicable to the college campus environment. He chooses six approaches based on the ability to make possible some sensible predictions concerning the outcome of person–environment relationships. Based on this premise, the following approaches to the environment are discussed by Walsh (1978): (1) Barker's (1968) theory of behavior settings; (2) the subculture approach (Clark and Trow, 1966); (3) Holland's (1973) theory of personality types and model environments; (4) Stern's (1970) need $\times$ press $=$ culture theory; (5) Moos's (1973, 1974) social climate dimensions; and (6) Pervin's (1968) transactional approach. The application of each of these approaches to the campus setting is particularly useful in enhancing our understanding of the interactions between students and their campus environment.

Still another approach to the conceptualization of the environment is Steele's work on physical settings and organizational development (1973), which provides a conceptualization for the functions of the physical environment. Steele's approach includes looking at the six functions that can be measured relative to the physical environment. These are (1) security and shelter, (2) social contact, (3) symbolic identification, (4) task instrumentality, (5) pleasure, and (6) growth. Elements within the environment can be assessed in relationship to each of these functions. For example, the lighting system in an environment may produce certain levels of security in addition to its relationship to the task it performs.

The application of Steele's work to the college campus is particularly useful in understanding problems associated with physical structures. For example, two students at the University of Missouri–Columbia utilized Steele's approach to formulate a response to a facility security problem (Barton and Rau, 1979). The campus's former field house was converted to a free play and intramural athletic facility. As the popularity of the facility grew with the student body, the field house also became attractive to the nonuniversity community population. Two specific problems of security arose: (1) the number of noneligible participants grew to the point that eligible members of the university community could not find available space; and (2) the number of locker thefts and unauthorized entries into the women's locker areas by nonelegible persons grew. The university's administrative response included increased security through the assignment of additional personnel, a tightening up of identification checks, and the posting of signs that unauthorized personnel would be prosecuted for trespassing. Although these measures were helpful and certainly confirmed the university's concern, they did not give special attention to the facility's unique physical environment.

Barton and Rau's approach was to apply Steele's (1973) conceptual framework to study the physical environment of the field house in relation to security. From their analysis they found six sets of double exit doors surrounding the main floor area. These doors were necessary as fire exits when the building was used as a basketball field house. It became apparent that many noneligible users of the facility gained access through these doors by simply knocking loudly and being let in by someone within the facility. The doors were locked from the outside but could be opened by a kick-bar lock release from the inside, an arrangement necessary for use as a fire exit. The simple solution of permanently locking the door was not acceptable to the fire marshal. Barton and Rau's (1979, p. 8) recommended solution was as follows:

> In order to guarantee security of the floor area we propose the following: maintain existing locking systems on the doors but augment them with an alarm device so that when they are opened for other than managerially-approved purposes an audible signal would sound requiring the attention of a facility employee to turn if off. Thus through peer pressure and a Skinnerian series of conditioning it would eventually deter unauthorized use of the door.

This approach takes into account both the unique physical properties of the environment and the people inhabiting it.

Perhaps the conceptualization of environment that contributes most to understanding the relationship of campus environment to student development is the work of Blocher (1974, 1978). Blocher (1974) combines the concept of life stage tasks with that of psychological needs to propose an ecological model of student development. The underlying assumption is that a sort of "ecological balance" or "dynamic equilibrium" between task demands and "psychological nutrients" is most conducive to growth (p. 362).

Blocher identifies three basic subsystems for the purpose of analyzing a given ecological system. The first is the "opportunity structure," which refers to the problems or situations available in the environment that stimulate the individual to address a particular developmental task. The "support structure" is the configuration of resources available to the individual for coping with stress. Those resources are both affective (supportive relationships) and cognitive (tools for understanding stress). Finally, the "reward structure" defines the reinforcers for effort expended.

Banning (1980) has translated Blocher's ecological model into a "Management Template for Campus Ecology," which is presented in Figure 1. The template provides a tool for mapping a campus environment along the dimensions of opportunity, support, and reward structures relative to a goal of the educational institution. Using Chickering's (1969) developmental vectors as desired student development outcomes, Figure 1 illustrates the template. As an example of its use, Figure 2 shows a possible entry for one developmental task.

Blocher (1978) further elaborated his ecological model by proposing a set of core conditions for fostering learning and student development. The conditions proposed by Blocher (1978, pp. 20–21) are the following:

**1** The learner actively engages the learning environment in a way that puts at risk significant psychological values as self-esteem, approval of significant others, or important aspects of existing self-concept. This is the condition of *involvement*.

**2** The learner is in a condition of mild disequilibrium or tension. A moderate degree of discrepancy exists between the learner's present coping behavior or cognitive structures and those demanded by the tasks of stimulation present in the learning environment. Generally the levels of stimulation in a learning environment are measurable in terms of variables such as novelty, complexity, obstructions, ambiguity, and intensity. At any rate, an *optimal mismatch* should exist between the learner and the requirements for mastery of those

| Developmental Vector | Ecology Structure | | |
|---|---|---|---|
| | Opportunities | Support | Reward |
| Achieving competence | | | |
| Managing emotions | | | |
| Becoming autonomous | | | |
| Establishing identity | | | |
| Freeing interpersonal relationships | | | |
| Clarifying purposes | | | |
| Developing integrity | | | |

**Figure 1** A management template for campus ecology.

| Developmental Vector | Ecology Structure | | |
|---|---|---|---|
| | Opportunities | Supports | Rewards |
| Managing emotions | Residence hall living | Student assistants<br>Conflict resolution workshops | Increased self-respect<br>More funds from damage deposits available for floor decorating |

**Figure 2** Illustrative management template item.

aspects of the learning environment that lead to instrinsic rewards such as feelings of competence and control. This is the condition of *challenge*.

3 The learner experiences a degree of empathy, caring, and honesty from other human beings in the learning environment. That is, the learner is touched by a network of positive human relationships. This is the condition of *support*.

4 The learner has available examples of functioning of performance slightly more advanced than his or her own and is able to observe these performances, see that they can resolve the task demands in the learning environment, and witness that they are rewarded. In the moral development research literature this is sometimes called "plus one modeling." It is termed here the condition of *structure*.

5 The learner has opportunities to practice the use of new cognitive structures and their related skills, and to receive clear, accurate, and

immediate information about his or her performance relative to the demands of the environment. This is termed the condition of *feedback.*

6 The learner is able to test actively new concepts, attitudes, and skills in a variety of natural settings and situations in which opportunities for improved relationships, problem solving, decision making, or appreciation can be directly experienced. This is the condition of *application.*

7 Finally, the learner is able to review, critically examine, and evaluate new learnings in a safe, reflective, and unhurried atmosphere in which the new learning can be reconciled and assimilated with past experiences. This is the condition of *integration.*

Blocher goes on to relate these seven conditions for growth to the subsystems of the environment: (1) the opportunity subsystem relates to the conditions of involvement, challenge, and integration; (2) the support subsystem can provide the essential conditions of structure and support; and (3) the reward subsystem provides the conditions of feedback and application.

The core learning conditions add an evaluative dimension to environmental mapping. As illustrated in Figure 2, the management template for campus ecology provides for a structural analysis of the environment relative to a key developmental task. It is possible to use the conditions for growth to make a more refined assessment of the degree to which the subsystems of opportunities, supports, and rewards are likely to facilitate maximum growth on a given developmental task. In Figure 3, a work sheet for this purpose is shown. The usefulness of these conditions for campus design is also apparent.

For purposes of illustration let us assume that "choosing a lifework" is the developmental task of interest. The first step from a campus ecology perspective is to identify all the resources in the environment (opportunities) that can impact on the development of students on this dimension. Remaining nonevaluative at this stage is useful. The task is to generate all the possible opportunities to impact on career development without regard to whether the possible opportunities are currently being used to their maximum potential. Answering the specific questions regarding the important conditions for student development provides the evaluative dimension as well as a stimulus for environmental redesign.

With regard to career development opportunities, vocational counseling and placement services will probably come to mind immediately. Certainly, the classroom, library, and academic advising would be add-

**Developmental task:** ______________________________

| Environmental resources | Core conditions: Involvement | Challenge | Support | Structure | Feedback | Application | Integration |
|---|---|---|---|---|---|---|---|
| | | | | | | | |
| | | | | | | | |
| | | | | | | | |
| | | | | | | | |
| | | | | | | | |
| | | | | | | | |

**Figure 3** Work sheet for campus ecology.

ed. Field placement, cooperative education, and work-study employment are typically available to some degree. The alumni(ae) office, campus speakers' program, peer advising, student government, and student activities also have potential for impact.

The next step is to assess the degree to which these opportunities are or can be used to provide the core conditions for student development. If, for example, counselors use a "test 'em and tell 'em" approach to vocational counseling, the condition of involvement is likely to be minimally met. On the other hand, a career development program that teaches self-assessment and career investigation skills incorporates conditions of involvement and challenge. Academic advising, when it is seen as a mentoring process, contributes to integration of new with past learnings.

Role models of various types provide the condition of having examples of advanced fucntioning or "structure" as defined by Blocher (1978). Successful alumni(ae), campus speakers, and faculty and staff members are often willing to talk with students who are considering a major in their fields. Having advanced students serve as peer advisors can be impactful, especially when there are common special factors involved such as race, sex, disability, age, or first-generation college student status.

Field placement, summer employment, work-study jobs, and student activities involvement are opportunities that can provide conditions of application and feedback when the student is helped to select an activity or job that is related to a possible major. The prospect of testing oneself in a possible lifework provides challenge and involvement also.

As is apparent from these few examples related to the one developmental task of choosing a lifework, Blocher's (1974, 1978) approach has much potential. The environment could be similarly mapped for each developmental vector or task in terms of opportunities available and the degree to which core learning conditions are provided. The resulting assessment can be a potent stimulus for environmental redesign.

## CONCLUDING OBSERVATIONS

The environment in all its complexity has tremendous impact on human behavior. To deny this impact is to discount some very common everyday experiences as well as a growing body of supportive research. To limit our attempt to understand behavior only to the person, or our understanding of campus behavior to students, is shortsighted and reflective of past trends. Bloom (1977) suggests that in fact the upper limit on the ability to predict human behavior solely on the basis of personal characteristics is relatively low. He suggests that person-only conceptualizations leave perhaps three-quarters of the variation in human behavior unexplained.

There are numerous ways to approach the conceptualization of the environment which have direct application to the campus. Although the approaches presented are not exhaustive, they do provide a "sample" of recent thinking and approaches. Increased application and utilization of these approaches should lead not only to a better understanding of the environment but also to an understanding of the role of the environment in fostering student growth and development.

## REFERENCES


Astin, A. W. Effect of different college environments on the vocational choice of high aptitude students. *Journal of Counseling Psychology*, 1965, **12**, 28–34.

Astin, A. W. *The College Environment*. Washington, D. C.: American Council on Education, 1968.

Astin, A. W. and J. L. Holland The environmental assessment technique: a way to measure college environments. *Journal of Educational Psychology*, 1961, **52**, 313–316.

Banning, J. H. Improving mental health services on western campuses: a regional action program. In B. L. Bloom (Ed.), *Psychological Stress in the Campus Community: Theory, Research, and Action*. New York: Behavioral Publications, 1975.

Banning, J. H. (Ed.). *Campus Ecology: A Perspective for Student Affairs*. National Association of Student Personnel Administrators Monograph, 1978.

Banning, J. H. Management of the campus ecology. In U. Delworth and G. Hanson (Eds.), *A Handbook for Student Services*. San Francisco: Jossey-Bass, 1980.

Banning, J. H. and L. Kaiser An ecological perspective and model for campus design. *Personnel and Guidance Journal*, 1974, **52**, 370–375.

Barker, R. G. *Ecological Psychology: Concepts and methods for studying the environment of human behavior*. Stanford, Calif.: Stanford University Press, 1968.

Barker, R. G. and P. V. Gump (Eds.). *Big School, Small School*. Stanford, Calif.: Stanford University Press, 1964.

Barton, B. and T. Rau Perception of the man-made environment (mimeo). 1979.

Berke, J. and V. Wilson *Watch out for the Weather*. New York: Viking, 1951.

Blocher, D. H. Toward an ecology of student development. *Personnel and Guidance Journal*, 1974, **52**, 360–365.

Blocher, D. H. Campus learning environments and the ecology of student development. In J. H. Banning (Ed.), *Campus Ecology: A Perspective for Student Affairs*. National Association of Student Personnel Administrators Monograph, 1978.

Bloom, B. L. *Community Mental Health*. Monterey, Calif.: Brooks/Cole Publishing Company, 1977.

Brown, R. D. Manipulation of the environmental press in a college residence hall. *Personnel and Guidance Journal*, 1968, **46**, 555–560.

Chickering, A. W. *Education and Identity*. San Francisco: Jossey-Bass, 1969.

Clark, B. R. and M. Trow The organizational context. In T. M. Newcomb and E. K. Wilson (Eds.), *College Peer Groups: Problems and Prospects for Research*. Chicago: Aldine, 1966.

Delworth, U. and G. Hansen (Eds.) *A Handbook for Student Services*. San Francisco: Jossey-Bass, 1980.

Delworth, U. and E. Piel Students and their institutions: an interactive perspective. In C. A. Parker (Ed.), *Encouraging Development in College Students*. Minneapolis: University of Minnesota Press, 1978.

Heilweil, M. The influence of dormitory architecture on resident behavior. *Environment and Behavior*, 1973, **5**, 377–411.

Holland, J. L. *Making Vocational Choices: A theory of Careers*. New Jersey: Prentice-Hall, 1973.

March, J. G. Higher education and the pursuit of optimism. Paper presented at 57th annual conference of NASPA. San Francisco: 1975.

Miller, T. K. and J. S. Prince *The Future of Student Affairs*. San Francisco: Jossey-Bass, 1976.

Moos, R. H. Conceptualizations of human environments. *American Psychologist*, 1973, **28**, 652–665.

Moos, R. H. Systems for the assessment and classifications of human environments: an overview. In R. H. Moos and P. M. Insel (Eds.), *Issues in Social Ecology*. Palo Alto, Calif.: National Press Books, 1974.

Moos, R. H. and P. M. Insel *Issues in Social Ecology*. Palo Alto, Calif.: National Press Books, 1974.

Morrill, W. H., E. R. Oetting, and J. C. Hurst Dimensions of counselor functioning. *Personnel and Guidance Journal*, 1974, **52**, 354–359.

Murrell, S. A. *Community Psychology and Social Systems*. New York: Behavioral Publications, 1973.

Pace, C. R. and G. G. Stern An approach to the measurement of psychological characteristics of college environments. *Journal of Educational Psychology*, 1958, **49**, 269–277.

Parker, C. A. (Ed.) Thirty-six faces of counseling. *The Personnel and Guidance Journal*, 1974, **52**, 354.

Parker, C. A. (Ed.) *Encouraging Development in College Students*. Minneapolis: University of Minnesota Press, 1978.

Pervin, L. A. Performance and satisfaction as a function of individual–environment fit. *Psychological Bulletin*, 1968, **69**, 56–68.

Rappaport, J. *Community Psychology: Values, research, and action*. New York: Holt, Rinehart and Winston, 1977.

Sauber, R. College adjustment and place of residence. *Journal of College Student Personnel*, 1972, May, 205–208.

Schroeder, C. C. and N. Freesh Applying environmental management strategies in residence halls. *National Association of Student Personnel Administrators Journal*, 1977, **15**, (4), 51–57.

Sells, S. B. Ecology and the Science of Psychology. *Multivariate Behavior Research*, 1966, (1), 131–144.

Steele, F. I. *Physical Settings and Organization Development*. Reading, Mass.: Addison-Wesley Publishing Company, 1973.

Stern, G. G. *People in Context*. New York: John Wiley & Sons, 1970.

Walsh, W. B. Person/environment interaction. In J. Banning (Ed.), *Campus Ecology: A Perspective for Student Affairs*. National Association of Student Personnel Administrators Monograph, 1978.

Western Interstate Commission for Higher Education. *The Ecosystem Model: Designing Campus Environments*. Boulder, Colo.: WICHE, 1973.

# 4

# Understanding Student–Environment Interaction

STEPHEN C. PAUL

The ACE research model outlined in Chapter 1 presents three types of variables that are expected to influence educational outcomes. Most student service workers would unquestioningly accept the importance of the student as an input variable in the educational system. They would even nod agreement to the proposition that the university environment is a critical part of the educative process. When asked concerning the meaning and importance of the role of the student–environment interaction as a contributing factor, the head nodding may well turn into head scratching. "Interaction" is a term which has an inscrutable, almost mystical ring to it. The purposes of this chapter are to (1) demythologize the concept of student–environment interaction by simply explaining its meaning, (2) provide background for the concept of student–environment interaction in terms of its history and development, (3) discuss the current relevance of person–environment interaction to higher education, (4) consider some applications of the concept on college campuses, and (5) suggest some new directions and applications for use of the concept in the future in higher education.

## THE MEANING OF INTERACTIONISM

Over the years, three major theoretical positions have been used to explain why people (including students) behave the ways they do. The first of those positions can be termed "personologism." The basic idea represented by that position is that a person's actions are principally directed by factors resideing within him/herself such as traits, dispositions, or psychic structures. From the perspective of the personologist, the individual carries stable internal factors from situation to situation and those factors result in consistency of behavior across varying settings (e.g., an "aggressive" person is aggressive whether in class or on a football field).

The second theoretical position can be referred to as "situationism." That point of view stresses that events or factors in the social or physical environment outside of the person control the behavior of the individual. A person is expected to be influenced by the specific situation in which he or she finds him/herself and, therefore, to change behavior from setting to setting (e.g., the same person who is aggressive on the football field will behave differently in the classroom).

The "interactionism" position contends that neither personologism nor situationism can completely account for complex human behavior. Therefore, it integrates the two positions, suggesting that the way in which both person and environment factors act together, or interact, determines how an individual will behave. An example can be drawn by combining the two earlier illustrations. A person who is more "aggressive" than others may be more of a terror than his teammates both on the football field and in the classroom, but he would be much more disposed to show that aggressiveness during practice than during a biology lecture. The basic notion of interactionism is not very mystical at all. The idea that both the person and the environment interact to produce behavior is attractive and reasonable.

## A BACKGROUND CONTEXT FOR INTERACTIONISM

When the idea of an interaction between the persons and the environment appears in most contemporary writing, it is introduced as a new discovery—a revelation. Actually, interactionism is an exciting old notion reintroduced. As a philosophical concern, the concept of an important interaction between a person and his/her environment dates back through the ages. Interactionism can be traced forward in time at least from Aristotle (Shute, 1973). More recent philosophical representations of the concept appear in the phenomenological thinking of philosophers like Merleau-Ponty (1962), who emphasizes the role of perception in the person–environment relationship.

Within the field of Psychology, interactionism has existed for several decades. Ekehammer (1974) has recently reviewed the long-standing historical background of interactionism in psychology and has helped restore a much-needed longitudinal context. He noted that Kantor (1924) was perhaps the first early proponent of the person–environment interaction perspective when he strongly advocated that all behavior should be studied as the mutual interaction of the organism and the various situations in which it behaves.

Lewin (1936) was the major psychological interactionist who has most strongly influenced the thinking of subsequent interactionist theorists over the years. He developed what he referred to as a "field" view which conceives of the situation, including the individual, as a whole. According to Lewin (1936, p. 12), ". . . In psychology one can begin to describe the whole situation by roughly distinguishing the person (P) and his environment (E). Every psychological event depends upon the state of the person and at the same time on the environment, although their relative importance is different in different cases. Thus, we can state our formula B=f(S) for every psychological event as B=f(PE)."

Several other notable psychological theorists contributed interactionistic theories which to some extent are retained in more recent elaborations. Tolman (1935) proposed a second equation in which behavior was seen as a function of stimuli, heredity, training, and the physiological state of the organism. Angyal (1941) used the term "biosphere" to connote a complex combination of biologic, social, and psychological components to comprise the total organism–environment system. Murray (1938) developed yet another interaction theory which has persisted over the years. Basically, he described the person in terms of his/her needs; in a parallel sense, he defined the environment in terms of its role in the frustration or satisfaction of needs, which he referred to as "press."

These "grand theorists" laid the theoretical groundwork for an understanding of the person–environment interaction. Their theories are most notable for their scope. Unfortunately, that very comprehensiveness made them very difficult to test empirically and very little research was carried out based on these early frameworks. Researchers continued to focus on either the person or the environment in isolation. As a result, the ideas of the early theorists largely were neglected over the intervening years and seldom are mentioned in recent interactional theorizing.

Two rather interesting developments seem to be responsible for the renewed interest in interactionism in psychology. One of those developments was the introduction of sophisticated analysis of variance statistical procedures as research tools. With the advent of those procedures, psychologists became able to partition the relative influence of behavior of the person, the environment, and the person–environment interation in an experimental situation. This advance was coupled with a heated debate among researchers regarding whether the person or the environment was principally responsible for behavioral outcomes. The personologists attacked the situationist position and the situationists assaulted the personologist viewpoint.

There were some key studies conducted throughout the course of the person–environment tug of war. One of the best known is one reported by Endler and Hunt (1966), who presented a sample of subjects with an anxiety inventory composed of eleven anxiety-evoking situations and fourteen modes of response indicating anxiety. The subjects were asked to rate the intensity of each response for each of the eleven situations. When Endler and Hunt compared the relative contributions of the three variance components, they found that either individuals or situations taken separately accounted for only 5 percent of the total variation for each behavior. Surprisingly, the interaction between the person and the environment contributed approximately 30 percent of the total variation in behavior.

Similar findings have been reported in a number of subsequent studies. Bowers (1973) reviewed several empirical studies that had employed analysis of variance procedures and that addressed the person–environment question. He reported that almost all those studies had shown that the interaction made a greater relative contribution to total behavioral variance than either individual differences or situational differences considered independently. the unexpected outcome of the struggle to document either the personologist or situationist position was to recognize the even more impressive effects of the interaction between those two parts of behavior. New trends in psychological theorizing (c.f. Mischel, 1973) are attempting to take those findings into account.

## RELEVANCE OF STUDENT–ENVIRONMENT INTERACTION TO HIGHER EDUCATION

A similar dialectic has developed on college campuses. Student personnel professionals have most consistently focused their attention on the adjustment of the individual student to the college environment. Banning and Kaiser (1974) pointed out that three separate assumptions have guided the work with the individual student: (1) some students should not be in college; (2) some students must alleviate personal problems in order to benefit from educational opportunities; and (3) some students must develop new skills in order to take full advantage of the college experience. The exploration of a myriad of student variables continues (see Chapter 2).

Students do vary greatly in any number of dimensions that may significantly affect the educational experience. Some of the salient dimensions that are frequently considered are year in school, major, living situation, ethnic background, race, and handicaps. No doubt some students are not adequately prepared to be in college and others do need to resolve problems or to develop new skills in order to take full advantage of available opportunities. A focus should be maintained on the individual.

However, in reaction to what they perceived to be a one-sided emphasis on the person, Banning and Kaiser (1974) became advocates of an environmental orientation. They bagan developing conceptual models to guide the assessment and redesign of campus environments to better match student needs. In theory and practice, they took the burden of educational outcome off the student and placed it on the environment (see Chapter 3).

The university environment is the primary educational, cultural, recreational, and social range of opportunity for most students. The impact of environmental factors such as library holdings, registration procedure, advisor accessibility, and residence hall accommodations seems indisputable. Over the last few years universities have become increasingly aware of the importance of the educational setting that they provide. They have had to use their environmental assets as sales points as recruitment has become more challenging.

The synthesis of the person (or student) and environment (or campus) positions has also taken place on campus. Although the evidence may not be accumulating as systematically on college campuses as in the research laboratories, nevertheless documentation is available supporting that the person–environment interaction is equally important in the college setting. In a recent overview chapter, Huebner (1979) reported that there is a great deal of data demonstrating that different testing methods, curricula, and teaching methods have different effects on different types of students. Huebner also summarized a body of research that has examined the impact of person–environment congruence or similarity on person behaviors. Generally, that literature suggests that congruence stimulates achievement, increases satisfaction, and augments successful coping practices. Conversely, Huebner's own work (1979) has led her to the conclusion that a poor fit between the person and the environment leads to increased stress. In combination, these results prompt a conclusion similar to that drawn from laboratory research. In order to maximally understand or influence educational outcomes, educators and student personnel professionals should attempt to take both person and environment factors into consideration.

Apart from the more complete view of the causes of behavior which the interactional perspective holds, there is an additional reason why it is especially well suited to the student personnel worker's role. The student affairs professional has a unique vantage point at the interface between the student and university. He/she is frequently charged with a concern for some aspect or aspects of the students' college experience (e.g., residence halls). Often that means that the student personnel professional either through formal assessment or less formal contact becomes aware of particular student characteristics, problems, and needs. He/she may be one of very few people on campus who actually deals with or is concerned about the student as an individual. In addition, as a member of the university professional community, the student personnel professional is also aware of university concerns.

This dual role is often a cause of misgiving, but it can also present unique opportunities to employ the interactional perspective. Mimimally, the student affairs professional is responsible for a subsection of the university environment (e.g., the residence hall) which he/she often has the power to directly influence. Maximally, he/she may also be involved in committee process or administrative decision making that has university-wide impact on aspects of the campus environment, broadening his/her influence further. In those roles and all others, the student affairs person can operate with both an awareness of student issues and needs and a corresponding awareness of the university issues, resources, and needs.

## APPLICATIONS OF THE STUDENT–ENVIRONMENT INTERACTION PERSPECTIVE ON COLLEGE CAMPUSES

The student–environment interaction viewpoint has been translated into several models that have been applied on college campuses. There seem to be two basic types of models that have been developed. The descriptive/research type has been developed chiefly to describe the relationship between the student and the environment or to test theoretical assumptions about variables thought to influence their interaction. The second set of models is referred to as the prescriptive/intervention type. This second type of model has been developed primarily to identify those elements of the person–environment interaction that can be modified to improve the nature of the interaction. The two types of models differ greatly in terms of the different purposes for which they were developed and the different methods they employ to accomplish those purposes.

### Descriptive/Research Models

Walsh (1973, 1975) provides extensive reviews and comparisons of the various interactional models that are classifed here as descriptive/research models. For that reason, they are not covered in great depth here. However, three major descriptive/research models are briefly summarized in order to examine how they have applied to the campus setting and to consider the extent of their usefulness.

***Personality Model*** Holland (1973) has developed an interactional model based on the premise that congruence between an individual's personality and the nature of the environment contributes to the satisfaction, stability, and achievement of the individual. He characterized individuals according to their compatibility with six basic personality types: realistic, investigative, artistic, social, enterprising, and conventional. The placement of the individual in relationship to the types is accomplished through the person's responses to the Vocational Preference Inventory, the Self-Directed Search, and scales from the Strong-Campbell Vocational Interest Blank. Environments are similarly characterized according to the combined self-reported preferences of members of a population on the same measurements.

The extensive research on the constructs of Holland's theory generally supports the existence of both the six personality types and the six environmental models. The findings have also supported his hypothesis that person–environment congruence (e.g., investigative person in a investigative environment) leads to heightened personal stability, vocational stability, satisfaction, and achievement.

***Needs/Press Model*** The model outlined by Stern (1970) is an extension of Murray's earlier theory (1938), which assumed behavior to be a function of the relationship between a person's needs and environmental press. This is the only applied model that directly draws on the classical theorizing discussed earlier in the chapter. As in Holland's work, the needs/press model adopts a common frame of reference for both the person and the environment. In order to depict the person, Stern created the Activities Index, an instrument that collects self-report responses in thirty need areas. The environmental press of a setting is inferred from the characteristic features or demands of the setting as reported collectively by persons in the setting on an instrument called the College Characteristics Index.

The needs/press model emphasizes the value of congruence between the person's needs and environmental press. Unfortunately, the research that has been done in an attempt to assess the effects of student–environment congruence on student satisfaction and achievement outcomes generally tends not to support the theory. However, there is some support for the notion that students who share a common need pattern tend to be found at colleges that have a similar press pattern.

***Transactional Model*** In a third model, Pervin (1968) has similarly proposed that it is preferable for an individual to be in an environment that closely matches his/her own personality characteristics. He expects a good match between person and environment to result in increased performance, greater satisfaction, and reduced dissonance in the individual. Pervin comments that the fit between the person and the environment is optimal when the conditions in the environment help the individual to move his/her perceived self toward his/her perceived ideal self. Within this framework, the best situation exists when the environmental potential for improvement is not too great, but still provides the individual with the opportunity for growth toward the ideal self.

The Pervin model describes the person based on his/her responses to an instrument called the Transactional Analysis of Personality and Environment. The individual makes ratings of his/her "actual self," "ideal self," and the college environment. A description of the interpersonal environment is drawn from the same instrument by combining the responses of a sample of members of the community. There is some equivocal research support for Pervin's hypothesis that greater congruence between the person and the environment leads to higher levels of self-reported satisfaction. The suggested link between person–environment congruence and achievement has not yet received empirical attention.

The descriptive/research models have specific applications on the college campus. One of those applications is the exploration of the person and environment factors that contribute to the interaction. Each model explores a specific set of person and environment variables (e.g., needs, press) and measures of outcome (e.g., satisfaction). Each model is based on a limited theoretical framework. None of the models represents a comprehensive student–environment interaction model. Although the research conducted within each model provides information about the relationship among the variables explored, there is no clear evidence concerning how important the selected factors are compared to the vast number of unexplored variables. Knowledge of other variables will have to be gained from other models or these models will have to be expanded to accommodate new variables before a comprehensive theory will emerge.

Other functions the descriptive/research models serve are related to their descriptive capabilities. The three models facilitate the comparison of different environmental settings on the same dimensions, allowing for comparisons between different campuses or between different areas or departments on the same campus. This information could be very useful to students (or faculty and staff) in selecting a new campus environment. Comparisons between student characteristics and similar environmental characteristics could be useful in terms of predicting compatability and subsequent satisfaction, involvement, and achievement.

All three descriptive/research models use the concept of person–environment congruence to depict interaction. The person description is compared with the description of the environment (combined individual reports) to determine the extent to which they match. Although there may be matches or mismatches on any of a number of other dimensions, these models can at least point to discrepancies on those dimensions they consider. What the descriptive/research models do not do is point out the broader range of possible discrepancies or suggest person or environmental changes that could be introduced to reduce existing discrepancies. Those are the purposes for which the prescriptive/intervention models were developed.

## Prescriptive/Intervention Models

The basic common characteristic among the prescriptive/intervention models is their focus on needed changes in the person–environment system. They have been developed specifically in order to guide an assessment and change process. Like the theories and models described earlier, they differ in terms of the particular ways in which they operationalize the person, the environment, and the person–environment interaction. However, they all hold the common view that the person, the environment, and the person–environment interaction must be considered as part of an intervention process. More attention and detail are allotted to the prescriptive/intervention models in this chapter since they appear to be the framework within which the student–environment interaction concept is currently being applied to the college campus.

Two prescriptive/intervention models have developed from a common ancestry. Their theoretical framework seems to have arisen chiefly from work stimulated at the Western Interstate Commission for Higher Education (WICHE). The perspective that grew from that stimulation came to be known as the ecosystem model. Early advocates of the ecosystem model (cf. Banning and Kaiser, 1974; Kaiser, 1972) began with a strong emphasis on environmental factors. They hoped to intervene on campuses by designing or redesigning campus environments to meet the needs of students rather than fitting students to existing environments. However, despite the environmental focus, these early conceptualizers recognized that educational outcomes depended on the transaction which takes place between students and the environment. Their ultimate aim was to produce increased congruence or fit between the student and environment elements of the interaction.

***The Ecosystem Model.*** The theoretical assumptions of the ecosystem perspective later were translated into a rudimentary applied model by Aulepp and Delworth (1976). That model is worth describing since most of the prescriptive/intervention applications to date have arisen from it. The Aulepp and Delworth ecosystem model is elaborated in five stages (see Figure 1) that are intended to lead to the identification and elimination of dysfunctional features of the environment and to the promotion of those environmental features that enhance student growth. These five stages can be applied to the entire campus or to subenvironments in the campus community.

Stage 1 of the ecosystem model entails obtaining commitment and support from those persons with ultimate administrative responsibility for assessing the environment. This stage also involves the establishment of a planning team composed of members of various constituent groups represented in the community of interest. The planning team approach ensures that differing perspectives are recognized and also lends credibility to any subsequent activities. In stage 2, this planning group generates a list of areas that they would like to assess, drawing from their unique and common perspectives.

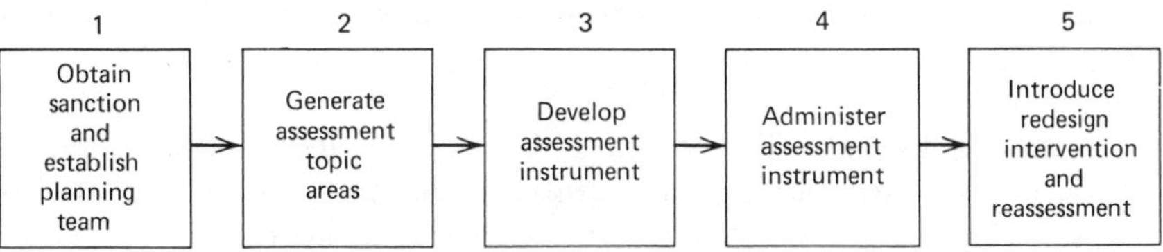


**Figure 1** Steps of the ecosystem model.

The assessment topics of interest generated in stage 2 are converted into an assessment instrument format in stage 3. One of several objective item formats is selected to produce questions concerning the topic area. In addition to the objective items, the assessment instrument gathers some useful data to guide the environmental redesign process. Using what has been termed the environmental referent format, students are asked to identify those objective items to which they respond most negatively. For those items, students are typically asked to indicate (1) what causes the problem and (2) what they would recommend be done in order to resolve the problem. Combined with the objective items, the environmental referent data point out needed change areas and some suggestions for directing that change.

The formal instrument is administered to a sample of the community population in stage 4. The collected data are then analyzed to identify those problem areas that are held in common by a sizable segment of the population. This information is considered as a part of stage 5 and redesign interventions are implemented to correct mismatches between the student population and the environment. Following the intervention period, the population is reassessed to determine whether existing problems have been remedied. This assessment redesign cycle subsequently becomes implemented on an ongoing basis by members of the community. The details of the entire assessment/redesign process are provided in a training manual prepared by Aulepp and Delworth (1976).

The basic ecosystem model, with some variations, has been applied to a number of different settings on college campuses. Huebner (1979) recently has compiled descriptions of the use of the model in two residence hall settings, a university medical school, the office of a dean of student affairs, and throughout an entire university system. Daher, Corazzini, and McKinnon (1977) have reported on the use of a modified ecosystem model in their Residence Environment Assessment Program. Conyne (1975) has introduced an innovative approach to the process in which he has had paraprofessional students (campus sensors) conduct regular identification of problem areas in their own community. Each of these applications appears to have been successful at reducing discrepancies in student–environment congruence and serves as an example of the assessment/intervention process derived from the ecosystem model.

***Ecomapping Model.*** The ecomapping model (Huebner and Corazzini, 1976) is a second approach to intentional campus design. The applied steps of the model are an outgrowth of a general theoretical framework in which the student is seen as the possessor of needs that must be met largely through external resources, the environment is conceived of as the potential source of those needed resources, and the student–environment interaction is discussed in terms of the congruence between needs and resources. In order to meet needs, the student engages in a process called "mapping." Through that process, the student identifies the various parts of the environment and attempts to act on the environmental parts (e.g., academic advisor) in order to fulfill the identified needs. The degree to which there are matches or mismatches between the student's needs and the student's successful location and utilization of resources to meet those needs determines congruence.

Huebner and Corazzini contended that earlier approaches to assessment and intervention from an interactive perspective have been limited by their singularity of method (e.g., questionnaire) or focus (e.g., phenomenological). They propose the use of various methods for assessment (questionnaire, interview, observation, etc.) and various content focuses of assessment (perceptions, behaviors, events, demographics, physical features) in order to present a more complete representation of the environment. Huebner and Corazzini have outlined a ten-step intervention process (see Figure 2) which differs somewhat from that used in the ecosystem model.

During step 1, the environmental design consultant is concerned with establishing a relationship with an administrative representative of the system and the establishment of an on-site design team. Step 2 of the ecomapping procedure involves creating a chart of the actual envi-

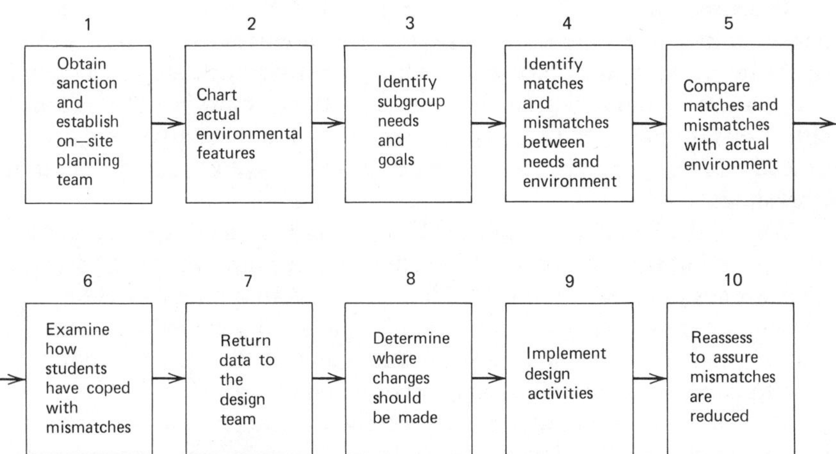


**Figure 2** Steps of the ecomapping model.

ronmental "topography," or a description of features of the environment. The perceived environmental topography is then charted by checking students' awareness and use of various physical features of the environment. In step 2, the focus is clearly on the environment.

In step 3 of the process, needs and/or goals for each subgroup are identified and differentiated in terms of importance. Information is gathered to describe the extent to which a need or goal is currently perceived to be met. Information is also collected from constituents concerning the extent to which the goal/need should ideally be met. This step constitutes the incorporation of the individual into the model.

Apparent matches and mismatches between the perceived environment and the goals and needs of the constituents are examined in step 4. In step 5, the apparent matches and mismatches are compared with the actual environment. Huebner and Corazzini suggest that some of those comparisons can be made by means of recording behavior and events, "walking through" the system, using confederates to test features, conducting interviews, and observing participants. They also recommend the collection of environmental referent data asking students what is responsible for the perceived mismatch and how that mismatch might be remedied. Step 6 uses similar environmental referent methodology to assess what students have actually done to cope with instances of perceived mismatch. The examination of matches and mismatches operationally represents the interaction of person and environment.

Steps 7 through 9 constitute the action steps of the ecomapping process. In step 7 the information collected via the various assessments is passed back to the on-site design team. The data are examined in order to determine where changes can and should be made in step 8, and based on its perception of what needs to be done and what they can do, the team plans and implements redesign activities in step 9. Huebner and Corazzini thought that those interventions could be in the form of either system changes (e.g., administrative edict to change registration procedure) or program development activities (e.g., career planning workshops).

The final step (step 10) in the Huebner and Corazzini model consists of reassessing the environment in order to determine whether perceived mismatches have been reduced. Ideally, the ecomapping model becomes an ongoing monitoring system which is continually cycled through. The aim of the consultant is to educate members of the environment to be able to carry out the assessment process independently.

The ecomapping model clearly attends to more variables than the ecosystem model. In that sense, it is much more comprehensive and theoretically rich. However, the added complexity makes the model very difficult and time-consuming to apply. As a result, there has been little actual use made of the model as a whole and those conceptual pieces which have been used are incorporated into the less cumbersome ecosystem model.

***The Multiple Perspective Model.*** The multiple perspective model (Paul and Huebner, 1978) is of a different genre from the first two prescriptive/intervention models. Rather than proposing assessment or intervention steps, it is a prescriptive model that can be used to visualize the interaction process. The conceptual framework was intended to represent the range of elements which are pertinent to the person and to the environment. Unlike any of the other models portrayed here, it attempts to view both the person and environment in terms of process. The multiple perspective model is depicted in Figure 3.

The model can be explained by briefly describing both person and environment elements and processes and then pointing out how the interaction transpires. The model does not adopt any particular theoretical orientation and any theoretical point of view (e.g., dynamic, learning theory) can be accommodated into the model where it fits. In this way, the model is meant to serve as an integrative framework for existing concepts as well as a heuristic vehicle for pointing to new ideas and their relationships with the old.

Person attributes or elements are contained in the box on the left side of Figure 3. Those elements include physical aspects, affective characteristics, motivational factors, cognitive characteristics, consistencies of behavior (personality), interpersonal behaviors, and social and cultural factors. They can be thought of as the products of development and the experiences that the individual brings with him/her into an environment, forming a unique composite for each individual. The elements influence the person's interactive process with the environment and also are affected by that interaction.

The multiple perspective model views the individual as a problem-solver who progresses through a series of eight steps in order to gather information about alternatives in the environment and then act to produce outcomes that are satisfying, need-reducing, and/or self-sustaining. Those steps are based on the basic problem-solving sequence outlined by D'Zurilla and Goldfried (1971). A particular individual may not pass through the eight steps in the same sequence under different circumstances, and different individuals may follow different sequences under similar circumstances. In this sense, the model is prescriptive rather than literal.

According to the model, environmental information is taken in by

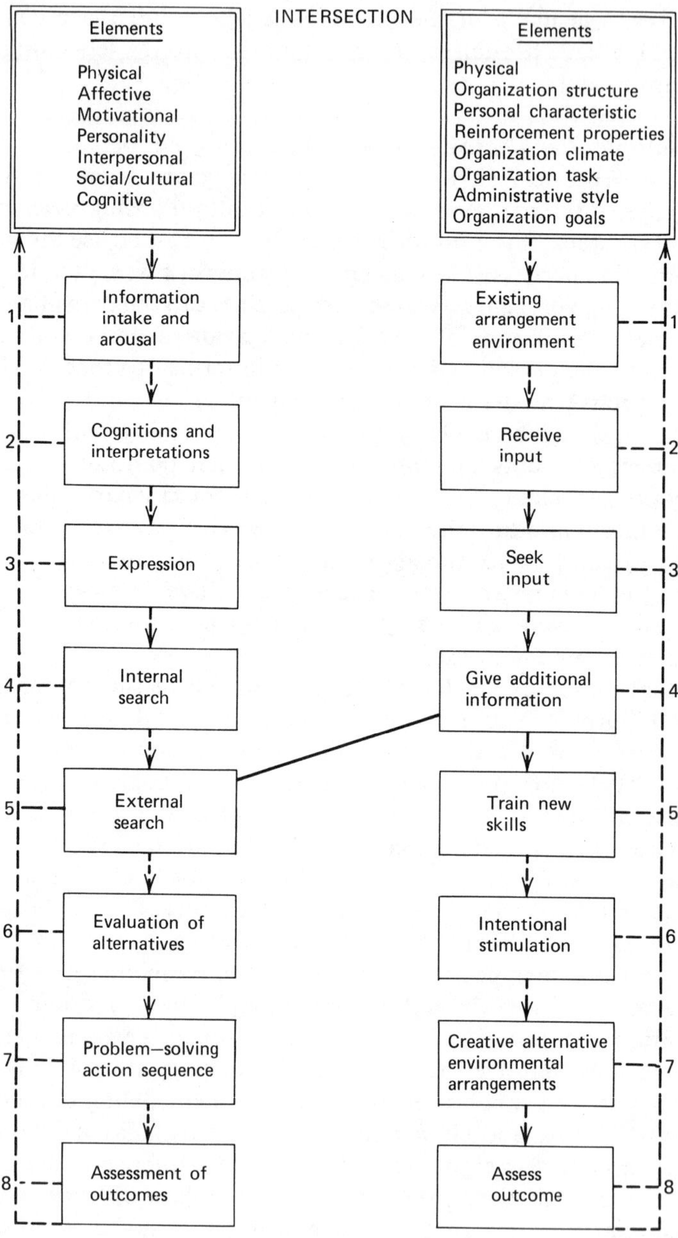




**Figure 3** The multiple perspective model framework.

the individual (step 1), and based on interpretations of that information (step 2) a problem or need may be recognized and perhaps expressed to others (step 3). If the problem is intense or persistent, alternative solutions may be generated by the individual (step 4) or sought out in the environment (step 5). The alternative solutions identified are weighed (step 6) and one of the alternatives may be applied (step 7). A thorough problem solver will consider the outcome of the attempted solution (step 8) and commence the process again if the outcome is unsatisfactory.

Although considerably less attention has been paid to identifying and describing important parts of the environment, several types of environmental elements have been explored. The elements listed in the box on the right side of Figure 3 are taken from Moos (1973) and James and Jones (1974). They include the physical features, organizational structure, personal characteristics of setting inhabitants, operating reinforcement contingencies, organizational climate, organizational tasks, administrative style, and organizational goals found within the setting.

The multiple perspective model suggests that the environmental process can be conceptualized in a sequence that parallels the person process. At the most passive level (step 1) the environment furnishes the existing arrangement of its elements as a context for behavior or even a constraining coercive influence on behavior (e.g., library). Agents in the environment may accommodate the expressions of members of the community (step 2) or more actively seek constituent expressions (e.g., suggestion box or needs assessment, step 3).

The remaining steps involve intervention activity on the part of the environment. Environmental agents may attempt to inform community members about aspects of the environment (step 4), train individuals in new skills (step 5), or change perceptions or attitudes about the experience in the environment (step 6). An even more impactful intervention may involve the actual addition, subtraction, or modification of environmental features (step 7). Finally, the outcomes of the environmental process are monitored to ensure environmental goals are attained (step 8).

The process steps for the person and the environment compatibly overlap and the way in which those two processes work together is thought of as their interaction. For example, a person's search for information corresponds with the delivery of information by a service provider (illustrated at their intersection in Figure 3). To enhance the interaction, either the person can be trained to do a better job searching out alternative resources or the service provider can be encouraged to improve information availability. Perhaps the most important implication of the model is that for any single problem interventions can be directed at several steps of the two processes simultaneously. People can be trained and service information can be improved. Simultaneous interventions are likely to be potent and recognize different person and environment causal factors resulting in a single problem. Unmet needs can be assessed in terms of where in the two processes breakdowns are occurring. Incomplete stages of either process may result in a reduced likelihood of need fulfillment.

One of the important steps in any assessment of student–environment interaction is the generation of assessment topics and questionnaire items pertaining to those topics. Typically, those activities are guided unsystematically by the interests of the investigator. The multiple perspective model points out the variety of factors that may be involved in the problem and can guide the assessor in systematic exploration of factors that may otherwise be overlooked. The model does not describe an assessment/intervention process in the way that the ecosystem or ecomapping models do. Rather, it provides the investigator with an integrative framework within which to visualize the complex system in which he/she is operating. As a result, this model supplements rather than replaces the earlier prescriptive/intervention models.

***The Human Competence Model*** Recently Gilbert presented an interaction model that both outlines the elements of the person and the environment and suggests an intervention procedure (1978). His human competence model is based on four theorems. The close tie between the implications of those theorems and the application of the model make the human competence model the best articulated of the models presented. In application, the model provides a guide for what is termed performance troubleshooting in a setting. Each setting is considered at its philosophical, cultural, policy, tactical, and logistic levels and a similar progression of three stages is applied at each setting level. In the first stage valued accomplishments, performance required to achieve the valued accomplishments, and exemplary standards for performance are identified. The second stage involves collecting measures to identify instances where there is a potential for improving present performance to the exemplary level. Finally, in the third stage, a framework called the behavior engineering model is used to guide changes in the environment of the setting or the people in the setting in order to bring performance to the exemplary level.

Gilbert's third theorem elaborates the interactional nature of his model as it guides interventions at the third stage. It states, "For any given accomplishment, a deficiency in performance always has as its immediate cause a deficiency in a behavior repertory (P), or in the environment that supports the repertory (E), or in both. But its ultimate cause will be found in a deficiency of the management system (M)." When an attempt is made to improve performance the focus is on improving behavior, but behavior is recognized to be a transaction between the person and the environment. From Gilbert's perspective, this suggests that the interventionist can alter the person's repertory, the environment, or both to improve inadequate performance. The choice becomes a pragmatic one of selecting the most effective approach.

In order to better understand what variables within that behavioral whole can be modified to improve performance, Gilbert breaks the whole into six component pieces of the behavior engineering model (see Figure 4). There are three components that are complementarily represented in both the environment and the person; (1) information, (2) instrumentation, and (3) motivation. The environmental forms of these

| | $S^D$ Information | R Instrumentation | $S_r$ Motivation |
|---|---|---|---|
| E Environmental supports | Data<br>1. Relevant and frequent feedback about the adequacy of performance<br>2. Descriptions of what is expected of performance<br>3. Clear and relevant guides to adequate performance | Instruments<br>1. Tools and materials of work designed scientifically to match human factors | Incentives<br>1. Adequate financial incentives made contingent upon performance<br>2. Nonmonetry incentives made available<br>3. Career-development opportunities |
| P Person's repertory of behavior | Knowledge<br>1. Scientifically designed training that matches the requirements of exemplary performance<br>2. Placement | Capacity<br>1. Flexible scheduling of performance to match peak capacity<br>2. Prosthesis<br>3. Physical shaping<br>4. Adaptation<br>5. Selection | Motives<br>1. Assessment of people's motives to work<br>2. Recruitment of people to match the realities of the situation |

**Figure 4** The behavior engineering model. From *Human Competence* by T. F. Gilbert. Copyright © 1978 by McGraw-Hill. Used with permission of McGraw-Hill Book Co.

three components are the data available (e.g., the course syllabus), the instruments present (e.g., course text), and the incentives provided (e.g., course grades). The corresponding person aspects are discrimination (e.g., recognizing course purpose), response capacity (e.g., reading text), and motives (e.g., desire for grade). All six components can be considered for any single behavioral act.

The human competence model proposes that there are a number of things that might be done to improve behavior efficiency in each of the six components and that there is a logical order for approaching interventions. Gilbert recommends that attention first be paid to environmental variables, since changes in them are likely to have more powerful effects and generally cost less to implement. The intervener begins by looking at how adequately data available in the environment guide performance and indicate how well the individual has performed. Gilbert sees information deficits as the most frequent cause of incompetence. Secondly, the intervener examines whether tools and materials in the environment are adequate and suited to their users. Thirdly, he/she examines incentives available in the setting to reward worthy performance. Finally, after correcting any environmental obstacles to competence, the intervener turns his/her attention to training of individuals in the setting. This systematic approach is meant to lead to more efficient interventions.

Gilbert has adopted what might be called a pragmatic maximization view of the person–environment interaction. Interaction results at the point where person and environment elements come together in a behavior. In this way, it is similar to the Paul and Huebner model. There is no intervening construct (e.g., congruence) between the person and environment components and the behavior. Their interaction is successful if it results in exemplary performance. If the performance is not exemplary, then some elements of either the person, environment, or both require modification. The human competence model focuses on ultimately valued accomplishments. Such a focus is as important in education as it is in industry.

In its full elaboration, the Gilbert model provides a simpler view of the elements of interaction than the Paul and Huebner model. It also offers an equally simple and reasonable approach to intervention. The evidence that Gilbert has accumulated in industrial settings suggests that the model successfully increases performance outcomes. The model's value on the campus remains to be tested, but there is no reason to believe it cannot be applied with equal success to improving performance on specific accomplishments there as well.

## IMPLICATIONS AND FUTURE DIRECTIONS

It is to be hoped that at this point, the head scratching over the meaning of the concept of student–environment interaction has stopped. There are abundant indicators that it is a valuable concept and that both person and environment, in combination, are important determinants of student behavior. This recognition results in both a major gain and a major loss. The gain is a richer and more complete view of what leads to student behavior. However, the relative simplicity of acknowledging only person or environmental influences on behavior is lost. It becomes necessary to extend our theorizing and our intervention skills to accommodate the additional complexity. It does seem that it is time we face that complexity directly rather than ignoring its existence.

Much of that complexity can be reduced. Often, the temptation has been to attempt to examine all the factors influencing all of the outcomes in broad settings. It makes much more sense at this early stage of development to concentrate on more circumscribed projects. Focus can be limited by selecting a specific problem to address (e.g., vandalism in residence halls) or a specific accomplishment to foster (e.g., pass math entrance test). Additional narrowing can be done by limiting both the setting (e.g., one college in the university) or the population (e.g., probationary students). Once the topic and the environment are narrowed, it is easier to consider the range of person and environment factors that may be interacting to produce the problem or accomplishment.

### Elements of the Student–Environment Interaction

The descriptive/research models have systematically investigated the impact of a narrow range of person and environment variables on student behavior. The prescriptive/intervention models have investigated a wider range of variables, but they have been less systematic in relating them to behavioral outcomes. They have been more concerned with optimizing outcomes by changing all the identified interfering conditions. The research on those variables that influence specific behavioral outcomes must be extended. That can be done in part by carrying out more theory-linked studies from within a descriptive/research type model. It can also be done by paying closer attention to the link between variables and behavior outcomes in the prescriptive/research models. In applying either type of model, it also would be useful to begin to identify the relative impact of different types of variables. It would then be possible to say that environmental variable A not only has been found to influence a behavioral outcome but also it influences that outcome more or less than person variable A or environment variable B. With this type of information, it would be possible to begin to focus on the most potent variables.

Investigation of the various person and environment variables has been aided by the development of those models that attempt to visually depict the interaction process. The multiple perspective model and the behavior engineering model both serve this purpose. They can be used heuristically to systematically explore potential person or environment contributors to any behavior outcome. However, the validation of these models will have to arise from research that experimentally confirms or disconfirms their assumptions.

### Outcomes in the Student–Environment Interaction

The early descriptive/research models related specific independent variables (e.g., match between person needs and environment press) to specific outcome measures (e.g., satisfaction). However, the later ecosystem and ecomapping intervention models seem to have accepted a more general assumption that congruence between person and environment is a desirable outcome in and of itself. They then attempted to reduce any mismatches between person and environment for any of the multitude of variables to which they attended in order to promote the outcome of congruence. There is no reason to automatically believe that person–environment congruence on untested variables leads to improvement on behavioral outcomes. It seems important to reintroduce the practice of measuring the impact of interventions on the actual measures of interest (e.g., performance) rather than an untested intervening variable (congruence).

Apart from the need to confirm the theoretical assumptions underlying the intervention models, there is a second, perhaps more pressing reason for measuring the behavioral outcomes. Student affairs professionals are more and more being asked to demonstrate outcomes that are valued by administrators and other members of the educational community. Administrators are concerned about impact on such outcomes as student retention, probationary status, and skills deficits. The student affairs professional is certainly free to conceptualize and measure any intervening outcome variables along the way to the final behavioral outcomes; however, it is the behavioral outcomes that matter.

Gilbert (1978) proposes that each intervention should be measured in terms of its impact on economic outcomes. That may have a very dissonant ring to those who work in "the helping professions." Nevertheless, he has a valid point. If student affairs personnel could demonstrate that their interventions result in substantial economic savings to the university (e.g., tuition preserved by fostering retention) there would be little question concerning their relevance. As new projects are propsoed, it is at least worth considering how direct measures of behavioral outcomes and their economic consequences can be measured. It may be a good policy to weigh intervention costs against expected tangible outcomes before beginning any new interventions.

## Integrating the Models

The models presented here have been developed for a number of purposes in reference to the central theme of student–environment interaction. The descriptive/research models test theoretical assumptions, the more prescriptive models propose the sets of untested person–environment relationships, and the intervention models are designed to improve the nature of the interaction between students and the environment. The models are not interchangeable; however, it would seem that by combining the advantages of the other approaches any of the individual models could be enhanced. It may even be possible to combine aspects of the models in ways that allow model applications to accomplish more than one purpose at a time. Some suggestions for integrating the models are made in this final section.

The human competence model provides a complete approach to assessment and intervention for those situations where there is a specific accomplishment to be improved upon (e.g., math performance). Through the use of that model, an exemplary performance is identified and interventions based on the behavior engineering model are carried out to bring the typical performance to the level of the exemplary. The final, valued outcomes are examined to determine if the performance has actually been improved.

There seem to be two useful ways of incorporating parts of other interaction models into the human competence model. First, it may be beneficial to include the earliest stage of the ecosystem or ecomapping models. That stage explicitly recognizes the highly political nature of systems interventions. In it, sanction and support for the assessment/intervention project are obtained from administrators, and representatives of the various constituency groups with something at stake in improving the outcome are involved. Including that stage does not in any way modify the sequence of activities carried out in the Gilbert assessment or intervention, but adding it is likely to make the process more palatable to members of the community. This political savoir faire would be particularly important in an educational setting where performance tends to be viewed very personally and not in the "company's" jurisdiction.

Another modification can be made in the human competence model that will allow it to serve a second purpose without disturbing its integrity. Because the model already introduces changes in person and environment variables and then measures primary outcomes (accomplishments), it can easily be used to gather preliminary information about the relationship of those variables and outcomes. Gilbert views the model as a pragmatic intervention model, but hypotheses are tested each time a variable is modified and an outcome is measured. The accumulated findings resulting from these "experiments" optimally would be guided by theoretical assumptions, but even if they are not, they can be fitted to existing assumptions or assumptions may arise from them. In any case, they should be reported.

The ecosystem model (see Figure 1) is a useful intervention framework intended to guide the examination of sources of dissatisfaction actually result from redesign efforts. Like the human competence model, it can be supplemented by aspects of other interaction models to make it more effective and to accomplish an additional purpose. The ecosystem model can be refined by including as a new second step the determination of important and valued setting outcomes (in addition to congruence) as suggested in the Gilbert model. With those outcomes in mind, the planning team members could then use the multiple perspective model to generate the content areas to be included an an assessment of factors that might be interfering with optimal outcomes.

Later in the application of the ecosystem model, the behavior engineering model can be consulted to recommend different approaches to reducing problems identified during the assessment phase. The addition of this systematic guide to intervention will be a helpful supplement to the ecosystem process. It currently lacks an elaboration of ways in which to approach interventions.

There is an evaluation phase built into the ecosystem model. Presently, that evaluation involves a reassessment of the constituents of the setting to determine whether perceived person–environment mismatches have been reduced through the implemented intervention. As noted earlier, it would be theoretically as well as pragmatically useful to build an evaluation of valued outcomes into the model as well. Those outcomes could be measured before and following an intervention in ways that would demonstrate more directly the effects of the intervention. This would also make it possible to examine the effects of the modified variables on the selected outcomes in a research sense, accomplishing a second purpose.

## CONCLUSION

This chapter has presented an overview of the area of student–environment interaction. It has reviewed the meaning and the development of the concept and its relevance to the student affairs professional. The area of student–environment interaction has been advanced primarily through the development and application of the descriptive/research and prescriptive/intervention models. Those models have been briefly described.

There is a need for both types of interaction models. This chapter has attempted to make clear their differences in terms of purposes and methods. However, it has pointed out their commonalities as well in order to encourage their integration in ways that will extend the field. The model-building work that has been done in the student–environment interaction area provides a good beginning. The area is still in its early childhood and there is room for new models, theoretical refinements of existing models, model testing, and new model applications. The results of early efforts in working with student–environment interactions suggest a challenging and a rewarding future.

## REFERENCES

Angyal, A. *Foundations for a Science of Personality*. Cambridge: Harvard University Press, 1941.

Aulepp, L. and U. Delworth. *Training manual for an Ecosystem Model: Assessing and designing campus environments*. Boulder, Colo.: Western Interstate Commission for Higher Education, 1976.

Banning, J. H. and L. Kaiser An ecological perspective and model for campus design. *Personnel and Guidance Journal*, 1974, **52**, 370–375.

Bowers, K. S. Situationism in psychology: an analysis and critique. *Psychological Review*, 1973, **80**, 307–336.

Conyne, R. K. Environmental assessment: mapping for counselor action. *Personnel and Guidance Journal*, 1975, **54**, (3), 150–154.

Daher, D. M., J. G. Corazzini, and R. D. McKinnon An environmental redesign program for residence halls. *Journal of College Student Personnel*, 1977, **18**, 11–15.

D'Zurilla, T. J. and M. R. Goldfried. Problem solving and behavior modification. *Journal of Abnormal Psychology*, 1971, **78**, 107–126.

Ekehammar, B. Interactionism in personality from a historical perspective. *Psychological Bulletin*, 1974, **81**, (12), 1026–1048.

Endler, N. S. and J. McV. Hunt Sources of behavioral variance as measured by the S–R inventory of anxiousness. *Psychological Bulletin*, 1966, **65**, 338–346.

Gilbert, T. F. *Human Competence.* New York: McGraw-Hill, 1978.

Holland, J. L. *Making Vocational Choices: A Theory of Careers.* Englewood Cliffs, N.J.: Prentice-Hall, 1973.

Huebner, L. A. (Ed.), *Applying the Ecosystem Perspective.* San Francisco: Jossey-Bass, 1979.

Huebner, L. A. and J. G. Corazzini Eco-mapping: A dynamic model for intentional campus design. *Student Development Staff Papers*, Vol. 6. Fort Collins: Colorado State University, 1976.

James, L. R. and A. P. Jones Organizational climate. *Psychological Bulletin*, 1974, **81**, 1096–1112.

Kaiser, L. R. Campus ecology: implications for environmental design. Unpublished manuscript. Boulder, Colo.: Western Interstate Commission for Higher Education, 1972.

Kantor, J. R. *Principles of Psychology,* Vol. 1. Bloomington, Ind.: Principia Press, 1924.

Lewin, K. *Principles of Topological Psychology.* New York: McGraw-Hill, 1936.

Merleau-Ponty, M. *The Phenomenology of Perception.* London: Paul, 1962.

Mischel, W. Toward a cognitive social learning reconceptualization of personality. *Psychological Review*, 1973, **80**, 252–283.

Moos, R. H. Conceptualizations of human environments. *American Psychologist,* 1973, **28**, 652–665.

Murray, H. A. *Explorations in Personality.* New York: Oxford University Press, 1938.

Paul, S. C. and L. A. Huebner Persons in their contextual systems or consumers in the market place. Paper presented at the Annual Convention of the American College Personnel Association, Detroit, Mich., 1978.

Pervin, L. A. Performance and satisfaction as a function of individual–environment fit. *Psychological Bulletin*, 1968, **69**, 56–68.

Shute, C. Aristotle's interactionism and its transformations by some 20th century writers. *Psychological Record*, 1973, **23**, 283–293.

Stern, G. G. *People in Context.* New York: John Wiley & Sons, 1970.

Tolman, E. C. Psychology versus immediate experience. In E. C. Tolman, *Collected Papers in Psychology.* Berkeley, Calif.: University of California Press, 1951. (Reprinted from *Philosophy of Science*, 1935, **2**, 356–380.)

Walsh, W. B. *Theories of Person–Environment Interaction: Implications for the College Student.* Princeton, N.J.: The American College Testing Program, 1973.

Walsh, W. B. Some theories of person/environment interaction. *Journal of College Student Personnel*, 1975, **16**, 107–113.

# II

# Interventions For Student Development

The "cube" model presented in Chapter 5 was the basis for a special issue of *The Personnel and Guidance Journal* in 1974 and received the Best Article of the Year Award for that volume. This model is designed to provide the vehicle for carrying out the roles for student services presented in Chapter 1, particularly the role of teaching students the skills they need to take advantage of the learning environment and the role of impacting on the educational environment. The model identifies whether the target of the intervention should be the individual or the environment. In addition, the model also attends to potential purposes for any intervention with either individuals or the environment. The purposes might be remedial, preventive, or developmental. Moreover, the model addresses various means for carrying out interventions. The method of the intervention may be either direct, such as administrative interventions or counseling and therapeutic interventions, indirect, utilizing consultation, training, or media.

In addition, this part addresses the importance of evaluating the effects or impact of any interventions that are carried out. Chapter 9, by E. R. Oetting, is a landmark discussion of program evaluation. This very readable step-by-step discussion of the evaluation process will make it possible for any student affairs professional to carry out an effective program evaluation project.

# 5
# A Conceptual Model of Intervention Strategies

WESTON H. MORRILL, JAMES C. HURST, AND E. R. OETTING

In recent years student affairs workers have produced a constant flow of new procedures designed to augment the educational experience. These include group programs, consultation, psychoeducational activities, training as modes of treatment, variations in administration, and environmental modification. The profession has grown over the years through the efforts of creative and hardworking individuals who have created programs and offices to respond to the recognized needs of individuals and institutions. A criticism of student affairs professionals, however, has been that we lack a clear conceptual way to tie all these programs and activities together with some unifying direction or purpose.

In this chapter a model is introduced that provides a means of conceptualizing the range of possible interventions and that is designed to provide a vehicle for carrying out the roles presented in Chapter 1. Although the model was originally designed to deal with counseling interventions, it is general enough to provide the same precision in defining interventions in all student development activities. In planning student development interventions, we must determine whether our most appropriate target would be individuals or the environments that

---

This chapter is a modification of the following previously published article: W. H. Morrill, E. R. Oetting, and J. C. Hurst. Dimensions of counselor functioning. *Personnel and Guidance Journal,* 1974 52 (6), 354-359.

affect individuals. We must also make decisions about the purpose of the interventions as well as about the best method for carrying out these interventions. The model provides a means for systematically addressing these questions and thereby serves as a means of conceptualizing, categorizing, and describing the potential activities of the student development specialist in a variety of settings.

The three dimensions of the model as depicted in Figure 1 are as follows:

1 **The Target of the Intervention:** The target of the intervention stated most simply may be either (a) the individual or (b) the environments that affect or influence the individual. The environments that affect the individual include (i) primary groups, (ii) associational groups, and (iii) institutions or communities.
2 **The Purpose of the Intervention:** The purpose may be (a) remedial, (b) preventive, or (c) developmental.
3 **The Method of the Intervention:** The method of reaching the target population may be (a) direct interventions by professionals or administrators with the target, (b) consultation and training of other

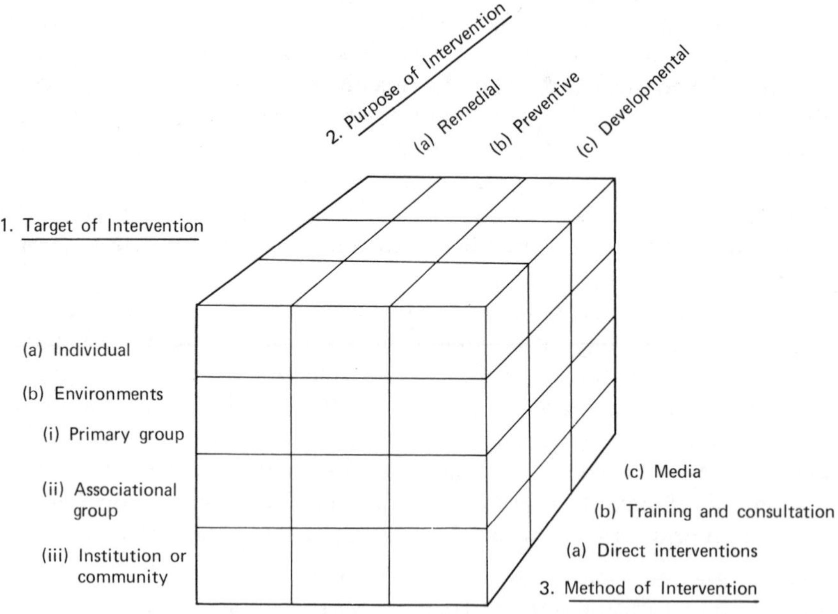


**Figure 1** Dimensions of intervention for student development. Copyright © 1974 by Morrill, Oetting, and Hurst.

helping professionals or paraprofessionals, or (c) the use of media in carrying out the intervention.

Any intervention has these three dimensions: who or what the intervention is aimed at, why the intervention is attempted, and how the intervention is implemented.

## THE TARGET OF THE INTERVENTION

The question of who or what should be the target of an intervention has not been asked until recently. The answer was traditionally assumed to be *the individual*; that is, the immediate objective was to produce positive changes in the individual student. Even most group programs do not reflect an effort to change the group as a functional unit, but rather to influence individuals within the framework of group methods. The target dimension introduces the possibility that interventions designed to impact on environments (groups, institutions, and communities) that in turn influence individuals may be primary goals in and of themselves. Environmental modification has become recognized as a viable intervention method in recent years. It has been long known that environments affect people's self-esteem, mood, and satisfaction (Moos, 1979). There is some evidence to suggest that people in less populated environments are less sensitive to evaluation, have more functional importance, engage in different programs, and assume more responsibility. Holland (1973) has proposed that vocational satisfaction, stability, and achievement depend on the congruence between a person's personality and the environments in which that person works. Furthermore, those environments in which there is a large hiatus between a person's need and the environmental resource can precipitate dysfunctional stress (Barker, 1978). In some instances, individuals become victims of their environment, or environmental casualties. Although Lewin (1935) suggested quite some time ago that behavior is a function of an interaction between personality and the environment, it has only been recently that environmental modification has been accepted as a legitimate intervention activity by professionals as a method of treatment. The early work in this area has focused on developing methodologies that can be used to characterize or typify environments. Recent directions have focused on the development of a technology that identifies major mismatches between individuals and their environment. Identification of environmental mismatches with a knowledge of precipitating events, coping mechanisms, and suggestions for change allow the student development professional to make those environmental modification interventions that can be productive of growth for large numbers of individuals. The area of environmental modification promises to be an exciting and rewarding one in the years to come (Banning, 1978). Ultimately, of course, such interventions effectively influence the quality of life of the individual (Martin and Horner, 1967).

For clarity in this model, the broad category of environment is broken down into somewhat more manageable parts. Thus the environmental targets depicted in the model include primary groups, associational groups, and then more broadly, institutions and communities. The primary goal of an intervention may be to alter the group structure or the organizational characteristics of an institution or community. The model suggests that the professional may choose to intervene with the individual or the environment.

## The Individual

The target of the intervention can be the individual, usually on either a one-to-one or small group basis. The attempt is to influence the individual through altering his or her knowledge, attitudes, perceptions, emotions, and responses.

## The Environments Affecting the Individual

***Primary Group.*** In many cases the target of the intervention might more effectively be the primary groups that affect the individual. "Primary groups," as the basic units of social organization, are the groups that are most influential for the individual. They are intimate, continuing personal associations on a face-to-face basis, and are determined by the degree of intimacy rather than physical or geographic proximity. Primary groups such as families, couples, or close friends strongly influence the individual's self-concept and behavior. The behavior of individuals in the primary group and their presence or absence from the group can profoundly influence the other members as well as the group itself. Interventions at this level attempt to alter both function and structure in primary groups (Jarvis and Stutzman, 1969; Linden, Goodwain, and Resnik, 1968).

***Associational Group.*** The target of the intervention may also be the associational groups to which individuals belong. Bierstedt (1970) uses the term "associational groups" to describe more organized groups based on choice or chance associations. Group members share a consciousness of similar interests, goals, or needs and join together in some organized way to pursue those interests. The distinction between this category and institution or community is that members of associational groups meet together with other members of the group. Examples of associational groups are classes, clubs, fraternities, student government groups, and the students on a dormitory floor. Interventions at this level include attempts to alter goals, communications patterns, interactions, organization, expectations, interdependencies, and methods of achieving goals (Preuss, 1967; Stark, 1964).

***Institution or Community.*** A more ambitious target of an intervention might be the institution and/or community. These environments differ from associational groups in that they do not involve any meetings or close association of the members of the group. However, members are aware of their membership in an institution or community. Examples include an individual school, a college, a professional school, a residential living system, a town or city, a neighborhood, church, state, or nation. Intervention at this level would include attempts to alter goals, communications, system linkages, power distribution, information flow, policies, and sanctions.

## THE PURPOSES OF THE INTERVENTION

The second dimension of the model deals with what the intervention is designed to accomplish. The function of a student development specialist may be the remediation of an existing problem, the prevention of a potential problem, or the promotion of developmental skills leading to positive and creative growth.

The range of this dimension suggests both a reactive and a proactive role for the developmental specialist. Under in loco parentis, most student affairs work was primarily reactive. That is, programming was designed to deal with a student after he or she had recognized a problem and had sought assistance. The purpose dimension embodies the recognition of the alternative roles of prevention and of promoting positive development. The purpose of the intervention can be remediation, prevention, or development.

### Remediation

Intervention at the remedial level generally occurs after something has gone wrong and damage has taken place. This may be the result of a discrepancy that exists between the skill of the student and the demands of the environment. Examples include depression and loneliness resulting from a lack of social and interpersonal skills, failure to make valid development decisions because of lack of information, or failure of a group to accomplish a definite task because of organizational or structural deficiencies (Abel, 1967; Kuehn, 1970; Stinnett and Niedenthal, 1968; Stephenson and Scarpitti, 1968).

## Prevention

Prevention is the result of predicting and providing. It is an effort to identify those skills that are needed now or that may be needed in the future and to provide a means for acquiring them. The intent is to anticipate future problems (Bloom, 1971; Bower, 1963; Sanford, 1965). This definition encompasses both primary and secondary prevention as described in the public health model (Brown, 1969). An example of preventive intervention might begin with the recognition that transition from high school to college is a traumatic experience for many students. Programs designed to decrease the casualties of this period could include such things as group programs to create primary group social support for individual students, precollege academic skill training to prepare the student for the transition, or the modification of institutional rules and procedures or even classroom environment when it can be demonstrated that they contribute to the problem. The overall objective here is to provide the skills that will be needed to adequately meet the environmental demands and/or modify unnecessary and debilitating environmental demands.

## Development

This category is different from the first two of this dimension in that it is not problem oriented. Whereas remediation refers to repairing damage after the fact, and prevention is designed to take steps early enough to avoid a problem, developmental interventions are designed to enhance the functioning and developmental potential of healthy individuals and groups (Cady, 1969; Danskin, 1965; Farnsworth, 1966; Foulds and Guinan, 1969; Morrill, Ivey, and Oetting, 1968; Oetting, 1967; Sanford, 1968). Such programs are often proactive, promoting the development of potential. Though related to prevention, development has the primary focus of promoting positive growth for all, not just those identified as having or about to have problems. Examples would include situations in which students are experiencing success and yet are not maximizing their potential not only to succeed but to excel.

## THE METHOD OF INTERVENTION

The method of working with or reaching the target of the intervention can vary depending on the intent or stage of the program. The limited number of professionals available in most settings has made it essential that some means of increasing their range of influence be developed. The method dimension is, in this respect, related to the target dimension, in that interventions with associational groups or institutions are also means of extending the range of influence of the professional. However, this dimension poses the question of how the actual intervention is presented to the target population. The student development professional can be directly, personally involved in providing the intervention; can be indirectly involved through consulting with or training other individuals to intervene with the target; or can utilize media as a vehicle for the intervention (such as newspapers, computers, programmed materials, books, television, audio tapes, and films). These three levels of method of intervention are outlined in the model.

### Direct Interventions

The direct interventions may vary depending on the job title or role of the professional involved. These may be administrative interventions or counseling or therapeutic interventions. An administrator such as a vice-president for student affairs, a director of housing, or a dean of students would often utilize administrative interventions. Through the direct power or authority of his/her role or title decisions can be made which affect individuals and environments. For example, students are admitted, placed on probation, or dismissed; policies are changed that affect the way institutions impact individuals; programs or offices are created that change the environment for students. These are examples of direct administrative interventions. Direct counseling or therapeutic interventions have utilized direct professional involvement with the target. There are situations in which professional skills and experience can be critical; for example, a person involved in critical stress frequently needs the highest level of help available. There are problems that require experienced judgment or skills that only extensively trained and qualified professionals can provide. There are other situations where the status of the professional is important, where it provides the political reassurance or personal charisma that is necessary for a particular program. The disadvantages of direct professional involvement with all targets include cost, both in money and in scarce professional time, the ability to deal only with relatively small numbers of students, and the resultant limit on reaching a wide variety of groups of students or providing a comprehensive range of programs.

## Training and Consultation

Through consultation and training of allied professionals and paraprofessionals, the student development specialist can affect the target population indirectly through other individuals. The underlying concept of consultation is that with limited resources and almost unlimited possibilities for student development interventions, professionals can have greater effect if they impact on people who in turn work with the student (Bindman, 1959; Caplan, 1963; Goldin, 1970; Newman, 1965; Seashore and Van Egmond, 1959).

Another important resource resides in the selection and training of paraprofessionals to work in a variety of settings (Carkhuff, 1969; Rioch et al., 1963; Zunker and Brown, 1966). The professional is involved in conceptualizing a program and in selecting and training the paraprofessionals who may then provide the service. This not only increases the student development work force, but paraprofessionals often are able to work with certain groups more effectively than professionals.

## Media

In addition to the traditional direct service and the more recent emphasis on consultation, training, and environmental modification, media are becoming an important tool in intervention for student development. There are numerous examples of the use of various communications media to extend and enhance the influence of direct service. These include such things as computer-assisted counseling (Super, 1970), programmed human relations training materials (Human Development Institute, 1969), video tape (Higgins, Ivey, and Uhlemann, 1970), and other media approaches such as newspaper articles and radio or television programs. Several universities are now offering self-help tapes that can be accessed by telephone. The topics for such tapes vary widely, including depression, suicide, and anxiety. These are all tools that can be used by a professional to offer direct service to individuals and groups. The body of research and literature about computer-assisted counseling indicate that this too may be a major development during the next few years.

## ASSESSMENT AND EVALUATION

Recognizing the range of potential alternative interventions highlights some critical needs. It forces us to make important decisions about the nature of the services that are going to be offered. We are faced with decisions of priority concerning the target to select for intervention, the purpose of intervening, and the most efficient and effective method to use. These issues clearly underline the critical need for a systematic assessment of institutional and individual needs in order to plan appropriate and effective interventions; the assessment must be followed by systematic evaluation of the effects of whatever programs are developed. There is evidence that many programs are not effective in achieving their goals, yet we are often guilty of offering programs year after year with no evidence concerning program impact.

The model for alternative interventions presented here not only provides a framework within which modes of intervention can be both classified and understood, but also implicitly prepares the user to *consider various targets, purposes, and methods so that the best all-around intervention procedures will be developed.* The process of planning intervention strategies should begin with an assessment of needs and the personal, environmental, and institutional conditions that limit potential. The model then provides a point of departure—a stimulus for creative thinking about alternative interventions; then evaluative research can be the feedback mechanism that leads to further implementation or change. Student affairs work as a profession simply cannot afford to function in the comparatively ineffective and limited ways of the past. Alternative developmental interventions that really meet the human needs of our society must be developed.

In the next chapters we consider each of the three dimensions—target, purpose, and method—separately, emphasizing examples of intervention at each level.

## REFERENCES

Abel, W. H. Group counseling and academic rehabilitation of probationary transfer students. *Journal of College Student Personnel,* 1967, **8** (3), 185–188.

Banning, J. H. (Editor) *Campus Ecology: A Perspective for Student Affairs.* Monograph of the National Association of Student Personnel Administrators, Cincinnati, Ohio, 1978.

Barker, R. G. *Habitats, Environments, and Human Behavior*. San Francisco: Jossey-Bass, 1978, pp. 1–16.

Bierstedt, R. *The Social Order* (3rd ed.). New York: McGraw-Hill, 1970.

Bindman, A. J. Mental health consultation: theory and practice. *Journal of Consulting Psychology*, 1959, **23**, 473–482.

Bloom, B. L. Strategies for the prevention of mental disorders. In J. Glidewell and M. Brown, *Community Issues in Contemporary Psychology and Preventive Mental Health*. New York: Behavioral Publications, 1971.

Bower, E. M. Primary prevention of mental and emotional disorders. *American Journal of Orthopsychiatry*, 1963, **33**, 832–848.

Brown, B. S. Philosophy and scope of extended clinical activities. In A. J. Bindman and A. D. Spiegal (Eds.), *Perspectives in Community Mental Health*. Chicago: Aldine, 1969.

Cady, L. V. Developmental guidance: one definition and rationale. *School Counselor*, 1969, **16** (3), 218–221.

Caplan, G. Types of mental health consultation. *American Journal of Orthopsychiatry*, 1963, **33**, 470–481.

Carkhuff, R. R. *Helping and Human Relations*, Vols. I and II. New York: Holt, Rinehart and Winston, 1969.

Danskin, D. G., C. E. Kennedy, and W. Frieson Guidance: the ecology of students. *Personnel and Guidance Journal*, 1965, **44** (2), 130–135.

Farnsworth, D. L. Developmental tasks of college students. In D. L. Farnsworth (Ed.), *Psychiatry, Education and the Young Adult*. Springfield, Ill: Charles C. Thomas, 1966.

Foulds, M. L. and J. F. Guinan The counseling service as a growth center. *Personnel and Guidance Journal*, 1969, **48**, 111–118.

Goldin, P. Preparing mental health professionals as race relations consultants. *Professional Psychology*, 1970, **1**, 343–350.

Higgins, W. H., A. E. Ivey, and M. R. Uhlemann Media therapy: a programmed approach to teaching behavioral skills. *Journal of Counseling Psychology*, 1970, **17** (1), 20–26.

Holland, J. *Making Vocational Choices: A Theory of Careers*. Englewood Cliffs, N.J.: Prentice-Hall, 1973.

Human Development Institute, Inc. *Basic Interpersonal Relations: A Course for Small Groups*. Atlanta, Ga.: Bell & Howell, 1969.

Jarvis, E. and F. Stuzman Evaluation and treatment of families at Fort Logan Mental Health Center. *Community Mental Health Journal*, 1969, **5** (1), 14–19.

Kuehn, J. L. Counseling the college student drug user. *Bulletin of the Menninger Clinic*, 1970, **34** (4), 205–215.

Lewin, K. *Dynamic Theory of Personality*. New York: McGraw-Hill, 1935.

Linden, M. E., H. M. Goodwain, and H. Resnik Group psychotherapy of couples in marriage counseling. *International Journal of Group Psychotherapy*, 1968, **18** (3), 313–324.

Martin, C. V. and G. C. Horner Social institutions as therapeutic communities. *Psychotherapy and Psychosomatics*, 1967, **15** (1), 44.

Moos, R. H. *Evaluating Educational Environment.* San Francisco: Jossey-Bass, 1979, pp. 1–22.

Morrill, W. H., A. E. Ivey, and E. R. Oetting The college counseling center: a center for student development. In J. C. Heston and W. B. Frick (Eds.), *Counseling for the Liberal Arts Campus.* Yellow Springs, Ohio: Antioch Press, 1968.

Morrill, W. H., E. R. Oetting, and J. C. Hurst Dimensions of Counselor Functioning. *Personnel and Guidance Journal,* 1974 52 (6), 354–359.

Newman, S. Administration project in school consultation: a preventative approach. *Psychology in the Schools,* 1965, **2**, 70–76.

Oetting, E. R. Developmental definition of counseling psychology. *Journal of Counseling Psychology,* 1967, **14**, 382–385.

Preuss, W. J. The development of interpersonal relations in a college freshmen girls' dormitory. Unpublished doctoral dissertation, University of Nebraska Teachers College, 1967.

Rioch, M. J., C. Elkes, A. A. Flint, B. S. Vsdansky, R. G. Newman, and E. Silber National Institute of Mental Health pilot study in training mental health counselors. *American Journal of Orthopsychiatry,* 1963, **33**, 678–689.

Sanford, N. The prevention of mental illness. In B. Wolman (Ed.), *Handbook of Clinical Psychology.* New York: McGraw-Hill, 1965.

Sanford, N. Education for individual development. *American Journal of Orthopsychiatry,* 1968, **38** (5), 858–868.

Seashore, C. and E. Van Egmond The consultant-trainer role in working directly with a total staff. *Journal of Social Issues,* 1959, **15** (2), 36–42.

Stark, M. Human relations activities as an educational program in a college residence hall. *Journal of College Student Personnel,* 1964, **6** (1), 18–20.

Stephenson, R. M. and F. R. Scarpitti Establishing a therapeutic milieu in a non-institutional setting for delinquent boys. *Corrective Psychiatry and Journal of Social Therapy,* 1968, **14** (1), 10–23.

Stinnett, R. E. and L. K. Niedenthal The use of indigenous volunteers in a rehabilitation living unit for disturbed college students. *Community Mental Health Journal,* 1968, **4**, 232–243.

Super, D. E. *Computer-Assisted Counseling,* New York: Teachers College Press, 1970.

Zunker, V. G. and W. F. Brown Comparative effectiveness of student and professional counselors. *Personnel and Guidance Journal,* 1966, **44**, 738–743.

# 6

# The Target of Intervention

**JAMES C. HURST, WESTON H. MORRILL, and E. R. OETTING**

Student affairs professionals are in the business of intervening. Traditionally, the intervention has been in response to one individual (a helpee) extending an invitation to another individual (the helper) to utilize skill and knowledge in affecting a change in some aspect of the helpee's life. Basically, when student development professionals attempt to implement their knowledge and/or skill for the benefit of others, they are intervening for the purpose of change.

With all due respect to the immense contributions that early human development theorists made to conceptualizing student development, their theory and practice provided a set for subsequent theorists and practitioners that seems to have limited the scope of intervention and may even have distracted human development practitioners from their most basic goal. It appears that the concept of one person being able to provide effective help for another person by talking with them face-to-face was so personally involving that it has been emphasized and has become an end in itself. The result has been the investment of a tremendous amount of energy and talent in how one person should talk to another to bring about the most effective change. Hundreds of volumes have been written on this topic alone. All of this is well and good in terms of what we have learned about this particular mode of intervention. The inherent danger, however, is that of perceiving the process as an end in itself to be maintained and protected as the only mode of intervention. An attendant danger is the narrow professional self-identification with individual or small group interventions to the exclusion of other effective, and frequently more efficient, modes of therapeutic intervention. These statements may seem extreme since sociologists and community and organizational psychologists have long seen the possibilities of intervening in social systems and institutions in order to affect individuals and their fundamental interactions. Student affairs professionals, however, through a limited self-definition, are slower to adopt other intervention strategies that may be more effective and efficient in specified situations.

The innovation of doing individual counseling and therapy in groups that emerged during the mid 1950s and early 1960s was indeed a step in recognizing the possibility of making interventions in ways other than on a one-to-one basis. The immediate focus of the intervention, however, remained the same—the individual person. At first glance the innovation of group counseling was a truly different mode of intervention. A closer look, however, revealed that the target of the intervention was the same, changing the individual. The technique gave the appearance of a different approach, but was fundamentally still people talking with each other. The model described here recognizes that interventions may be legitimately made at points of impact other than with the individual. The first dimension of this model is titled *target of intervention* and specifies two possible targets that a student development specialist might attend to in an effort to intervene for change. These targets are the individual and the environment. To provide some specificity, the environment is divided into primary group, associational group, and institution or community.

## THE INDIVIDUAL AS TARGET OF INTERVENTION

As noted above, interventions designed to impact the individual have received the lion's share of attention since the time of Freud. Traditional training for counseling, advising, discipline, and health care deal almost exclusively with making the intervention on a one-to-one basis, with the professional interacting with the student so that individual change of behavior occurs. Regardless of whether the intervention is for the purpose of remediating a behavioral deficit, preventing a problem through teaching prerequisite knowledge and skills, or simply working in a developmental way to help an effective person become even more effective, the traditional intervention target was still the individual.

A counseling center that places a counselor in the residence halls so that students can have greater access to the counselor may term that an "outreach" effort. The individual is still, in fact, the target of the intervention. The counseling center that places a counselor in the student center or a married students' complex to help individuals attain a better adjustment is still making individual interventions. In both these activities the target for the intervention is the individual student and, regardless of the purpose or method used for the intervention, if the individual remains the focus, the classification of intervention remains as "individual" in the target dimension of the model.

The direct and individual intervention is ordinarily perceived as the cornerstone from which other targets or methods of intervention may emanate. This is probably the case partly because the body of research concerning this target of intervention is so much more extensive than any of the others. It is also probably the case because of tradition. It is expertise in intervening with the individual that provides the basic identity for most human development practitioners both in and outside of higher education. Training programs in intervention strategies usually reflect this circumstance by insisting that all students acquire a basic competency level in individual and small group interventions. Interventions with the individual then are usually viewed as the cornerstone for applied student development programming.

In many respects it is appropriate for the individual intervention strategy to provide the foundation for other intervention strategies. Whether the target is the individual or the environment, the goal of student affairs professionals is to enhance the functioning and quality of life of the individual. We target the environment because of its impact on individuals. In these respects we can indeed view individual interventions as a cornerstone and foundation on which to build the rest of the structure.

## THE ENVIRONMENT AS TARGET OF INTERVENTION

Lewin as early as 1936 was stressing the importance of taking into account both the person and the environment in understanding and predicting behavior. Murray (1938) also addressed his attention to the environment with his needs/press theory of personality. Yet even with these early beginnings, most of the efforts of student affairs professionals have been only on the person side of the equation, often ignoring the environment. The usual approach taken when we wish to improve the quality of the graduates of institutions of higher education has been to select students who are more like our goal for graduates and not change the environment to influence that quality. This procedure worked well until declining enrollments and civil rights legislation somewhat mandated a change. Even so, a recent example highlights our difficulty in breaking set and looking beyond the individual in effecting change. Hirschberg and Itkin (1978) reported in a study of graduate students success in psychology, among other findings, that "only 35% of the women . . . obtained a degree, whereas 68% of the men had obtained their degree" (p. 1090). The authors discussed the problem of selection and proposed a multiple-hurdles model. They did not even suggest the possibility that there are aspects of the departmental environment that might differentially affect attrition rates by sex. Perhaps a more positive sign for the future is that at least three individuals called attention to that obvious oversight in the comments section of the *American Psychologist* (Wittig, 1979; Sherrill, 1979; Sollod, 1979).

The purpose of the target dimension is to clearly suggest consideration of the environment as well as the person as targets for intervention. One of the difficulties, however, is that environment is such an inclusive term that the model breaks it down into separate parts for ease in consideration. Thus consideration progresses from the most basic environmental unit, the primary group, through associational groups to institutions and communities.

## Primary Group

The primary group is the basic unit of social organization. It is that group (or groups) that has the greatest impact and influence on individual behavior. Characteristics that define a primary group are intimacy, frequency of interaction on a face-to-face basis, strong interpersonal sanctions concerning accepted or unaccepted behavior, and ongoing or continuing associations. Primary groups have a strong influence on the development and continuation of the individual's self-concept, with the group being an integral part of an individual's self-identification and social role adoption. If even one member of the primary group is absent, that absence is noted through observation and modified behavior patterns and interactions of the group. The prime example of the primary group is the conjugal family in American society and consanguine family in other societies. When a child moves into adolescence, the primary group usually expands to a small but tightly knit group of peers. Later in life, the primary group may cut across family lines to include that of the spouse. Intervention at the primary group level includes efforts to alter communication patterns and interaction systems, intra- and interpersonal perceptions, the status structure in the group, reward or punishment contingencies, and patterns of dependence and independence.

A large body of literature exists that deals with intervention strategies at the primary group level (Gurman and Kniskern, 1978). Some of these strategies have been developed specifically for primary group intervention such as marriage and family counseling strategies. Others are simply adaptations of strategies and theories designed to deal with individual interventions, but are then applied to primary group interventions. Alfred Alder's work has been adapted by a number of his proponents to deal with primary group intervention. Sonstegard and Dreikurs (1967) wrote of primary group counseling as it exists in a school setting and how interventions may be made with teachers, parents, or directly with students as possible components of a primary group. *Adlerian Family Counseling* (Dreikurs, 1959) is a manual designed to training the reader in the organization of a family counseling agency based on Adlerian principles. *The Challenge of Parenthood* (Dreikurs, 1958) emphasizes parent–child interaction and ways to modify that interaction as an example of a primary group intervention. *Paring* (Bach and Deutsch, 1970) is a good example of an effort to work with communication and interaction patterns as they relate to the development of such things as intimacy, fighting, dependence, and feedback. Emphasis on communications as the raw material of primary group intervention is also the underlying framework of Haley in his *Strategies of Psychotherapy* (1963) and *Techniques of Family Therapy* (1967), which he wrote with Hoffman. Jackson (1968,) also *deals* with the basic elements of communication and applies them exclusively to marriage and the family. Many others (Messer, 1970; Satir, 1967; Zuk and Boszormenyi-Nagy, 1967) have made significant contributions to this area.

Many of the more well-known and traditional individual therapy processes have also been adapted to primary group intervention modes. Transactional analysis as defined and described by Berne (1961, 1967) lends itself well to primary group intervention inasmuch as it is a theory based on communication in an adaptation of a psychoanalytic style position. The popularization of Berne's position by Harris (1969) has helped to make transactional analysis household conversation in many families across the country. In addition, Carkhuff (1971), Perls (1951, 1969), and Rogers (1959, 1965) have all made efforts to adapt their theoretical position to interventions with primary groups. Their programs were all initially developed with a one-to-one helper/helpee paradigm in mind. The adaptation of these theories is useful in conceptualizing intervention strategies with primary groups.

Any discussion of the effectiveness of individual intervention will eventually deal with the inherent difficulty of changing an individual's behavior if the 1 or 2 hours of contact a week are being counteracted by the student's immersion during the rest of the week in a destructive primary group milieu. This is especially critical for adolescents and young adults in their formative years. The theories and conceptualizations noted above have grown out of an initial focus on the individual toward a focus on the primary group that played such an important role in the formation of the character of the individual. Common sense suggests that a modification of the primary group itself may be prerequisite to individual behavior change that is expected to be permanent. The method of the actual intervention in most instances still relies on the verbal interaction between professionals and students, but greater attention is given to diagnosing and modifying transactions and reward and punishment schedules manifested in the interpersonal interactions of the primary group.

The feasibility of primary group intervention with students on college and university campuses may be limited by several factors. First, the fact that students' families may reside hundreds of miles from the campus often makes such an intervention impractical. Second, not all students develop circles of friends on campus that are close enough and intimate enough in their interactions to be classified as primary groups. Both these factors would appear to be determined at least in part by whether or not the campus is a low residence environment as opposed to one that has a high incidence of student residents. A third factor is the size of the population of married students residing either off campus or in married student housing on campus. The stress of attending school while married has been documented through the relatively high frequency of married students seeking out counseling. In such an instance the involvement of the student's spouse is often recommended and in some cases imperative.

The traditional intervention, in which the 50 minute hour is the primary mode of activity, must sooner or later attend to the difficulties noted above in trying to bring about a change in behavior during one contact hour competing against hundreds in which the student is immersed in a primary group. Under these circumstances the most effective work is with the student's primary group in order to modify the punishment or reward system, develop an emotional support system, create new channels of communication, realign and/or reestablish dependence allocations, or any other modification that may be in the best interest of the student's goals. A good argument for primary group intervention can be made not only because this approach may well enhance the educational process, but also build a maintenance system to assist the student in the continuation of more effective and productive behavior patterns. It is obvious that a primary group may experience change as a result of one of its members being the recipient of an individual intervention. In this case, however, the intent has been to modify not the primary group but the individual, with the difference that emerges in the group being incidental. Conversely, in the primary group intervention the focus is on the basic characteristics and patterns of the primary group itself with changes in the individual members of the primary group occurring as a result of the differences in the primary group. This of course does not rule out intentionality in planning for individual change through intervention with the primary group structure.

Although a true primary group may be relatively rare on campus there are still a number of primary group interventions possible. Examples are marital and premarital counseling, inviting the student's family to the campus office to diagnose and treat according to observed interactions among family members, designing a dorm to facilitate the formation of primary groups, training the student to be an agent in modifying the interaction patterns within his/her family, utilizing small groups in order to create a model of a family through role playing, and other techniques followed by teaching the group members procedures for creating constructive primary groups as a support system for the members of the groups. Creativity and innovation are called for in developing new approaches for primary group interventions on the college campus perhaps more than any other strategy. This is one of the potentially most powerful intervention tools and a good deal of attention is called for in adapting it to the university or college setting.

## Associational Groups

Associational groups are those in which group members share a consciousness of similar interests and/or needs and join together with some organizational structure to pursue these common interests or needs. Bierstedt (1970) further characterizes the associational group as one in which all members may come together relatively frequently, often with the ability to recognize other members of that group through personal acquaintance. The associational group may be as small as a six to eight member seminar or as large as an entire freshman class. It may be as closely knit and interdependent as a drill team or as loosely organized as a particular dorm or residence hall. It is distinguished from the primary group in such ways as the absence of one particular member not having an impact on the total group, the personal feelings of the other members of the group not having as much valence with regard to sanctioning of personal conduct, and the primary group playing a much more central role in the member's definition of self. The associational group may be distinguished from the next level of intervention, institution, or community in that the associational group may and often does meet together with the entire membership present; there is much greater commonality in at least one critical variable such as age, sex, interests, and educational level; and the organizational and communication pattern is much simpler and less bureaucratic. Whereas an intervention at the individual level may have a significant effect on the primary group of which that individual is a member, it would in all likelihood have little or no impact on an associational group or institution or community. This of course would not be true if the individual who is the recipient of the individual intervention is a key person in the institution or associational group.

An associational group intervention may be made through an effort to modify the group administrative or governmental operating procedures. An example would be an intervention to establish a democratic decision-making process in a residence hall in place of one that is automatic. The result of this kind of an intervention may be a greater degree of participation of residents in designated activities, and thus more participation and satisfaction in the activities themselves. In addition, the residents may express less frustration and stress and show less resistance to the living rules in a residence hall. Here the focus of the intervention would be on the associational group, not on an individual within that group.

Another possible example of an associational group intervention might be the identification and modification of covert reward and punishment systems. Efforts to discover the reasons for a particular fraternity or sorority having a significantly lower academic performance might reveal that academic pursuits are interfered with, that members are chided for studying, or that social activity is seen as more important and good grades are seen as having little value. In this case an intervention might entail having all the members and pledges participate in a goal-setting session and then pointing out that in most cases the covert reward systems were dissonant with the goals of college graduation and success in beginning a career.

A third type of associational group intervention could involve training key people in the administrative or governmental structure of the group. For example, a wide variety of student organizations could be provided with the leadership skills to better accomplish the goals of providing a more effective support system designed to enhance members' success if the leaders are trained in communication procedures and effective methods of organization and implementation. In some cases this type of intervention may at first be perceived as an individual rather than an associational group. The distinguishing features, however, are that the intent would be not just to provide key personnel with skills for their personal edification, but rather to teach them the skills needed to provide for more effective functioning of the associational group.

Other methods of making interventions at the associational group level are environmental manipulation, such as facilitating the membership's geographic proximity; establishing communication links through the use of a micro-lab; enhancing frequency of interaction through the development of projects or more frequent meetings; identifying an issue that is perceived as having urgency by the entire membership; facilitating the development of goals or altering present goals of the group, and working to alter the method of goal attainment.

A sizable body of literature exists concerning associational group intervention. The bulk of this work has not been done within the framework of human development theory, but rather in sociology and industrial psychology. The study of associational groups provides a point of interfacing between the disciplines of psychology and sociology with the specific point of contact being the overall topic of group dynamics. Bonner (1959), March (1965), Mills (1967), Reeves (1970), Shaw (1971), and Zander (1971) are examples of authors who have dealt in detail with the topic of group dynamics. The industrial psychology–organizational development approach is represented by Argyris (1970), Blake and Mouton (1964), Blake, Shepard, and Mouton (1964), Bradford, Gibb, and Benne (1964), Davis (1967), Dickson and Roethlisberger (1966). Reports of actual associational group interventions have been written by Bloom (1965), De Ordio (1968), Powell et al. (1969), Schauble (1970), Moore, Hinkle, and Forrest (1972), Morrill and Banning (1973), and Morrill, Oetting, and Hurst (1975).

## The Institution or Community

The target of an intervention may also be either an institution or a community. These differ from associational groups in that they do not necessarily involve any meeting where all the members are present. Members are aware of their membership as part of an institution or community; however, the membership is usually very informal and if a member or a number of members were to disappear, their absence would not likely be noticed by the entire institution or community. Also, membership in an institution or community has much smaller valence with regard to influencing and sanctioning the beliefs and behavior of the member. An institution or a community probably includes as part of its composition associational groups, primary groups, and obviously many individuals. Examples of institutions or communities are an individual school, a school system, a town or city, a neighborhood, a religious organization, professional organizations such as the American Personnel and Guidance Association, a state, or even a nation. Intervention strategies at this level of intervention are obviously different from those at the individual or primary group level and yet there are also some basic similarities. Interventions at this level include attempts to alter the goals, communication patterns, system linkages, power distribution, information flow, sanctions, rewards, and leadership styles (Morrill, Oetting, and Hurst, 1972). In general, interventions at this level occur with the perception that the institution or community is the "client" and the diagnostic, treatment, and assessment activities are directed toward the institution or community (Kelly, 1966). A number of individual personality theories have taken cognizance of the impact of the individual's environment on personality development. In essence these theories may be perceived as ecological approaches to the psychology of personality. Murray (1938) proposed a theory of personality that used a model for the relationship between the individual and their environment. In Murray's model the person is viewed as one having a complex system of needs that interface and interact with environmental presses. In this system much can be said about congruence or discrepancies with regard to these needs and presses. Lewin (1951) stressed the impact of what he called "field theory" in his explanation of personality. The field he is referring to is simply the larger environment, which may be considered to include the institution or community. Angyal (1941) also talked of personality in organismic terms in which he described reciprocal interaction between the organism and the environment. Gordon (1970) identified three core dimensions that he believed were essential to investigate if the understanding of the development of personality was to occur:

1 **The Balance between Congruence and Incongruence:** It is necessary to maintain a maximum of congruence with just enough incongruence between the person and the environment for optimal tension and to ensure that interaction will not become static.
2 **The Constancy/Chance Dimension:** The interaction between the person and his environment must be sufficiently consistent to allow for orientation, while also maintaining a certain level of, or capacity for, change to keep the ecosystem dynamic.

3 **The Collective/Idiosyncratic Need Balance:** There must be a relative balance between the needs of the group and those of the individual.

Kaiser (1972a) made an effort to more clearly delineate the differences between traditional models for intervention to bring about a change of behavior and what he described as the ecological model:

| Traditional Models | Ecological Model |
|---|---|
| Follows the medical model to explain client distress | Follows the socioenvironmental explanations of client distress |
| Has remedial orientation | Has prevention and development orientation |
| Focuses on pathology in the individual | Focuses on pathology in the environment |
| Interacts in limited ways with the social system | Has close liaison with social systems |
| Reaches limited proportion of the population | Can influence, at least potentially, a large proportion of the population |

This ecological model has as its thesis that there is a reciprocal relationship between the person and the larger environment such as institution or community. In a sense it is an application of the theories of Murray, Lewin, and Angyal.

In addition to the theoretical positions cited above there is also much empirical evidence supporting the interdependence of the two variables. As early as 1925 Park and Burgess indicated that their research suggested that behavior was indeed a function of the urban environment. Finally, Barker (1968) represents a growing number who proposed that individuals and their environment must be seen as a single psychological entity rather than two separate entities. Work is continuing in an effort to identify those environmental variables that have a direct correlation to the development of social and/or personal dysfunction and maladjustment (Kaiser and Sherretz, 1978).

***Institutional and Community Diagnosis.*** One of the similarities between individual or primary group intervention and interventions attempted at the environmental or community level is that the intervention must be based on some kind of assessment or diagnosis. Interventions made without this first step are haphazard and may or may not have the desired result. At present there are four basic approaches to diagnostic assessment of an institution or community. The first of these is the *demographic approach.* This approach is primarily descriptive with information gathered that describes the various characteristics of the institution or community. Astin (1962) utilized the demographic approach and identified five factors descriptive of college environment as affluence, size, masculinity, homogeneity of offering, and technical emphasis. Although the demographic approach to assessment may be considered as a basic point of departure, it may well miss some of the more covert dimensions of an environment.

The *perceptual approach* to environmental assessment emphasizes the members' perceptions of their particular environment. Whereas the demographic approach is essentially descriptive, the perceptual approach is phenomenological. The underlying philosophy is that what the members perceive is to them reality and therefore impacts on their beliefs, attitudes, and behavior. Pace (1969) authored The College and University Environment Scales (CUES) as one example of this approach.

The *behavioral approach* is an effort to identify actual behaviors that occur in an environment rather than the perceptions of what is occurring. Chickering (1970) seems to favor this method in that what is actually taking place is seen by him as providing the most immediately useful and powerful information for program planners and decision makers. One technique to get at this is a paper and pencil approach in which respondents describe what they do, such as in Astin's (1971) Inventory of College Activities (ICA). Carruth and Comer (1972) also describe *unstructured student interviews* as providing extremely useful information relative to actual behavior in the environment.

Finally, the multi-method approach unifies the strengths of all three techniques above in that it is a combination of all three. This approach utilizes a multi-method questionnaire to provide the investigator with all three types of information. Some specific instruments designed as multi-method instruments are *College Student Questionnaire* by Peterson (1968), *Questionnaire on Student and College Characteristics* by Centra (1970).

***A Model for Institutional Intervention.*** One example of a procedure for intervention into an institution or community is that which Kaiser calls ecosystem design process. He describes this as an attempt to create a campus environment that will foster student growth and development. Kaiser's model has four basic components. The first of these is an ecosystem-design philosophy which takes into account the transactional relationship that exists between the individual and the environment and then postulates that an intentionally designed environment can be most congruent with individual freedom and development. Second, he describes an ecosystem-design methodology with two basic components. The first is a self-selection method in which the designer creates a diverse campus environment structured to appeal to different kinds of students. The second method is one in which the student is studied individually and then based on this study the campus environment is created with features designed to appeal to these student profiles. Third, an ecosystem design process contains seven sequential steps for the actual design process (Kaiser, 1972b, 1972c):

**Step 1:** Select the institutional values that are to be pursued.

**Step 2:** Translate values into environmental goals.

**Step 3:** Design environmental programs to accomplish goals.

**Step 4:** Fit environmental programs to the students, faculty, staff, and administration.

**Step 5:** Measure student, faculty, staff, and administration perceptions of programs and the environment in general.

**Step 6:** Monitor student, faculty, administration, and staff behavior in the program.

**Step 7:** Feed back data to designers to discuss findings with appropriate campus members.

This process (steps 1 through 6) has produced a data base on which judgments of what to do are based. A feedback loop now exists to take the designers back to what values exist so that the process can start again at step 1.

Kaiser (1972a, 1972b) identifies three types of designs for an environment. The first is a *compensating* design for the purpose of remediating a deficit or handicap that exists among the members of the environment. The second type he calls a *facilitating* environment and attends primarily to providing a range of opportunities so that individuals can enhance existing competence. The third type of design is called a *potentiating* one, which has as its purpose stimulation of the development of dormant abilities possessed presently only as potentials by the individuals in the environment.

This then completes a brief description of one person's conceptualization of how an institutional or community intervention may be made. There are obviously others that should be attended to relative to actually bringing about an intervention at this level through designing an entire environment.

***The Interventionist.*** At the institutional–community level the interventionist may be either an outside or inside person or agency. An outside consultant is defined by Lippitt (1959) as meeting these three criteria: (1) a professional helper (consultant) (2) who works together with a help-seeking system (client) in a voluntary and temporary relationship (3) in which the consultant assists the client in solving immediate or potential problems. The advantages of having an interventionist be external to the system are first that outsiders are likely to be more objective in the absence of having vested interests within the environment and second that they are relatively free from repercussions from their work in the environment. Finally, outsiders can provide modeling for on-campus action committees that normally act as mediators in campus disputes (Ferguson, 1968). The disadvantages of having an outsider attempt the intervention are that outsiders may lack information that an insider has, are more likely to be perceived with suspicion than an insider, and will be seen as an unknown entity to the members of the environment in which the intervention is to be made. Other writers (Carkhuff, 1969; Ferguson, 1968; Lippitt, 1959; Schein, 1969; and Walton, 1969) have written concerning the goals and general principles of effectiveness concerning the outside interventionist.

An internal person or agency may also bring about changes in an institution or community. All the disadvantages of the external interventionist are conversely to the advantage of the internal. Just as in the case of the associational group, a particular intervention may have as its focus the physical environment, the communication pattern, policies and administrative procedures, individuals in the power structure, associational groups within the institution or community, job definitions and role in the power structure, organizational structure, norms and sanctions of behavior, and interpersonal relationships among key people.

## SUMMARY

The individual intervention is historically the cornerstone of all therapeutic interventions designed to modify human behavior. Interventions with primary groups, however, may in some cases be far more effective as well as more efficient than individual interventions. More recently the advantages of more large-scale interventions impacting associational groups and even a whole institution or community are deemed possible and in some cases advisable. It is through the interventions at these larger levels that whole systems which are counterproductive to human development may be modified. Expertise in intervention strategies at all four levels is probably too much to ask for in any one individual. However, it is not too much to ask that the expertise exist in various members of the staff of a particular student affairs division. In this way a student affairs program can acquire a reputation as having the capability of making interventions at whichever level is most appropriate. In this way individuals, primary groups, associational groups, or an entire institution or community may be perceived as a legitimate target of intervention.

## REFERENCES

Angyal, A. *Foundation for a Science of Personality*. New York: Commonwealth Fund, 1941.

Argyris, Chris *Intervention Theory and Method: A Behavioral Science View*. Reading, Mass.: Addison-Wesley, 1970.

Astin, A. W. An empirical characterization of higher educational institutions. *Journal of Educational Psychology*, 1962, **53** (5), 224–236.

Astin, A. W. Two approaches to measuring students' perceptions of their college environment. *Journal of College Student Personnel*, 1971, **12** (3), 169–173.

Bach, G. R. and R. M. Deutsch *Pairing*. New York: Avon Books, 1970.

Barker, R. G. *Ecological Psychology*. Stanford, Calif.: Stanford University Press, 1968.

Bennis, W. G., K. D. Benne, and R. Chin *The Planning of Change*. New York: Holt, Rinehart & Winston, 1961.

Bennis, W. G. Theory and method in applying behavioral science to planned organizational change. *The Journal of Applied Behavioral Science*, 1965, **1** (4), 337–361.

Bennis, W. G. *Changing Organizations*. New York: McGraw-Hill, 1966.

Berne, E. *Transactional Analysis in Psychotherapy*. New York: Grove Press, Inc., 1961.

Bierstedt, R. *The Social Order*. New York: McGraw Hill, 1970.

Berne, E. *Games People Play*. New York: Grove Press, Inc., 1967.

Blake, R. R. and J. S. Mouton *The Managerial Grid*. Houston: Gulf Publishing Co., 1964.

Blake, R. R., H. A. Shepard, and J. S. Mouton *Managing Intergroup Conflict in Industry*. Houston: Gulf Publishing Co., 1964.

Bonner, H. *Group Dynamics*. New York: The Ronald Press Company, 1959.

Bradford, L. P., J. R. Gibb, and K. D. Benne *T-Group Theory and Laboratory Method*. New York: John Wiley & Sons, 1964.

Carkhuff, R.R. *Helping and Human Relations* (2 vols.). New York: Holt, Rinehart and Winston, 1969.

Carkhuff, R. R. *The Development of Human Resources.* New York: Holt, Rinehart, and Winston, 1971.

Carruth, J. F. and P. E. Comer Outreach by structured interview. In W. H. Morrill (Ed.), *Preliminary Report: Outreach-Developmental Programs in College Counseling.* Grant No. RO1 MH 18007, National Institute of Mental Health, 1972.

Centra, J. A. The college environment revisited: current descriptions and a comparison of three methods of assessment. *College Entrance Examination Board Research & Development Reports,* RDR-70-71, NO. 1, Educational Testing Service, Princeton, N.J., 1970.

Centra, J. A., T. Harnett, and R. E. Peterson Faculty views of institutional functioning: a new measure of college environment. *Educational & Psychological Measurement,* 1970, **30** (2), 405–416.

Centra, J. A. and R. L. Linn On interpreting students' perception of their college environment. *Measurement and Evaluation in Guidance,* 1970, **3** (2), 102–110.

Chickering, A. W. The Experience of College Questionnaire. *The impact of Colleges on Students.* Paper presented at The American Association for the Advancement of Science, Washington D.C., Dec., 1970.

Davis, Keith *Human Relations at Work: The Dynamics of Organizational Behavior.* New York: McGraw-Hill, 1967.

De Ordio, Joseph *Residence Halls Staff Development,* Outreach Programming Report Form, Kansas State University, Manhattan, Kans., 1968.

Dickson, W. J. and F. J. Roethlisberger *Counseling in an Organization.* Boston: Graduate School of Business Administration, Harvard University, 1966.

Dreikurs, R. *The Challenge of Parenthood* (rev. ed.). New York: Duell, Sloan & Pearce, 1958.

Dreikurs, R., R. Corsini, R. Lowe, and M. Sonstegard *Adlerian Family Counseling.* Eugene: University of Oregon Press, 1959.

Faris, R. E. L. and H. W. Dunham *Mental Disorders in Urban Areas.* Chicago: University of Chicago Press, 1939.

Ferguson, C. K. Concerning the nature of human systems and the consultant's role. *Journal of Applied Behavioral Science,* 1968, **4** (2), 179–195.

Gordon, E. W. Perspective on counseling and other approaches to guided behavior change. *Counseling Psychologist,* 1970, **2** (2), 105–114.

Gurman, A. S. and D. P. Kniskern Research on marital and family therapy: progress, perspective, and prospect. In S. L. Garfield and A. E. Bergin, *Handbook of Psychotherapy and Behavior Change.* New York: John Wiley & Sons, 1978, 817–902.

Haley, Jay *Strategies of Psychotherapy.* New York: Grune & Stratton, 1963.

Haley, J., and Hoffman *Techniques of Family Therapy.* New York: Basic Books, 1967.

Harris, T. A. *I'm OK—You're OK—A Practical Guide to Transactional Analysis.* New York: Harper & Row Publishers, 1969.

Hirschberg, N. and S. Itkin Graduate success in psychology. *American Psychologist,* 1978, **33**, 1083–1093.

Jackson, D. D. *Communication, Family, and Marriage,* Palo Alto, Calif.: Science and Behavior Books, 1968.

Kaiser, L. E. Campus ecology: implications for environmental design. Report for the

WICHE Task Force II—Epidemiology, *Campus Ecology and Program Evaluation,* 1972a, Boulder, Colo.

Kaiser, L. E. The ecological perspective: mapping and designing the students' educational community. Preliminary report for the WICHE Task Force II—Epidemiology, *Campus Ecology and Program,* 1972b, Boulder, Colo.

Kaiser, L. E. The ecosystem model: designing campus environments. Report for the WICHE Task Force II—Epidemiology, *Campus Ecology and Program,* 1972c, Boulder, Colo.

Kaiser, L. E. and L. Sherretz Designing campus environments: a review of selected literature, Chapter 6, Student–campus environment dysfunctions. In J. H. Banning, (Ed.) *Campus Ecology: A Perspective for Student Affairs.* NASPA Monograph, Cincinnati, Ohio: 1978, pp. 100–106.

Kelly, J. G. Ecological constraints in mental health services. *American Psychologist,* 1966, **21** (6), 535–540.

Lewin, K. *Principles of Topological Psychology.* New York: McGraw, 1936.

Lewin, K. *Field Theory in Social Science.* New York: Harper & Row, 1951.

Lippitt, R. Dimensions of the consultant's job. *Journal of Social Issues,* 1959, **15** (2), 5–12.

March, J. G. Changing interpersonal and intergroup relationships in organizations. *Handbook of Organizations.* Chicago: Rand McNally & Company, 1965.

Messer, A. *The Individual and His Family: An Adaptational Study.* Springfield, Ill.: Charles C Thomas, 1970.

Mills, T. M. *The Sociology of Small Groups.* Englewood Cliffs, N.J.: Prentice Hall, 1967.

Moore, M., J. E. Hinkle, and D. Forrest An experimental social center in university-owned married housing. *Journal of College Student Personnel,* 1972, **13** (2), 145–150.

Morrill, W. H. Institutional assessment and counseling outreach. Grant proposal submitted to the National Institute of Mental Health, 1973.

Morrill, W. H. and J. H. Banning *Counseling Outreach: A Survey of Practices.* Boulder, Colo.: Western Interstate Commission for Higher Education, 1973.

Morrill, W. H., E. R. Oetting, and J. C. Hurst Dimensions of counseling intervention. Technical Report #1, Colorado State University, Fort Collins, Colo.: National Institute of Mental Health, 1972 (RO1 MH 18007-01a1).

Morrill, W. H., E. R. Oetting, and J. C. Hurst *Nine Outreach Programs.* Fort Collins, Colo.: Colorado State University Press, 1975.

Murray, H. A. *Explorations in Personality.* New York: Oxford, 1938.

Pace, C.R. *College and University Environment Scale*: Second Edition: Technical Manual. Princeton, N.J.: Educational Testing Service, 1969.

Park, R. E. and E. W. Burgess *The City.* Chicago: University of Chicago Press, 1925.

Perls, F. S. *Gestalt Therapy.* New York: Dell Publishing, 1951.

Perls, F. S. *Ego, Hunger and Aggression.* New York: Random House, 1969.

Peterson, R. E. *College Student Questionnaire Technical Manual* (rev. ed.). Princeton, N.J.: Educational Testing Service, 1968.

Powell, J. R., S. A. Plyer, B. A. Dickson, and S. D. McClellan *The Personnel Assistant in College Residence Halls*. Boston: Houghton Mifflin Co., 1969.

Reeves, E. T. *The Dynamics of Group Behavior*. New York: American Management Association, Inc., 1970.

Rogers, C. A theory of therapy, personality and interpersonal relationships as developed in the client-centered framework. *Psychology: A Study of Science*. New York: McGraw-Hill, 1959.

Rogers, C. *Client-Centered Therapy*. Boston: Houghton Mifflin, 1965.

Satir, V. *Conjoint Family Therapy*. Palo Alto, Calif.: Science and Behavior, 1967.

Schauble, P. *Video Tape—A Powerful Tool*. Report to the American College Personnel Association, Commission III Workshop, March 17, 1970 (Program entitled: "What's Happening in Residence Hall Student Staff Training?").

Schein, E. H. Score one for process consultation. *Journal of Applied Behavioral Science*. 1968, **4**, 348–350.

Schein, E. H. *Process Consultation: Its Role in Organizational Development*. Reading, Mass.: Addision-Wesley, 1969.

Shaw, M. E. *Group Dynamics: The Psychology of Small Group Behavior*. New York: McGraw-Hill Book Company, 1971.

Sherrill, R. On selection and "deselection." *American Psychologist*, 1979, **34**, 798.

Sollod, R. N. Are more hurdles needed? *American Psychologist*, 1979, **34**, 799–800.

Sonstegard, M. and R. Dreikurs *The Teleoanalytic Approach to Group Counseling*. Chicago: Alfred Adler Institute, 1967.

Walton, R. E. *Interpersonal Peacemaking: Confrontations and Third Party Consultation*. Reading, Mass.: Addison-Wesley, 1969.

Wittig, M. A. Graduate student success: sex or situation? *American Psychologist*, 1979, **34**, 798.

Zander, A. *Motives and Goals in Groups*. New York: Academic Press, 1971.

Zuk, G. H. and I. Boszormenyi-Nagy *Family Therapy and Disturbed Families*. Palo Alto, Calif.: Science and Behavior Books, 1967.

# 7

# The Purpose of Intervention

E. R. OETTING, WESTON H. MORRILL,
JAMES C. HURST

The purpose dimension of the "cube" is concerned with what an intervention is trying to accomplish: remediation, prevention, or development. If the program or treatment is concerned with repairing damage that has already been done, you are engaged in remediation. If you are trying to keep a potential problem from occurring sometime in the future, you are involved in prevention. If you are not concerned with a specific future problem, but are trying to develop skills and abilities so that the future will be better than the past has been has ever been, you are engaged in a developmental intervention.

Student affairs professionals in the past have usually been reactive: they have reacted to requests for help or responded to problems in the organization only after the problem has become severe enough so it is easily recognizable. The intent of the purpose dimension is to increase awareness that the objectives and goals of an intervention should be proactive as well, preventing problems from occurring and developing greater human and organizational potential.

There is a classic poem by Joseph Malins (1936) called "A Fence or an Ambulance." The people of a small town kept falling over a cliff, so they all got together and developed a good ambulance service. Then some fanatic suggested another solution: building a fence. The poem illustrates part of the purpose dimension. If the purpose is remediation, then an ambulance is required. If it is prevention, then a fence is needed.

Actually, neither solution is complete. Even if there are good prevention programs such as the fence, there is still a need for remediation. The fence on one cliff will not keep people from falling off another cliff. Furthermore, the ambulance and the fence are not the only alternatives. Building a lot of fences not only doesn't keep people from falling off cliffs, but it may also prevent them from learning skills that they need for personal fulfillment and survival. This leads us to the third part of the purpose dimension, development. Defining the purpose as developmental would lead to teaching people the physical skills that they need to deal effectively with their environment. It is not aimed at preventing people from having a problem, but at expanding their personal limits and potential. People would learn climbing techniques, and develop balance and agility. They would be stronger, enjoy using their bodies, and be able not only to avoid falling off cliffs, but perhaps to climb mountains.

All three purposes must be met in the real world. Remediation programs are needed for those who are in trouble, prevention to reduce future problems, and developmental programs to increase potential.

## REMEDIATION

The focus of remediation is to move an individual or a group of individuals who are experiencing problems toward effective present functioning. Remediation is needed when an individual or a group is in trouble. They may not have the skills to meet the demands of the environment, or the environment in some way cannot meet their needs. The pain caused by this discrepancy may be great enough to cause the individual to drop out of the environment or seek some kind of therapeutic intervention. The breakdown could be a communication problem, a problem of inadequate skills, or a poor match of needs. It could be occurring in the present only, or it could be built on a long history of failures building up over the years.

Providing remediation for students is, and will in the near future continue to be, a major service of student affairs professionals. For example, estimates of prevalence of emotional disorders range from 10 to 25 percent of the population (Reid, 1970). Counseling centers on various college campuses report that up to 10 percent of the student population seek help for the remediation of identified problems at some time during their college career (Farnsworth, 1966). These figures make it clear that remediation activities will continue to require a significant portion of resources.

The role of student affairs professionals in discipline and academic standards has emphasized remedial activities. When students violate some rule or sanction of the institution, disciplinary action may be taken. The goal is to rehabilitate and change, not to punish. In a similar vein, academic standards programs operate to identify students whose academic grades fall below a certain acceptable level and then notify the students of probationary status in an effort to effect improvement of grades. It should be pointed out that this also has a preventive component in that attention is called to inadequate work with a goal of preventing continuing failure.

There is a generalized model, based on the Minnesota Model of Work Adjustment (Dawis, Englund, and Lofquist, 1964), that can be useful in diagnosing a remedial problem. It helps identify exactly what the problem is and provides clues about what can be done about it. Figure 1 illustrates the model. It shows a person–environment interaction. The environment has certain requirements that relate to the individual: if the person has capabilities that meet those needs, he or she is viewed as satisfactory. The person too has needs: if the environment can meet those needs, the person is satisfied. If there is a mismatch, and either the need of the person or the requirements of the environment are not being met, then there is a problem that needs remediation.

The student in academic trouble is an example of a mismatch. The school environment has academic requirements that are not being met by the student's capabilities for studying and taking exams. Since the requirements are not likely to change, remediation has to focus on either changing to another environment that does not make the same demands or changing the capabilities of the student so the requirements can be met. The term "capability" is used because it is the actual behaviors that count, not the student's potential: it is what the student does, not what the student might be able to do.

Another example of a mismatch might be an unhappy minority student, ready to leave the school. The dissatisfaction on the student's part indicates that the person has needs that are not being met by the environment. What are those needs? An interview might show that the student feels uncomfortable, different from other students in the dormitory and classroom, isolated and lonely. Can the dormitory situation be changed? Can a support group including other minorities be found? Can the needs be met in some other way? The model does not solve the problem, but it helps isolate what parts of the problems are crucial and how you might approach remediation.

A quick look through the books or the journals of any student affairs professional would identify materials dealing with the topic of remediation: therapy, counseling, parking problems of commuter students, con-

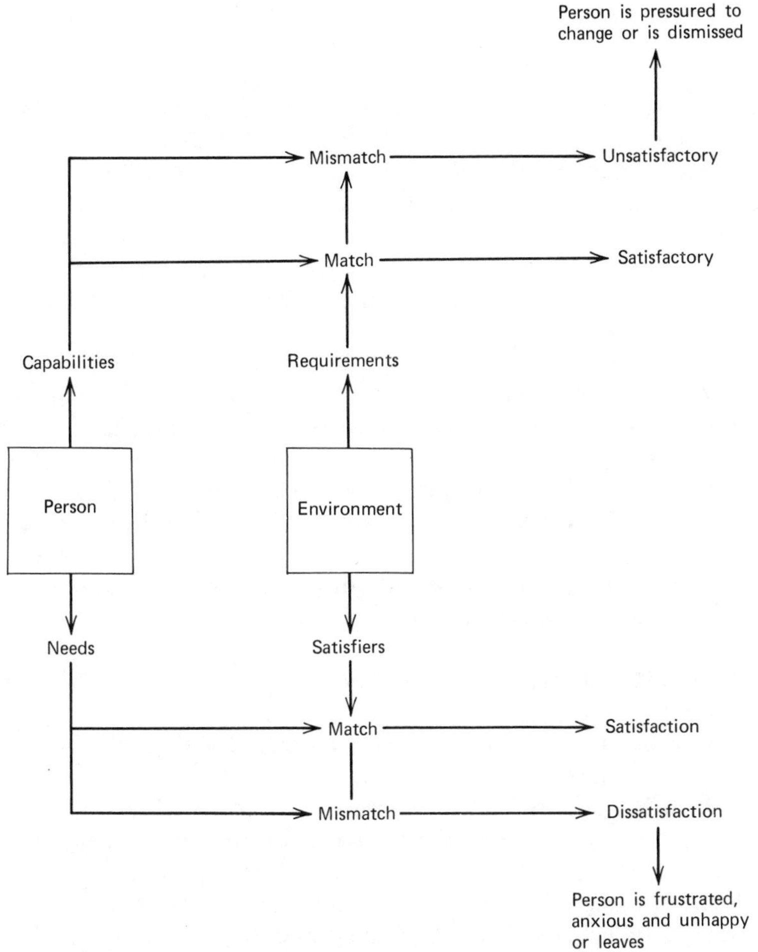


**Figure 1** A general adjustment model for diagnosing problems needing remediation.

dominium conversions and student housing problems, solving organizational communication problems, building access for disabled students, finding financial aid for middle income families, and many other such topics. Journals and professional meetings are full of papers about remediation of identified and existing problems. Since much of the literature in student affairs deals with remediation, we need not expand further on it here.

## PREVENTION

Almost all professionals agree with the need and desirability of preventive services, yet most feel some degree of frustration and lack of skill in creating and carrying out preventive programs. Bloom (1970a) reported that more than 90 percent of the mental health professionals from seventy-five western U.S. universities believed that preventive interventions were at least as important, if not more important, than traditional clinical remedial services. Yet more than 70 percent of these same respondents indicated that their mental health services were not providing preventive services.

Student affairs professionals have been somewhat more successful in providing preventive services by anticipating environmental demands on students and providing programs in advance of these demands. College orientation programs often have a strong preventive emphasis. One aim is to provide experiences that will prepare students for the demands of college. In a similar vein, placement testing and differential course selection has a preventive aspect in that efforts are made to place students in courses that are consistent with their previous training so that they can progress sequentially and not experience failure.

### The Public Health Model of Prevention

Prevention has been, for many years, identified with the public health model of prevention (Leavell and Clark, 1953). An understanding of the public health model will show where it overlaps with the "cube." The public health model includes three levels of prevention: primary, secondary, and tertiary. The tertiary level is essentially the same as the remediation category of the purpose dimension of the cube: we do not consider it to be prevention. Primary and secondary prevention are slightly different styles of prevention and both would fall under the cube's general category of prevention. They are discussed in the following paragraphs. The cube's developmental dimension, however, is intended to transcend the notion of illness, disease, or problems. Its focus is on promoting or expanding potential, and it is not covered by the public health model of prevention.

The purpose dimension of the cube, then, is similar to the public health model of prevention. It is broader, however, since it includes developmental interventions. The cube also uses the label remediation instead of the rather confusing term tertiary prevention. It does not make fine distinctions between other types of prevention, grouping them all in the one category. Examining how others have made such fine distinctions, however, may be useful in helping the student affairs professional identify possible preventive interventions.

*Primary prevention*, in the public health model, refers to preventing a problem or disease from occurring. Ruenberg (1953) makes an even finer distinction, splitting primary prevention into two types: primary and presumptive-primary. A true primary prevention prevents people from having a problem: there is usually hard evidence that it directly affects that problem. A presumptive-primary prevention is one that presumes to prevent distress, but there is only indirect evidence that it really prevents the ultimate problem from occurring.

An example of a primary prevention in student affairs would be a program run in conjunction with an active economically disadvantaged recruiting system. The system is designed to recruit students who would not ordinarily have attended college. Many of these students have poor academic skills. A primary prevention program would offer study skills, note taking, exam taking, and other academic skills during the summer and first year of college. The skills would, it is hoped, directly affect the students' ability to get better grades.

Other examples of a primary prevention would be a placement office providing specific training in job interviewing to prevent failure to get a job, or the medical service offering polio vaccination, or training in cardiopulmonary resuscitation. All directly prevent a possible future problem.

Presumptive-primary interventions are less direct. The counseling service might offer engaged couples a program in "how to fight." Fighting constructively is presumed to lead to a better marriage adjustment but there is little solid evidence that the "how to fight" training actually improves later marital adjustment.

A campus police program helping students mark their social security numbers on all valuable goods might presumably help reduce thefts. A retreat for members of the student affairs community might increase communication and friendliness and prevent later organizational problems. The programs are preventive, but they are somewhat indirect—they treat something that ought to be related to the final outcome, not the final outcome itself.

Reid (1970) proposed that on the college campus prevention be directed toward identifying and counteracting harmful circumstances in the environment that are stress producing and that might contribute to the incidence of failure and/or mental disorders in students. He also pointed out the need to identify and reinforce those factors that help students resist pathogenic influences in the environment, and stressed the importance of crisis intervention counseling for students. As an example, the staff at one university discovered that an unusually high incidence of distress was exhibited by freshman males who lived off campus. On the assumption that university residence halls provided needed support for young students, the university moved to require freshman males to live on campus. In another instance, efforts were made to establish procedures to allow students to deal with their feelings of lack of control or influence on their environment by appointing ombudsmen to help students deal with their complaints about faculty or institutional practices.

*Secondary prevention* deals primarily with early case finding and treatment before the problem becomes irreversible. In the medical field the Pap test, chest X-ray for tuberculosis, and self-examination for breast cancer are examples of secondary prevention. The object is not to prevent the occurrence of the disease, but to diagnose and identify the disease early so that corrective action will be effective.

Ruenberg (1953) includes psychotherapy and counseling with children and adults as examples of secondary prevention, but we would see this as remediation if the pain or problem was already obvious to the client. Reid (1970) indicated that colleges should develop a means of identifying and reaching out to maladjusted or troubled students rather than waiting for them to seek help. He cites the need for working with faculty and residence hall staff to train them to identify and refer disturbed students. He also suggests the possibility of utilizing screening tests or a routine evaluation of all students whose grade point average falls below a certain point.

If a faculty member interviewed all students who did poorly on a first examination and referred those with examination anxiety to an anxiety reduction program, it would be an example of secondary prevention. Early identification might allow treatment of the problem before the person failed the course.

Another example of secondary prevention is a program that was developed to help young women whose personal appearance and lack of self-confidence was likely to hinder their social adjustment. After the first few weeks of school the dorm floor aides identified young women that they thought might experience later difficulty. Several of these young women were then asked casually if they would like to join a group that would have weekly meetings on topics such as dress, makeup, social skills, and weight control. All volunteered enthusiastically. The program included both content, provided by local experts, and spinoff discussion sessions provided by a psychologist. It worked very well, leading to improvement in self-concept and sometimes radical changes in personal appearance.

## The Targets of Prevention

Under the medical model of prevention, it is suggested that prevention can be accomplished by addressing one of three possible targets. When talking about medical disease, the possible targets are (1) the host of the disease or the individual, (2) the agent of the disease or the organisms that transmit the disease, or (3) the environment that fosters or facilitates the disease-producing circumstances. In the area of prevention of failure in college or emotional problems we know little or nothing about the agent. Therefore, the literature in the area has tended to focus on the two concepts of affecting the host or individual and affecting the environment. Caplan (1964, p. 56) refers to the two prevention approaches of social action and interpersonal action. "The first of these aims is to produce changes in the community; the second has the goal of changing the particular individual." Caplan and others (Bloom, 1970b) talk about these levels of prevention that are compatible with the *Target* dimension of the cube model. If the prevention target is the individual, the strategy is to provide the individual with the coping mechanisms to withstand stress and thus prevent the occurrence of problems. If the target is the group or institution, two strategies are possible: one would be to directly change the target so that it is more effective in itself, the other would be to identify stress-producing aspects of the group or the institution that affect the individual and reduce the stresses to prevent problems.

Because of their background and training student affairs professionals have tended to focus on the person. Counseling helps the person adjust. Training helps the person develop skills. Teaching helps the person learn important knowledge. Unless we use care, there will be a tendency to focus our prevention efforts only on the person—to implicitly accept the premise that the person has to adjust to the environment. The adjustment model that was discussed earlier in the chapter in relation to remediation programs can also help evaluate potential prevention programs. It shows adjustment as a person–environment interaction, and emphasizes looking for possible changes in both the person and the environment.

Arsenian (1965) outlines sources of burdensome tension and proposes some general areas of support that suggest interesting different prevention possibilities. He proposes that every person has a "breaking point." Once stress crosses over that point, disorganization or mental illness is possible. The level of this threshold is different for every person and is influenced by both heredity and environment. He lists a series of sources of stress, including heredity, loss, ideological stress, conflict, and life cycle problems. The list suggests a variety of different possibilities for preventive actions.

Arsenian's proposed action for overloading in the area of heredity is to improve genetic stability and provide special services for offspring of unstable lines. There are useful prevention programs in this area, for example, blood type matching to prepare for a possible "blue baby" and amniocentesis and genetic advising. Practical examples in student affairs are rare. Any student affairs program based on identifying people as inferior hereditary stock would be morally repugnant, and the side effects of such a program on both individuals and society would be so damaging that no possible benefit would be worth it. We can, however, offer special services for people with problems that may be partially hereditary, but are more often due to early physical injury, for example, access to buildings for the physically disables and special programs to help the learning disabled compensate.

The suggested action for loss would be finding replacements and substitutes, compensations designed to meet the need of those who have loss. A "big brother" or "big sister" program might, for example, be planned to temporarily compensate for the loss of close peer contacts experienced by incoming students. At one private women's college, a senior student becomes a secret supporter, a "fairy godsister" of each freshman. Mysterious caring notes and small presents provide personal support during the period of making new friends.

Ideological stress could be prevented by clarification of reality. This can be an important area for student affairs professionals. In the college setting many young people meet, for the first time, faculty and other students with radically different attitudes and values. Some have great difficulty dealing with other ways of thought and with the resulting changes and inconsistencies in their own values and beliefs. A number of prevention programs might be possible. Dorm aides could, for example, be trained to recognize ideological stress and help students talk about and think through value conflicts. The student center could be architecturally designed to encourage "bull sessions." Special programs could be devised where students are shown a step-by-step method for identifying and working through such conflicts. Faculty could be sensitized to typical ideological questions and could include potentially useful material in lectures and discussion sections.

Arsenian suggests a similar approach to dealing with conflict: learning a variety of decision skills. Special programs could be offered through student radio, video tape, or the student center, for example, showing how to deal with different types of conflict. Approach–approach conflicts, for example, can often be resolved by an act of imagination. The student is told, "Imagine it is the future and that you have actually made one of the choices. Then look carefully at how you feel. Now imagine that you have actually made the other. How do you feel now?" The answer to the conflict often becomes apparent. Approach–avoidance conflicts often involve relations with other people. Assertiveness training may be very useful in resolving those types of conflicts. In avoidance–avoidance conflicts, the person may need practice in staying in the situation long enough to find the best solution. A later section in this chapter discusses psychological education, programs that could include this kind of content.

Life cycle problems should be countered with adequate preparation for each stage and provision of transitional supports. Students, for example, pass through a series of stages while in college, stages marked by different ways of viewing the world. As consultants to faculty, the student affairs professional could help them understand the stages that the students are going through, and help faculty find ways of providing support and encouragement during the process. People working with disciplinary problems also need insight into these stages so they can better understand the point of view of the students they are trying to help.

## DEVELOPMENT

The purpose dimension also includes those programs that are designed to enhance the functioning and development of "normal" individuals. Bloom (1970a) reported that almost 90 percent of the respondents from mental health agencies in seventy-five western U.S. universities believed that a university mental health program should deploy a significant proportion of its resources in working with normal students. Some authors have proposed health promotion as one means of accomplishing primary prevention (Brown, 1969). By our definition, prevention is an attempt to remedy or prevent a future problem. It is problem oriented. Development goes beyond this. Though it may also prevent, that's not the goal; the goal is the expansion and enhancement of potential.

Oetting (1967) proposed a definition of mental health as the ability to utilize the developmental tasks available in the environment for personal growth. Oetting suggested that instead of just treating problems after they emerge, we should determine whether students are able to use the college environment for personal, intellectual, or social development and then provide programs that either prepare the students so that they can use the environment or create changes in the environment so that it provides the developmental experiences the students need to maximize their potential.

Similar concepts were presented earlier by Danskin, Kennedy, and Friesen (1965) outlining variables affecting educational outcomes. They proposed the concept of ecology in considering the networks of interactions between students and their environments. They suggested a radical shift toward more developmental functions. The goal would be developmental; it is not to treat or prevent problems, but to increase the potential of the students.

They suggested that working under the ecological frame of reference would mean taking a very different approach to the job. They wrote about counselors, but freely adapting their ideas to the student affairs professional would mean that student affairs professionals would have to do the following:

1 Free their thinking from traditional approaches, and travel in uncharted directions.
2 Decrease time spent in one-to-one talking with students.
3 Decrease investment in traditional programs that evaluate people and categorize them.
4 Spent less time planning future programs for students and more time exploring current student experiences. Let the future flow from being alive to present experiences.
5 Invest more resources in observation of and systematic research into the learning (and social development) climate of the school. Put more time into reflecting, discussing, and writing, without the pressure to do the highly visible traditional student affairs functions.
6 Greatly enlarge the scope of contacts with teachers, administrators and others influencing the life of students, and become a "human development" consultant.

Other authors have suggested the need for counselors to consider alternative roles that are more developmental in nature (Foulds, 1972; Warnath, 1969). Morrill, Ivey, and Oetting (1968) proposed a developmental role for the college counselor in the provision of outreach programs. Layton, Sandeen, and Baker, in the *Annual Review of Psychology* (1971), challenged counseling psychology to assume its responsibility and become more creative and active in providing experiences that will stimulate positive development of students who are not focusing on their problems.

Prince, Miller, and Winston (1974) have provided useful materials for assessing and enhancing individual student development. Their work on developmental tasks and the developmental task inventory provides specific tools for working with individual students in a developmental framework. They reviewed the literature on developmental tasks and, based on developmental theory, proposed three functions to increase the effectiveness of students affairs professionals in facilitating the development of college students:

1 Assessing behaviors the student has already developed.
2 Formulating the student's behavioral objectives.
3 Selecting behavioral change strategies (p. 8).

The Student Developmental Task Inventory (SDTI) and a Student Developmental Profile and Planning Record* were created to facilitate these functions. The SDTI is an assessment instrument designed for use with college students to sample behaviors that students can be expected to demonstrate when they have satisfactorily accomplished certain developmental tasks. The instrument focuses on three major developmental tasks, with three subtasks for each of the major tasks:

1 **Developing Autonomy**

Subtask A. Developing emotional autonomy
Subtask B. Developing instrumental autonomy
Subtask C. Developing interdependence

2 **Developing Mature Interpersonal Relations**

Subtask D. Developing tolerance
Subtask E. Developing mature peer relationships
Subtask F. Developing intimate relationships with the opposite sex

3 **Developing Purpose**

Subtask G. Developing appropriate educational plans
Subtask H. Developing mature career plans
Subtask I. Developing mature life-style plans

---

*Available from Student Developmental Associates, 110 Crestwood Drive, Athens, GA 30601.

This instrument appears to have considerable promise in assessing developmental tasks and providing the means for establishing goals, objectives, and plans for accomplishing developmental tasks.

## Psychological Education

Another promising area for consideration in the area of developmental interventions is that of providing psychological education. Mosher and Sprinthall (1970) proposed psychological education in the schools as a means of promoting individual and human development. They cited the need for curriculum to promote personal and social competence in adolescents during times of change. They outlined several assumptions that underlie their work in psychological education. These include the belief in the value of self-knowledge and the assumption of developmental tasks and developmental stages. They cite the work of Erikson (1959) and Kohlberg (1969) as indicating personal/social developmental stages and stages of moral development as important concepts in considering psychological education. They propose that education in these areas requires active intentional effort by psychologists. Erikson's theory is particularly striking since one of the aspects of adolescent development is a recapitulation and reworking of all earlier stages. He points out the critical importance of this developmental stage to future growth.

Ivey and Alschuler (1973) indicate that psychological education involves taking initiative in deliberately teaching aspects of mental health to larger groups. Education, rather than remediation, is proposed with a primary goal to increase individual's intentionality. This is related to the developmental career counseling proposed by Ivey and Morrill (1968) and Morrill and Forrest (1970) aimed at providing individuals with the skills needed to influence their own development. Psychological education provides the vehicle for accomplishing this goal.

Alschuler and Ivey (1973) also indicate that the internalization of a skill, idea, or value is the desired outcome of psychological education. This denotes a developmental progression by the student. The "content" of education becomes a part of his or her behavioral repertoire rather than unrelated facts to be recalled for a test. As a human developmental consultant, the student affairs professional can become involved in the ongoing educational process to promote and facilitate the internalization of the material or content. One example by a counseling center was the development of a program to assist instructors in large lecture courses to provide students with a means for both understanding and internalizing the material. This program involves the use of a semistructured group discussion guide designed to relate the course material to students' previous learning and to their own personal experience. The Education Through Student Interaction (ETSI) procedure (Kitchner, 1979) has been utilized in a number of settings and appears to be useful in helping students internalize the content of education.

The May 1973 issue of *The Personnel and Guidance Journal* provides a useful beginning for professionals who wish to increase the scope of their developmental programming through psychological education.

## Developmental Environments

Insel and Moos (1974) underline the importance of interventions in environments as well as with individuals. They indicate that, "Like people, environments have unique personalities. . . . Some people are supportive; likewise, some environments are supportive" (p. 179). A WICHE publication (1973, p. 13) suggested that people might become "environmental brokers" by helping individuals identify the environments that they need for growth. Perhaps more help should be offered to people in choosing environments. Residence halls with different lifestyles and many small, distinct areas in the student center are examples. Morrill and Hurst (1971) indicated that the most sophisticated approach might be that of teaching the student the skills they need in order to modify their own environment so that it will better meet their developmental needs. This would be the logical extension of the notion of intentionality.

One of the most successful of the developmental programs that have actually been run is the International Democratic Community created at the University of Connecticut by Burns Crookston (1974). He worked within the dormitory system of the university. The goal of the Community has been to develop citizens who can translate our democratic ideals into effective social and political action. The Community is an environment that is specifically created to increase the assets and skills, the developmental potential, and so forth, of normal students. Unlike so many programs that somehow disappear after their creator leaves, the program is self-maintaining and is still functioning despite his death.

The purpose dimension of the cube shows that working as a student affairs professional requires far more than merely responding to and handling problems as they occur. Much of our work will still be remedial—people will continue to have problems and we will have to deal with them. But we should not just keep on fishing the bodies out of the stream and giving them artificial respiration. Someday we should go upstream and find out just who is throwing them in. Alternatively, we might drain the stream, give swimming lessons, provide water wings, and try to think of some other *really* creative ways of changing people and environments.

## REFERENCES


Alschuler, A. S. and A. E. Ivey Getting into psychological education. *Personnel and Guidance Journal*, 1973, **51** (9), 682–691.

Arsenian, John Toward prevention of mental illness in the United States. *Community Mental Health Journal*, 1965, **1** (4), 320–325.

Bloom, B. L. Characteristics of campus community mental-health programs in Western United States 1969. *Journal of the American College Health Association*, 1970a, **18** (3), 196.

Bloom, B. L. Current issues in provision of campus community mental-health services. *Journal of the American College Health Association*, 1970b, **18** (4), 257.

Brown, B. S. Philosophy and scope of extended clinical activities. In A. J. Bindman and A. D. Spiegel (Eds.), *Perspectives in Community Mental Health*. Chicago: Aldine, 1969, 41–53.

Caplan, Gerald *Principles of preventive psychiatry*. New York: Basic Books, 1964.

Crookston, Burns B. The intentional democratic community in college residence halls. *Personnel and Guidance Journal*, 1974, **52** (6), 382–389.

Danskin, D. G., C. E. Kennedy, Jr., and W. S. Friesen Guidance: the ecology of students. *Personnel and Guidance Journal*, 1965, **44** (2), 130–135.

Dawis, R. V., E. W. Englund, and L. H. Lofquist *A theory of work adjustment*. Minnesota Studies in Vocational Rehabilitation: XV. Minneapolis: Industrial Relations Center, 1964.

Erikson, E. H. Identity and the life cycle. *Psychological Issues*, 1959, **1**.

Farnsworth, D. L. *Psychiatry, education, and the young adult*. Springfield, Ill.: Charles C Thomas, 1966.

Foulds, M. L. The experiential-Gestalt growth group experience. *Journal of College Student Personnel*, 1972, **31** (1), 48–52.

Insel, P. M. and R. H. Moos Psychological environments. *American Psychologist*, 1974, **29**, 179–188.

Ivey, A. E. and A. S. Alschuler Psychological education: an introduction to the field. *Personnel and Guidance Journal*, 1973, **51** (9), 591–597.

Ivey, A. E. and W. H. Morrill Career process: a new concept for vocational behavior. *Personnel and Guidance Journal*, 1968, **46**, 644–649.

Kitchner, K. S. *Instructors Manual for Education Through Student Interaction*. Fort Collins, Colo.: Rocky Mountain Behavioral Science Institute, 1979.

Kohlberg, L. Stage and sequence: The cognitive developmental approach to socialization. In D. Goslin (Ed.), *Handbook of Social Theory*. Chicago: Rand McNally, 1969, 347–480.

Layton, W. L., C. A. Sandeen, and R. D. Baker Student development and counseling. *Annual Review of Psychology*, 1971, **22**, 533–564.

Leavell, H. R. and E. G. Clark *Textbook of Preventive Medicine*. New York: McGraw Hill, 1953.

Malins, J. A fence or an ambulance. In H. Feldman (Ed.), *The Best Loved Poems of the American People*. Garden City, N.Y.: Doubleday, 1936.

Morrill, W. H. and D. J. Forrest Dimensions of counseling for career development. *Personnel and Guidance Journal*, 1970, **49**, 299–305.

Morrill, W. H. and J. C. Hurst A preventative and developmental role for the college counselor. *The Counseling Psychologist*, 1971, **2** (4), 90–95.

Morrill, W. H., A. E. Ivey, and E. R. Oetting The college counseling center: a center for student development. In J. C. Heston and W. B. Frick (Eds.), *Counseling for the Liberal Arts Campus*. Yellow Springs, Ohio: Antioch Press, 1968.

Mosher, R. K. and N. A. Sprinthall Psychological education in secondary schools: a program to promote individual and human development. *American Review of Psychology*, 1971, **22**, 533–564.

Mosher, R. L. and N. A. Sprinthall Psychological education in secondary schools. *American Psychologist*, 1970, **25**, 911–924.

Oetting, E. R. Developmental definition of counseling psychology. *Journal of Counseling Psychology*, 1967, **14** (4), 382–385.

Prince, J. S., T. K. Miller, and R. B. Winston Student development task inventory. Athens, Ga.: Student Development Associates, 1974.

Reid, K. E. Community mental health on the college campus. *Hospital and Community Psychiatry*, 1970, **21** (12), 387–389.

Ruenberg, E. M. The prevention of mental disease. *Annuals of the American Academy of the political and social sciences*, 1953, **286**, 158–166.

Sanford, N. The prevention of mental illness. In B. Wolman (Ed.), *Handbook of Clinical Psychology*. New York: McGraw-Hill, 1965, 1378–1400.

Warnath, C. F. Service agency consumer views internship in counseling psychology. *Counseling Psychologist*, 1969, **1** (1), 37.

Western Interstate Commission for Higher Education. *The ecosystem model: designing campus environments*. Boulder, Colo.: WICHE, 1973.

# 8
# The Method of Intervention

WESTON H. MORRILL, E. R. OETTING, AND JAMES C. HURST

In the foregoing chapters, the target and purpose of intervention were discussed. The purpose of this chapter is to discuss the methods by which interventions may be carried out. The method of intervening with the target may be (1) direct interventions by professionals or administrators with the target, (2) consultation and training of other helping professionals or paraprofessionals, or (3) the use of media in carrying out the intervention.

The method of working with or reaching the target can vary depending on the goals and the intent of the intervention. There are a variety of ways that student affairs programs can be operated. The principal ingredient in this dimension is the concern about expanding the range and scope of services given by the limited availability of professional staff. The limited number of professionals in most settings makes it essential that some means of increasing their range of influence be developed. The student affairs professional can attempt to deal either directly with the target population or environment or indirectly by consulting with other care givers or training paraprofessionals to provide the direct services. In addition, both the range and the nature of the services can be expanded through the effective use of a variety of media.

The method dimension is related to the target dimension in that efforts to work with groups and institutions are also means of expanding and extending the range of influence of the professional. However, this dimension poses the question of how the actual intervention is presented to the target.

## DIRECT INTERVENTION

Direct interventions provided by student affairs professionals has and will continue to be the basic intervention method. However, the direct intervention methods may vary depending on the job title or role of the professional involved. These may be administrative interventions or counseling or therapeutic interventions. An administrator such as a vice-president for student affairs, a director of housing, or a dean of students would most likely utilize direct administrative interventions. The very nature of their job descriptions and the authority and power vested in these positions make possible decisions that directly affect individuals and environments. For example, adminstrative decisions about admissions standards, procedures, and policies greatly affect both individuals (who are admitted or not admitted) and the environment of the institution in terms of numbers and types of individuals making up that environment. A decision to not require the standard freshman admissions examination for older returning students directly affects such students returning to school. Many of these students lack "academic self-confidence" and avoid the feared entrance exams. The changed policy provides a stimulus to overcome those fears of failure and many students who would not otherwise take the risk apply and become students. Colleges are finding that once over that hurdle, these more mature students do very well academically. Thus the administrative decision has the impact of directly affecting many individuals and eventually their confidence in themselves. This also affects the college environment. Astin and Holland (1961) clearly demonstrated that one of the variables affecting the college environment is the mix of types of students making up that environment. A discussion in a freshman sociology class takes on added meaning if it includes mature, returning students along with the 18-year-old typical freshmen. The added breadth of the exchange is important. Similarly, the inclusion of culturally different students enhances the educative quality of the environment. This is only one example of the major impact direct administrative interventions can have. Most student affairs administrators could cite both positive and negative examples of the effects of direct administrative interventions. Examples such as creating academic advising centers, selling beer in the union, eliminating or adding services, and changing parking regulations have direct impact on individuals and environments. A goal would be to anticipate the impact of such direct administrative interventions with more planning.

Direct counseling or therapeutic interventions involve professionals in direct interaction with the target. This is most often the method used when the target is the individual. Bergin and Lambert (1978) reviewed recent outcome studies of direct therapeutic interventions and concluded that there is growing empirical evidence supporting the value of this method of intervention. Training in individual approaches to counseling and therapy provides an important cornerstone for student affairs professionals. A direct intervention is important and necessary in situations where the person involved is in critical stress. There are problems that require the experienced judgment or skills of a fully qualified professional. However, the traditional model of weekly face-to-face therapy may not be the best model for many students. For example, Munoz (1972) indicated that this was not appropriate for most minority students. The traditional model of professional help is based primarily on an Anglo-American, middle class value. Other disadvantages of direct professional involvement with all targets are related to the restricted range of impact and services that can be provided by the limited number of available professionals. The cost in both money and time for direct therapeutic intervention makes total reliance on this method unfeasible economically. If professionals deal with clients only on a face-to-face, individual or small group method, the number of individuals actually given service is very small. Requests for services and waiting lists make it essential that methods be found that are more economical of professional time and extend the influence of their services. Another reason that total reliance on direct service by professionals may not be wise is the finding that some client needs and problems can be better met by members of the target population trained as paraprofessionals.

Since there have been innumerable volumes written about direct service counseling and psychotherapy, this topic is not expanded here.

## CONSULTATION AND TRAINING

Through consultation with and training of allied professionals and paraprofessionals, the counselor can affect the target population not by direct interaction but through other individuals. This section briefly reviews the literature in the area of consultation and in the area of training paraprofessionals.

Berlin (1964) summarized the trends and history of mental health consultation through the early 1960s. According to his summary, the consultant's role in the 1930s and early 1940s was that of offering technical advice and information and providing education for mental health workers. In 1947, Jules Coleman stressed the need for the consultant to attend to needs of consultees, reasons for seeking help, their feelings, and concerns. Other writers in the 1950s stressed the therapeutic role of the consultant in helping the consultee deal with internalized conflicts, anxieties, and feelings.

Gerald Caplan and the Laboratory of Community Psychiatry at Harvard presented the landmark statement on mental health consultation in 1963 which has had significant influence on mental health consultation. Because of its significance, it is reviewed briefly here. His model has been restated in a more recent book (Caplan, 1970).

Caplan defines consultation in "a quite restricted sense to denote the process of interaction between two professional persons" (1963, p. 470). The consultee invokes the help because of a particular work problem that he is experiencing. The professional responsibility for the client remains with the consultee. The consultant may offer help in the form of diagnosis, clarifications, suggestions, or advice on treatment, but the consultee is free to either accept or reject this help. An important aspect of the consultation is to help the consultee deal more effectively not only with the current concern but also with similar problems in the future without the aid of the consultant. Caplan proposed that a significant proportion of the professional's time should be spent in relation to mental health and mental disorders. He also stressed the value of consultation in providing an opportunity for a relatively small number of consultants to exert a broad effect on the community.

Caplan described four types of mental health consultation. These are client-centered case consultation, consultee-centered case consultation, program-centered administrative consultation, and consultee-centered administrative consultation.

### Client-centered Case Consultation

In this type of consultation the client of the consultee is the primary focus of attention. The major goal is to help the consultee find the best method of treatment for the client. A secondary goal is to increase the knowledge of the consultee so that he/she can deal effectively with the same type of clients in the future without continued consultation.

### Consultee-centered Case Consultation

In this type of consultation, the primary focus of the consultant is the consultee, not on the client. Although the desired ultimate outcome is to improve the consultee's handling of the current and subsequent cases, the primary endeavor of the consultant is to assess the nature of the consultee's work difficulty and to help him/her work this through. Caplan outlines four major categories of difficulties that might inhibit the consultee's ability to work effectively with his client. These are (1) lack of understanding of the psychological factors in the case, (2) lack of skill or resources to deal with the problems, (3) lack of objectivity or inability to utilize his or her particular knowledge and skills with a particular client, and (4) lack of confidence and self-esteem.

### Program-centered Administrative Consultation

The primary focus of the consultant in this type of consultation is on making a specialized assessment of the current administrative program or policy predicament, then making a recommendation for resolving the difficulty. The focus is upon the problems of an organization or institution and the recommendation of changes to improve the administrative functioning of the unit.

### Consultee-centered Administrative Consultation

In this type of consultation, the goal is to improve the personal–administrative functioning of the consultee. This type of consultation is very similar to the consultee-centered case consultation. The primary focus is the consultee and the assessment of his difficulty in the work situation.

Caplan has provided a useful model for understanding the nature and process of consultation. More recent writers, however, have criticized his approach as being rather conservative and narrow by retaining its focus on the sick individual as the primary point of reference (Nagler and Cooper, 1969). Nagler and Cooper provide an interesting conceptual framework for levels of change which extends Caplan's model and complements the cube model under discussion. They propose differential goals and means of consultation for three different target levels for the consultation. The target levels they suggest are (1) the client or patient, (2) community caretakers, and (3) the social system. Signell and Scott (1971) also build on Caplan's concepts and add systems consultation concepts.

Gallessich (1974) presents a training plan for teaching consultation skills and reviews a variety of issues related to consultation models. She deals with the target of the consultation, the medium for change, and the method and role of the consultant. She also includes the notion of advocacy consultation for social systems intervention. This type of consultation based on social action concerns has explicit reform values. Unlike most consultants, the advocacy consultant is proactive and often works without the invitation or full sanction of organizations. As such, there are special problems associated with this type of consultation.

## Training

Another related indirect method of intervention is that of training others to carry out mental health and care-giving functions. Some aspects of consultation include training of the consultee or groups of consultees. The major innovation in the delivery of mental health services in the recent past has been the utilization of paraprofessionals as deliverers of mental health care. This is the primary category of training that is reviewed briefly here.

Sobey (1970) reported on a study of 10,000 nonprofessionals working in 185 National Institute of Mental Health sponsored projects in the United States. One of the major findings is that the nonprofessionals are utilized not simply because professional manpower is not available, but rather to provide new services in innovative ways. Delworth, Sherwood, and Casaburri (1974) in a monograph on student paraprofessionals in higher education reviewed studies indicating that paraprofessionals have been effective in working with chronic mental patients and emotionally disturbed children, in school, community, and antipoverty programs, and in a variety of university counseling and student services programs.

Delworth, Sherwood, and Casaburri (1974, p. 13) proposed a three-pronged rationale for the utilization of paraprofessionals:

1 Continued offering of service at reduced cost. The work of available professionals can be expanded by hiring paraprofessionals to take over part of the job, thereby freeing professionals for more appropriate tasks.
2 More effective offering of service through special skills and identification with peers.
3 Regular, systematic input into the system by members of the population to be served.

The utilization of paraprofessionals or nonprofessionals in a variety of student office settings has increased considerably in the last few years. The "new careers" movement (Pearl and Riessman, 1965) provided stimulus in this direction.

Numerous authors have written in the area of the utilization of paraprofessionals. It appears that for programs to be successful there must be critical attention to the selection, training, and supervision of paraprofessionals (Riessman, 1967). The development of hundreds of crisis and hot-line centers throughout the United States has been significant and characteristic of the change in the delivery of mental health services to people in need. Paraprofessionals (trained and supervised by profes-

sionals) have played a key role in the development and operation of such centers (Delworth, Rudow, and Taub, 1972).

## INTERVENTIONS UTILIZING MEDIA

A major new thrust in recent years has highlighted the potential utilization of a variety of media for creative interventions. These include telephone information services, programmed counseling and human relations training materials, use of television in training and treatment, structured anxiety treatment packages utilizing audio tapes, computerized and computer-assisted registration, advising, testing, and counseling, and a variety of biofeedback applications. These approaches expand both the number and scope of programs offered by student affairs professionals. The computer-assisted counseling and the biofeedback applications may very well revolutionize some aspects of the guidance and mental health fields.

Magoon (1964) introduced jukeboxes with occupational information records into strategic university locations as a means of providing career-related information for college students. The authors are aware of several university counseling centers offering educational and occupational information about the university academic areas utilizing cassette audio recordings of interviews with professionals and workers in various fields. This use of media is relatively inexpensive and easy to utilize.

There have been a number of programs designed to enhance or facilitate individual and small group interventions utilizing media. Gilbert and Ewing (1971) compared the effectiveness of a programmed *Self-Counseling Manual* and normal precollege counseling interview. Though the subjects rated the regular counseling more favorably, the findings support the use of programmed counseling as an adjunct to or a substitute for face-to-face counseling.

Silk (1972) described a variety of specific uses of video-tape recordings in brief joint marital therapy. In his descriptions, video-tape recordings are used as an adjunct to regular marital therapy. Higgins, Ivey, and Uhlemann (1970) described a programmed approach to teaching behavioral skills utilizing video recording, modeling, programmed instruction, and video feedback.

There have been a number of programs utilizing audio tape recordings for use in media-assisted therapy and self-directed groups, (Human Development Institute; Solomon, Berzon, and Davis, 1970). These programs utilize stimulus materials presented by audio tapes for clients or for leaderless or paraprofessional facilitated dyads and groups.

Hilf et al. (1971) experimented with the use of machine-mediated interviews with psychiatric patients. The interviews were conducted by means of remotely located teletypes connected with a computer. The authors suggest that this novel technique might prove useful for treating patients who are unable to communicate through usual face-to-face method (mutism). Another practical application which they suggested is that of diagnosis and treatment of individuals at locations remote from treatment facilities (e.g., rural areas)

Suinn (1972) has developed a tested automated systematic desensitization treatment package available on audio cassettes. Programs for test anxiety, math anxiety, and generalized anxiety management are available. These programs, utilizing media, have been tested and found to be effective in treating debilitating anxiety.*

Elwood (1972) demonstrated the potential value of computers in individual intelligence testing. They designed and constructed a totally automated procedure for the administration of the WAIS. They obtained test–retest reliabilities above .90. The potential freeing of professional time by this method is apparent.

Bernstein and MacLennan (1971) described a community intervention utilizing media. Their project involved consultation with the staff of a radio station which later progressed to community involvement. The consultant collaborated in setting up a twenty-part documentary series and a community action program on drug abuse.

***Media in Training*** Two innovative approaches to training counselors that utilize media have also been extended to the training of paraprofessionals and teaching clients specific skills. Both approaches have utilized television recordings in the process. The interpersonal process recall (IPR) (Kagan, Krathwol, and Farquhar 1965; Kagan and Schauble, 1969) utilized the recording of interviews and then the use of these recordings in a semistructured recall process in training. Kagan has extended the IPR program of teaching human interaction or human relations skills into a variety of settings. Microcounseling (Ivey et al., 1968; Ivey, 1971) has been utilized in a variety of training settings. The microcounseling format utilizes video-recorded modeling tapes, programmed instructional materials and taped brief interviews for feedback in learning specific counseling and human relations skills. Research evidence has supported the use of both these media approaches in teaching human relations skills.

*These programs are available for purchase from RMBSI, Inc., Box 1066, Fort Collins, Colo. 80522.

***Computer-assisted Counseling*** A major thrust in the area of career development counseling has been the use of computers in career-assisted counseling. There have been a number of pilot and experimental programs reported in the literature in the past few years (Cooley, 1964; Loughary, Friesen, and Hurst, 1966; Super, 1970; and Tiedeman, 1967). Although there are variations in the intent and scope of the various computer-assisted programs, they all are designed to facilitate the information and data retrieval and information processing aspects of counseling for career development. In these systems, the computer is not designed to replace the counselor, but to assist, broaden, and extend the growth and decision process of counseling. Myers (in Super, 1970) identified three primary purposes for the major systems which are under development. At present, although they are primarily experimental and demonstration projects, they are designed (p. 112):

1. To extend the influence of the counselor by providing individual client access to date,
2. To stimulate and supplant the counselor in aspects of fostering decision-making, and
3. To demonstrate the efficacy of certain ways of restructuring the schools.

The advantage of the computer is that it can accept, store, analyze, and display information rapidly and accurately. This allows the student to explore as many alternatives as possible in a short time span. Minor, Myers, and Super (1972) describe one of the systems currently under investigation. The system has three phases. The student can enter any of the stages depending on his level of vocational development. The counselor plays a critical role in the process of student entry into the system. In this system the student interacts in a conversational manner with the computer through the use of a typewriter keyboard.

The objective of Phase I of the system is to broaden the student's knowledge of occupational alternatives and his own multipotentiality by an exploratory process. In Phase I, the student learns how his tentative decisions relate to his personal attributes. The system begins by teaching the students a classification system to aid in thinking about the world of work and multiple opportunities. The student then begins by exploring his or her tentative career preferences. The student describes the kinds of activities and work conditions that appeal to him or her and the computer lists and defines compatible occupations. When the student ends this process, the computer provides him or her with statements of the relationships between these occupations and his school data profile and self-concept profile that has also been entered. The computer also lists and names the occupational fields that have not been mentioned by the student but are compatible with the school information and the self-concept profile.

After this preliminary exploration, the student chooses specific occupations for analysis in greater depth. This portion of the program both provides information about the occupations and relates this information to the student's specific characteristics. Work sample games are utilized to acquaint the student with the nature of the work. The computer presents brief problem-solving situations for the occupation and the student interacts with the computer to solve it. The computer also presents information about the duties, training requirements, employment environments, competition, career growth potential, salary, and methods of entry. In addition, the program helps the student analyze the occupation to determine if the values and requirements are in keeping with his self-concept, learning ability, grade point average, and interests, for example. Finally, in Phase I the system analyzes all the student responses and provides a summary for the student. This report also includes an analysis of the high school courses that relate to the occupations that were considered. The summary reports are printed and can be retained by the student for review with the counselor and parents.

Phase II is most appropriate for those students who are planning some post-high school education and can best think in terms of curriculum preferences. This phase makes relationships between educational and vocational exploration possible.

Phase III can be used by the student in his search of post-high school educational opportunities and locations. The system helps the student analyze various alternatives in light of both curriculum objectives and personal preferences. The personal preference variables include such things as geographic location, size of school, and type of school. The system provides work sheets that indicate the schools that satisfy curricular objectives, degree of selectivity, entrance requirements, and costs, as well as the personal preference items.

The authors conclude that the system should help the student be more efficient in career and vocational exploration. The amount of information that is available at the student's fingertips is increased many times. The counselor should be able to spend time working at a higher level of individualized, diagnostic problem solving with each student, since the student is prepared for those steps and the time-consuming presentation of information and alternatives is handled by the system.

In addition, the system could provide a means for curriculum revision and change. "By reviewing students' plans recorded in the system, the administrator should be able to gain new insights into how well the curriculum being offered meets their needs" (Minor, Myers, and Super, 1972, p. 180). This would provide an example of an institutional, developmental, media intervention.

***Media and Biofeedback*** A final area that utilizes media or technology to broaden and enhance the alternative intervention possibilities is that of biofeedback. Danskin and Walters (1973) briefly review some of the objectives and applications in the biofeedback area. They stress the value of biofeedback procedures in providing the client with the ability to "guide his own destiny by internal self-control" (p. 633). This utilization of biofeedback is related to the concept of "intentionality" discussed in the section on developmental interventions. Zaichkowski and Kamen (1978) found changes toward an internal locus of control in subjects who were given biofeedback whereas this was not found in meditation.

Biofeedback involves instrumentation to provide direct feedback to individuals on certain of their ongoing physiological processes. These physiological processes include such things as muscle tension, heart rate, temperature, and brain waves. This information is fed back directly to the individual so that he/she can learn to regulate these processes.

Danskin stresses the value of learning to regulate one's own physiological processes as contributing to an individual's sense of personal agency and thus self-concept. Biofeedback has been used to teach clients to control their own reactions to stress. This has included headache control, high blood pressure, and other physiological reactions. In addition, biofeedback has been used in desensitization of phobic or anxiety reactions, providing access to unconscious material, as an alternative to drug use, increasing attention and concentration, and numerous other applications. The use of media offers expanded opportunities for creative interventions. Heisel (1977) describes a variety of devices and techniques as well as equipment that can be used in biofeedback.

## REFERENCES

Astin, A. W. and J. L. Holland The environmental assessment technique; a way to measure college environments. *Journal of Educational Psychology,* 1961, **52** (6), 308–316.

Bergin, A. E. and M. J. Lambert Evaluation of therapeutic outcomes. In S. L. Garfield and A. E. Bergin (Eds.), *Handbook of Psychotherapy and Behavior Change: An Empirical Analysis,* New York: John Wiley & Sons, 1978.

Berlin, I. N. Learning mental health consultation history and problems. *Mental Hygiene,* 1964, **48**, 257–266.

Bernstein, S. B. and B. MacLennan Community psychiatry with communication media. *American Journal of Psychiatry,* 1971, **128** (6), 722–727.

Caplan, G. Types of mental health consultation. *American Journal of Orthopsychiatry,* 1963, **33**, 470–481.

Caplan, G. *The Theory and Practice of Mental Health Consultation.* New York: Basic Books, 1970.

Coleman, J. R. Psychiatric consultation in casework agencies. *American Journal of Orthopsychiatry,* 1947, **10**, 548–566.

Cooley, W. W. A computer measurement system for guidance. *Harvard Educational Review,* 1964, **34**, 559–572.

Danskin, D. G. and E. D. Walters Biofeedback and voluntary self-regulation: counseling and education. *Personnel and Guidance Journal,* 1973, **51** (9), 633–638.

Delworth, U., E. H. Rudow, and J. Taub *Crisis Center Hotline: a Guidebook to Beginning and Operating.* Springfield, Ill.: Charles C. Thomas, 1972.

Delworth, U., G. Sherwood, and N. Casaburri *Student Paraprofessionals: A Working Model for Higher Education.* Student Personnel Series No. 17. Washington, D.C.: American College Personnel Association, 1974.

Elwood, D. L. Automated WAIS testing correlated with face-to-face WAIS testing: a validity study. *International Journal of Man—Machine Studies,* 1972, **4** (2), 129–137.

Gallessich, J. Training the school psychologist for consultation. *Journal of School Psychology,* 1974, **12** (2), 138–149.

Gilbert, W. M. and T. N. Ewing Programmed versus face-to-face counseling. *Journal of Counseling Psychology,* 1971, **18** (5), 413–421.

Kagan N., D. Krathwol, and W. Farquhar IPR-interpersonal process recall: stimulated recall by video tape. Research Report No. 24, East Lansing, Mich.: Michigan State University, Bureau of Educational Research Services, 1965.

Kagan, N. and P. Schauble Affect simulation in interpersonal process recall *Journal of Counseling Psychology,* 1969, **16**, 309–313.

Heisel, D. M. *The biofeedback guide: affiliating with excellence.* New York: Gordon & Breach, 1977.

Higgins, W., A. Ivey, and M. Uhlemann Media therapy: a programmed approach to teaching behavioral skills. *Journal of Counseling Psychology,* 1970, **17**, 20–26.

Hilf, F. D. et al. Machine-mediated interviewing. *Journal of Nervous and Mental Disease,* 1971, **152** (4), 278–288.

Ivey, A. E. *Microcounseling: innovations in interviewing training.* Springfield, Ill.: Charles C Thomas, 1971.

Ivey, A. E., C. Normington, C. D. Miller, W. H. Morrill, and R. F. Hasse, Microcounseling and attending behavior: an approach to prepracticum counselor training. *Journal of Counseling Psychology,* 1968, **15**, 1–15.

Loughary, J. W., D. Friesen, and R. Hurst, Autocon: A computer-based automated counseling simulation system. *Personnel and Guidance Journal,* 1966, **45**, 5–15.

Magoon, T. Innovations in counseling. *Journal of Counselor Psychology,* 1964, **11** (4), 342–347.

*Media-Assisted Therapy.* Human Development Institute, 450 East Ohio Street, Chicago, Ill., 60611.

Minor, F. J., R. A. Myers, and D. E. Super An experimental computer-based educational and career exploration system. In J. M. Whiteley and A. Resnikoff (Eds.), *Perspectives on Vocational Development.* Washington, D.C.: American Personnel and Guidance Association, 1972.

Munoz, D. G. Issues related to working with minority students. Paper presented at American Psychological Association Convention, Honolulu, Hawaii, September, 1972.

Myers, R. A. Computer-aided counseling: some issues of adoption and use. In D. E. Super, *Computer Assisted Counseling.* New York: Teachers College Press, 1970.

Nagler, S. and S. Cooper Influencing social change in community mental health. *Canada's Mental Health,* 1969, **17**, 6–12.

Pearl, A. and F. Riessman *New Careers for the Poor.* New York: Free Press, 1965.

Riessman, F. Strategies and suggestions for training non-professionals. *Community Mental Health Journal,* 1967, **3** (2), 103–110.

Signell, K. A. and P. A. Scott Mental health consultation: an interaction model. *Community Mental Health Journal,* 1971, **7** (4), 288–302.

Silk, S. The use of videotape in brief joint marital therapy. *American Journal of Psychotherapy,* 1972, **26** (3), 417–424.

Solomon, L. N., B. Berzon, and D. P. Davis A personal growth program for self-directed groups. *Journal of Applied Behavioral Science,* 1970, **6** (4), 427–452.

Sobey, F. *The Nonprofessional Revolution in Mental Health.* New York: Columbia University Press, 1970.

Suinn, R. *Anxiety Management Training* (cassette tapes). Fort Collins, Colo.: Rocky Mountain Behavioral Science Institute, 1972.

Super, D. E. *Computer Assisted Counseling.* New York: Teachers College Press, 1970.

Tiedeman, D. V., et al. *Information System for Vocational Decision Making.* Annual Report, Cambridge, Mass.: Harvard University Graduate School of Education, 1967.

Zaichkowski, L. D. and R. Kaman Biofeedback and meditation: effects on muscle and locus of control. *Perceptual & Motor Skills,* 1978, **46** (3), 955–958.

# 9
# A Guide to Program Evaluation

E. R. OETTING

This chapter is a simple, step-by-step guide to setting up an evaluation plan. It is aimed at only one kind of evaluation problem, testing whether a clearly defined short-term program works. It is written for the practicing professional in student services who has had some graduate courses in research, is working in the field, and now would like to start evaluating what he or she is doing. It should also be very useful to someone who would like to evaluate a program for a master's thesis or doctoral dissertation. Some of the material in this chapter has been discussed in previous publications (Oetting, 1976a; Oetting, 1976b; Oetting and Cole, 1978). The steps in evaluation are summarized in Table 1.

There is an underlying philosophy: the idea that evaluative research is always aimed at getting practical and useful information that will help in making decisions about a program. In evaluation we may be interested in why things work, but our real goal is to find whether they work.

## Step I: SHOULD THERE BE AN EVALUATION?

The obvious answer is, "Of course. We should try to find out whether every program is effective." I have given that answer myself. It is in general true, but there are situations where evaluation is not appropriate. Evaluative research is not done for its own sake; it is a practical tool, and sometimes, like any tool, it is not really useful. Will the

**Table 1 Evaluative Research: Steps in Doing an Effective Evaluation**

| | |
|---|---|
| Step I | Should there be an evaluation?<br>Determine the possible benefits and the costs in money, staff time and human relations. |
| Step II | Involve people in the evaluation.<br>Ask administrators, staff, and people like those receiving the program to help plan, run, and interpret the results. |
| Step III | Establish the program goals.<br>Decide in broad, general terms what you want to accomplish. |
| Step IV | List the specific aims.<br>For each goal, list the specific aims that, if accomplished, would meet that goal. |
| Step V | Make the specific aims observable.<br>Build outcome measures for each specific aim. First seek a direct measure, then an "off-the-shelf" measure. If not available, "build your own" measure. Maximize first the validity, then the reliability of the measure. |
| Step VI | Select a research design.<br>Use Table 2 to select the best feasible research design. Work to answer "yes" to each question. |
| Step VII | Plan the program.<br>Plan and schedule the overall program, including evaluation. |
| StepVIII | Monitor the program.<br>Make sure that the program runs as planned, is potent, and that research data are collected. |
| Step IX | Analyze and interpret the results.<br>Use both inferential and descriptive statistics. Involve administrators and staff in interpretation. |
| Step X | Prepare the report.<br>State what was done, why, and the results. Focus on the data needed for decisions. |



expected results of the evaluation really be worth the cost and effort of obtaining them?

If your organization is not able to use evaluation results to actually change programs, evaluation is likely to be wasted. But the best way to change that is to show people that a good evaluation is useful. If you are going to try to change the system, though, keep two things in mind.

First, involve people in the evaluation from the planning stage on. If they participate in the evaluation, they are much more likely to use it than if the results are suddenly dumped on them after the fact. Second, for your first effort pick a program that can be evaluated easily and well. Put everything you have into it so the outcome measures are good ones and the research design is sound. A poorly planned evaluation, or one whose results are subject to multiple interpretations, may make the system even more rigid and less susceptible to feedback.

The cost might be too high to make evaluation worthwhile. Suppose, for example, some staff join a faculty bowling league to establish personal contacts. Evaluating the results might take a lot of staff time and might damage exactly what is being accomplished. The cost of the program is very low, the possible cost of evaluation high.

Another program, such as a parent's day, could be so firmly established or so much a part of the system that it cannot be reasonably changed. Testing its effectiveness would not be worth the cost. Still another program might be so new and changing its goals so rapidly that by the time the results are in, they relate to something that no longer exists. A new peer drug counseling program might be an example. Planned and run by students, it is in continual flux. Waiting until it stabilizes would be wise.

To decide whether an evaluation should be done, consider first how the evaluation results would be used and who would use them. What benefit could they have? What would be the costs in money, staff time, and human relations? Are the benefits worth the cost? If not, instead of an evaluation see the later section in this chapter on program monitoring.

## Step II: INVOLVE PEOPLE IN THE EVALUATION

It is easy to sabotage an evaluation. During a major test of a federal program the disadvantaged clients were to be *randomly* assigned either directly to jobs or first to training. The relative success of the two groups would determine how millions of dollars would be spent. A few months later the project director found a counselor out in the street, lining people up: "Do you want a job or training? Job? Move up a space. Training? Get in line behind her." It may have been very humanistic, but the groups would not be matched and the results would tell very little about which was the best approach to use. If the project counselors had been involved in planning the project and had shared in deciding how people would be assigned, they might have helped the research, not interfered with it.

The evaluator must help people learn that evaluation does not only provide evidence that lets administrators make the decisions that they already wanted to make, threaten their jobs, or limit what they want to do. It can actually help them, showing others that they are doing their jobs, improving services, and increasing communication. Administrators, staff, and representatives of the clients all should be involved in planning the evaluation. Share the goals with them and learn about their goals too. Work together to plan every stage. It not only helps to prevent sabotage, but the eventual evaluation results are more likely to be used.

## Step III: ESTABLISH THE PROGRAM GOALS

Decide what the program should be trying to accomplish. State it in fairly broad, general terms, but don't make the statement so broad that it is meaningless. First state the goals of the program, then test them by asking whether that goal would also be true for three other programs; teaching, the Girl Scouts, and psychotherapy. "To improve adjustment," for example, does not meet the test. It could be a goal of all of them. Make the goal specific enough to define your program as something different from any of these three and it will usually be a useful statement.

## Step IV: LIST THE SPECIFIC AIMS

Take each one of the general goals and try to separate it into several specific aims. One goal of a parent–teachers organization, for example, might be to increase parents' involvement in school affairs. Specific aims might be (1) to increase the number of parents voting on school bond issues, (2) to increase the number of questions parents ask about school programs, or (3) to improve the quality of questions asked at school board meetings.

A program might have several different parts that, although all contributing toward a major goal, have separate specific aims. It is very valuable if the specific aims are different enough so that they can be examined separately. You might be able to find out not only whether the program worked, but what parts were effective. For instance, a program designed to help adolescent girls improve their interpersonal interaction might have one part that deals with parent interactions and another that focuses on peer relations. Specific aims such as "increased communication with parents about school activities" and "improved quality of friendship" could show different results, suggesting that one or another part of the program was effective.

## Step V: MAKE THE SPECIFIC AIMS OBSERVABLE

This may be the single most difficult aspect of evaluative research. How do you make the specific aims of the program measurable or observable? If you can get a good measure of the aim, then you can usually tell whether a program works. There are still a few other considerations taken up in the later sections on design and program monitoring, but unless this first problem can be solved, no evaluation is possible.

Outcome measures fall roughly into three groups: *direct measures, "Off-the-shelf" measures*, and *"build-your-own" measures.*

### Direct Measures

Can the specific aims of the program be directly observed, counted, or measured in some way? When the information obtained is accurate, a direct measure is the best one to use for an evaluation. The measure is related directly to the program goals, since it is a specific aim of the program. A change in it would show everyone that the program was effective. No change would mean that the program did not meet the aim, and if you are concerned about the aim, you must do something further.

Obviously, direct measures are very powerful and useful, but there are still dangers that you have to consider. If whatever you are trying to change occurs *only rarely*, that change is usually not a very useful outcome measure for your program. For example, it would take decades to find out whether you had really changed the suicide rate if there were only one or two suicides every 5 years.

Another direct measure that may not show a change is one that, though it might be influenced by your program, is also influenced by so many other things that it is very resistant to change. Overall grade average, for example, is an outcome that is hard to change. General ability, study habits, teacher attitudes, courses taken, course loads, and many other factors may influence the average. Changing only one thing, such as motivation, might help students and still not change the overall grades enough so that the change could be demonstrated. Grades, and other outcomes of this kind, are not always bad criteria. If there is a special group whose *primary* problem is lack of motivation, if that is the main thing that is causing poor grades, then an effective motivation program could change grades enough so that it would show.

Once you choose a direct measure, make sure that the information you collect is accurate, that there is no way that it could be biased. Try to make it as objective as possible. An actual count of the number of people entering the room is better than a judgment of "crowded/not crowded." A photograph of a study area would allow more time to make an accurate count of the number of students looking out the window than an observer simply watching them. An independent observer might be more accurate than one who had a vested interest in success or failure. When possible, use several methods and check them against each other.

When there is a control or comparison group, collect the data in the same way as for the experimental group. If a student checked on noise level in study hall for one group, it would not be comparable to a teacher checking the same thing for another group. At least two things would be different. The student would probably have a different idea about what constitutes noise, and the presence of the teacher with an obvious check sheet would change the noise level.

The timing of the sample is also very important. Make sure that it is the same for the experiment and the comparison. If you were trying to reduce smoking in the park across the street, you might count the number of smokers at a particular time before and after your program. If, however, you did it at two different times of day, the comparison would be meaningless. Even the same time might be a problem if, in the meantime, class schedules changed or it started to snow!

A good test to make, before starting the actual project, is to pick out the specific aim, decide exactly what data you will collect, and how and when you will collect it. Then sit down with a group of colleagues and see if you can think of ways in which you could distort that information to make it look as though the program had either succeeded or failed. Then try to find ways to plug the holes.

### "Off-the-Shelf" Measures

When the specific aim is not directly observable, the next possibility that should be checked is whether the aim can be measured by a published test or scale. Suppose the aim is "to improve vocational adjustment." That aim is rather broad, and you might want to consider narrowing it, but you might also look at the literature to see what kinds of scales people have used to measure "vocational adjustment." Refer to *The Seventh Mental Measurements Yearbook* (Buros, 1972), *Meas-*

*ures of Social Psychological Attitudes* (Robinson and Shaver, 1973), *Measures of Occupational Attitudes and Occupational Characteristics* (Robinson, Athanasiou, and Head, 1969), or *A Sourcebook of Mental Health Measures* (Comrey, Backer, and Glaser, 1973). The local university library, ERIC, PASAR, or the Smithsonian (see reference notes for addresses) may be able to provide you with a computer search at a very reasonable cost that would identify articles on the topic. A recent article or a personal request to the author could provide you with scales or measures that are exactly what you need.

After you have found a test or two that seem applicable, check them carefully. The title of a test may not mean the same thing to the author as it does to you. Look at the items. Do they measure what you think of as the goal of your program? Or, if the items do not seem clearly related to the goal, is there evidence in the literature that shows they do relate to the goal? All the items on the MMPI depression scale, for example, do not obviously relate to depression, but the literature shows that the scale is a good measure of certain kinds of depression. Without that kind of evidence, if the items do not match *your* goals, look for another measure.

After making sure that the test or scale really relates to your goals, check the language used in the test. Is it too difficult? Does it "talk down" to those who will be taking it? Will taking the scale seem reasonable to the program's clients? If a test is denigrating, inappropriate, or confusing, or seems irrelevant, the clients may not cooperate and your results will be worthless. Clients almost always start with a very cooperative attitude; they want to help and enjoy taking tests. But if the testing goes on and on, or if they just can't understand why you would be asking these things, your relationship with them can go downhill very fast. This will not only hurt the evaluation, but can damage the program as well.

After making all these considerations, ask whether the test or scale is reliable and valid, that is, whether the score obtained is consistent and accurate. The answer is easy if the test or scale has been used successfully in programs very much like yours. If it has worked and has shown differences between groups that had a program like yours and those that did not, then it is likely to be sufficiently reliable and valid for your use.

If the instrument has not been used to test programs similar to yours, evaluating it is more difficult. You have to look at the evidence, the studies that have been done, and decide for yourself just what the instrument measures. This can be a difficult and complex task. Find out how and for what reason the scale was developed, what it correlates with and does not correlate with, and decide whether it is consistent with your specific aim.

Will your group score somewhere near the middle of the scale? If they score near the "positive" end, you may not be able to show a change. If they score near the "negative" end, some movement toward the mean would be expected even without a program, and to prove that the program worked, you may absolutely have to have a control group.

When a reliability figure is reported, how should that be interpreted? In general, the higher the reliability, the better the measure will be at detecting either a small change or a change in a small group of people. Arbitrary figures can be dangerous. There are many different ways of measuring reliability and the reliability interacts with many factors in the design. So treat the following statements with caution; but, if the reliability is in the .90s, the measure could be useful in many situations, even with fairly small groups. If the reliability is in the .70s, you will need both fairly distinctive changes and quite a few subjects to demonstrate that the results did not occur by chance.

### "Build-Your-Own" Measures

Perhaps it is a sign of how creative we are in developing new programs that we can so rarely find a good, pretested, "off-the-shelf" measure that exactly assesses the specific aim of our program. It leaves us forced to build something of our own. If you are going to build a scale to measure your outcome, it is essential that you have very clear specific aims for your project. Put down, on paper, the exact specific aims. Then try to say why and how your program should influence that aim.

The next step, which I have found very effective, is to gather a group of colleagues and brainstorm ideas about how that aim can be measured. For example, I bring in a friend who is expert at running brainstorming sessions so I can be part of the idea group. Together we create long lists of useful, funny, and ridiculous ideas. (The ridiculous idea is sometimes exactly the one that pays off. In one classic brainstorming session about what to do with a campus building, the idea "burn it down" was the one that eventually paid off. The building was destroyed and the area used for parking.)

I then take the whole list back to my office and start to work on it. I try to group the ideas into clusters with similar basic content, and sometimes organize those clusters into larger supergroups. Then I try to turn the ideas in a cluster into a practical set of items or way of measuring the aim.

At this stage it is important to keep your thinking simple. The more directly you can state a question, and the more obvious the relationship between what you are measuring and the specific aim, the better it is likely to work. Don't build long and convoluted chains of logic. For example, suppose you have a media program aimed at better eating habits. If the young people build better habits, the overweight ones will lose weight. If they lose weight they will look better. If they look better they will date more. So we will compare number of tickets sold to the school dance before and after the program. If this sounds like a strange chain of logic, it is no worse than some that I have encountered, even in my own thinking. Keep to ideas that are simple and close to what you want to change.

Also, stay as close as possible to the immediate goals of the program. Long-term or extended goals are valuable, and in some cases should be examined, but the chances that they will actually be influenced enough so that you can detect the change are minimal.

Are you using judges? If so, try to build an anchored rating scale (Campbell, 1970; Thorton and Oetting, 1980), one that has clear descriptions of typical behaviors that make that point. Compare the following scales. Which one would be easier and more accurate for judges to use?

### Typical Item

Rate personal relations between ethnic groups during lunch period.

1. Very bad
2. Poor
3. Fair
4. Good
5. Excellent

### Anchored Rating Scale

Rate personal relations between ethnic groups during lunch period. (Mark anywhere on the line.)

| 1 | 2 | 3 | 4 | 5 |
|---|---|---|---|---|
| No mixed groups, many direct hostile interactions. | Few or no mixed groups, some hostility. | Some mixed groups, cautious interactions. | Some to many mixed groups, respectful interactions. | Much mixing, friendly, carefree interactions between all groups. |

If at all possible, use more than one judge and train them thoroughly ahead of time. The training should always focus on making *accurate* judgments. You can train judges to be consistent with each other, but unless they are rating what you need to have evaluated, the consistency is useless.

Are you building a rating scale or test for the program clients to take? Be careful to avoid response biases that might produce answers that have nothing to do with what you are trying to measure. For instance, would the tendency to say "yes" lead to a score that is not meaningful? Would the tendency to want to give socially desirable answers prevent getting an accurate measure? Try to find several ways to measure each specific aim so that biases associated with a particular kind of item can be avoided. Consider including items that look at attitudes, feelings, and behaviors.

Get some people who are like the program's clients to take the instrument and debrief them. Ask them how they responded to the items, that is, what the items meant to them. Finally, have other professionals in your field check the content of your items, preferably without telling them ahead of time just what you are trying to measure. See if they can deduce your specific aim from the instrument you are going to use. If all these tests work out, you can be reasonably certain that you have some content validity.

Until you test your measure in action, you will have no other evidence of validity. But ask yourself, "If I do *not* get a change on this instrument as a result of the program, will I be convinced that the program failed?" If the answer is "yes," you can proceed with considerable confidence.

All the early work on an instrument should be concerned with its validity, that is, how well it will measure what you want it to measure. Once you feel that you have an instrument that is going to be valid, it should be rechecked to improve its reliability.

Check each item for ambiguous language or structure. Can it be rewritten more simply? An early form of one of our drug use surveys included the question, "If you were going to use alcohol, how likely would your friends be to do something to discourage you?" Later we changed the question to read, "Would your friends try to stop you from drinking beer or wine?"

Make sure that every item is easy to understand. One place where you can have difficulty is in trying to construct equal numbers of positive and negative statements. The negative statements can end up very artificial and hard to understand. "Are you not interested in how things work?" is a peculiar question. It is better to have clear questions and some imbalance in the proportion of positive and negative statements than to obsessively balance the numbers with confusing questions.

It is usually better to have a range of responses, not just "true–false" or "agree–disagree." Our practical experience suggests that five alternatives give good discrimination without being clumsy.

The item format must fit the question. Some questions call for specific responses. For example,

When do you drink beer or wine?

__________ I do not drink

__________ Just on weekends and holidays

__________ During the week and on weekends or holidays

__________ Almost every day

Some questions are most efficient in a checklist. A lot of information can be obtained very rapidly.

Why do you or might you use marijuana? (Check all that apply.)

__________ Never use it

__________ I like the feeling I get

__________ Part of being at a party

__________ Makes me less nervous

__________ Nothing else to do around here

We have had very good luck with a semantic differential format with older children and young adults. If you pick the adjective pairs carefully, you can get a lot of very precise information quickly. It is much faster to read a pair of words than to read a question and a list of responses. For example, the Concept–Specific Anxiety Scale (Cole and Oetting, 1968) gives a very accurate rating of anxiety using twelve items like the following two:

How I feel when I [the concept can be anything from taking an exam to seeing a snake].

Me

calm ______ : ______ : ______ : ______ : ______ : nervous

My hands

wet ______ : ______ : ______ : ______ : ______ : dry

These are only three of the many, many types of items that people have used. They are included as examples to encourage you to try to find the kind of item that will be most useful in your project, and to prevent getting stuck on a set of "agree–disagree" or "like–dislike" responses.

Finally, consider the length of your instrument. Increasing the length of the instrument increases the reliability, *if* all the items are equally good. Once you have used your best items, adding poor ones will not help. Further, if the instrument is too long, the clients or the judges are likely to get tired or bored and start marking casually or at random.

If you can, do some pilot work with your instrument before using it in your project. If you can run your program for a small group and see whether the instrument shows a change, it is very valuable. If not, can you give the instrument to a class or other group of volunteers? You can at least find out whether items that are supposed to measure the same thing are consistent with each other, and if items that are supposed to measure different things are not correlated. If you can give the measure twice, with a gap between, you can even find out whether the scores are consistent over time.

While doing that, consider whether there should be natural differences among people in the group if the instrument is working. For example, a "math interest" scale should surely relate to choice of major, an "aggressive behavior" scale to sex, an "economic security" scale to socioeconomic status, and so on. It is easy to check and see if there are relationships. If the pilot testing shows low reliability or does not fit your theory, back up and try to find the flaw in either your logic or in the instrument. Then try again. If the items are internally consistent with each other and reliable across time, and if they show differences where you would expect them, you can proceed with reasonable confidence.

## Step VI: SELECT A RESEARCH DESIGN

Once you know how you are going to measure the outcome of your program, it is time to plan the project so that you will get the information you need. All too often practicing professionals have been wary of research design. When they took the course in graduate school it either emphasized complex statistics or spent hour after hour criticizing designs, leaving the impression that it was nearly impossible to do good research. But nearly all evaluative research uses only relatively simple research designs; there just isn't room in the real world for elaborate and complex research plans. Nearly all the time, the research designs that are going to be useful to you come from a fairly short list.

Some of the designs on that list are very efficient. They will give you a very clear answer about the effectiveness of your program. Others are weaker—there may be several possible explanations for the results other than the effect of the program. But even the weaker design can be useful.

The trick is to use the most efficient design possible. But when you are forced by practical constraints to use a weaker design, go ahead and do the research anyway, using the best design you can. The results can still be very useful. A weaker design means that your results could have an alternative explanation, but you can consider that alternative possibility when it comes time to use the results to make decisions. You *must*, of course, treat the results with appropriate caution, but as long as the cost of the evaluation is reasonable, even a weak research design is far better than guessing whether a program works.

A decision matrix is given in Table 2. It will not work for everything, but will probably be useful for over 80 percent of your evaluative research. It is designed to encourage you to use the best possible research design for your problem. Every question that you can answer "yes" improves your chances of having a good design. The following paragraphs discuss the questions asked in the matrix:

1. *Are you testing a clearly defined program and are you concerned with either whether it works or how well it works?* This first question is asked only to make sure that this table applies to your problem. There are, of course, a lot of very complex evaluative research problems; questions such as which parts of a program are effective, or whether education is meeting its goals. It would be impossible to deal with all these questions in a short chapter. But most evaluative research is not that complex. Usually we are testing a new program, for instance,

an orientation program, a dorm facility, or a life planning workshop. Those kinds of programs can almost always be tested within the framework of some relatively simple research designs. It is those designs that we discuss here.

If your problem is more complex, or if you have questions about theoretical issues, you will have to seek expert help. Remember, though, that the consultant's ideas and goals may not be the same as yours. Many consultants are primarily interested in scientific inquiry; they are used to planning studies to find out *why* something works, to answer theoretical questions. They may not have a good feel for the kind of information that you need to make decisions. Make sure that the results of whatever study is planned will provide you with the answer to the questions, "Does it work?"

2. *Is the program to be tested still in the future?* If possible, start planning the evaluation when you start planning the program. If the program has already been run, it is hard to get really good information, but you can sometimes learn enough to be of some use in making decisions. If the program is already finished, go to Question 7 on the matrix and see whether you have a natural experiment, one that was not planned but that can still provide you with useful information.

3. *Can a comparison group be found?* A control or comparison group is very valuable. With some kinds of programs, the procedure is easy. If there are two sections of a class, you can work with one and use the other as a comparison. If there are 100 volunteers, you can choose fifty and have fifty wait. In other situations, a comparison group is difficult to find. There may be only a few people who want or need the program at your school—too few to divide into two groups. The program might be aimed at the whole school, not just a part of it. Can you find some ingenious way of getting a comparison group? How about a sister institution, with students and program much like yours? How about friends in the same profession, each of whom could find you a few comparison clients? *It is worth a great deal of effort to try to find a way to compare the effect on your clients with a group who did not get your program!*

There are three general kinds of comparison groups. Each kind answers a different question. Decide which of the following questions you want answered. If you want more than one answered, then use more than one comparison group.

3a. *Does the program work?* If that is the question, use a no-treatment or waiting-list control, that is, a group that receives no treatment during the period that your program is running. The waiting-list control group is slightly different from the no-treatment group. People on a waiting list know that they are going to get treatment and there may be some implicit communication that they are not to change until it occurs. It is, nevertheless, a very efficient type of control group. Since services are often limited, there are frequently people on a waiting list anyway, and, ethically, you are not denying treatment to anyone just to run your evaluation. (A waiting list for suicide prevention, however, would obviously have ethical and practical consequences.)

3b. *Does the program work better than the usual system (or better than another program)?* If that is the question, use the regular program or the alternative program as a control group. You may be in a situation where everyone has to get some kind of program, or where you have two alternatives to choose from. The problem is that, if the regular program is effective at all, it is often very difficult to demonstrate clearly that yours is better. Most outcome research comparing similar methods of treatment finds only minor differences between them. You might, therefore, also want to include a no-treatment or waiting-list control. It would at least show that both treatments had some effect, and you can reach a decision based on cost. Of course, if you are convinced that the present program is doing no good at all, it would make a very good control group.

3c. *Does the program work because of its content or just because a program was given?* If that is the question, you would want to use a pseudo-treatment (placebo) control group. This question is often not as important to service-oriented people as the preceding two questions. They want to help, and if the content is less important than simply paying attention to some people, they are willing to do it. But if the evaluation question really is whether the *content* of the program is important, this type of control group is essential. The pseudo-treatment group must have all the characteristics of the real program. It should be as exciting, interesting, and involving, take as long, demand as much effort, and if the outcome of the program would be obvious to the clients, seem as if it would work. In medicine you can give a sugar pill or saline injection, but in this kind of program, it is more difficult to run a control. It might seem very hard to devise a program that meets all of these requirements and yet doesn't work. In fact, is the program you are running as good as the placebo?

The pseudo-treatment method is more likely to be used when you are at the stage where you are examining individual parts of a program instead of the whole thing. You might change them to a placebo one at a time and see if it makes a difference. It probably won't, by the way. The expectancy of the subjects and the commitment of the staff are such powerful determinants of a program's effects, that they often overcome any minor differences due to content.

4. *Can you use random assignment?* If the people in the experimental group start out different from those in the comparison group, how can you tell whether the outcome is due to the program or occurs only because the groups were different in the first place? Obviously, you can't! You might be able to logically demonstrate that the groups should be the same. You could logically show that whatever differences exist should not be important in terms of program effects. But the *best* way of making sure that the groups are the same is to randomly assign people to the groups. That way, even if there is some differential program effect that you do not know about, it should be balanced between the two groups and have no overall effect. (The section on blocking, below, adds even more certainty, but notice that the final step in blocking is still random assignment.)

All too often, people whose primary commitment is to provide service feel that random assignment is somehow impersonal or even unethical. Staff hear about the new program and immediately know that it is just what John or Susan needs. It is hard to resist the pressure to get their clients in, particularly since you too know the program is a good one. But help them to see the long-term importance of really knowing whether a program does work. Without that knowledge, you may run the program but not really be helping all the future clients just like them, or without that evidence even an effective program may not be around to help anyone.

Randomized assignment can be done. Boruch, McSweeney, and Soderstrom (1977) cite more than 300 studies with random assignment in schools and other institutions. Random assignment is worth a great deal of effort because it protects you against most of the potential alternative explanations that might have led to your results.

5. *Before assignment, can you sort people on characteristics that might relate to program impact?* Would your program have a greater or lesser effect because of age, sex, intelligence, or college major, for example? If you expect the program to influence some people more than others, make sure that you have the same proportion of each type of person in the program and in the comparison group. Use blocking to match people on the important characteristics and to assign one person

of each pair *randomly* to each group. That way the groups will be as much alike as possible, and the random assignment still takes care of any important difference that you may not have thought of.

If you have very large groups and random assignment, blocking is probably not needed. When you have a small program, it could be very important. Suppose there are ten people in the program, ten in the comparison group, and only four males altogether. Even with random assignment, about one time in sixteen you would get all four males in the same group. That might change your results. Matching for sex and randomly assigning one of each pair would assure two males in each group.

6. *Do you have really good outcome measures?* This is an important question because it determines whether you should have a pretest or whether you can use a post-test-only design. The post-test-only design is cleaner. If you give a pretest, the results could somehow be influenced by the pretest instead of the program. For example, taking the pretest might suggest to the clients how they are expected to change and could make them respond differently to the program. Any serious practitioner should read Campbell and Stanley's 1966 review of advantages and disadvantages of various designs.

At first, it would appear that you should always use the post-test-only design, but this is not necessarily true in applied research. When random assignment is not used, you need a pretest to make sure that your groups are similar on the outcome measure before they start the program. Besides, you may be less concerned about whether taking a pretest helped lead to a difference between the groups. If it did, it might just be a good addition to the program.

Most importantly, though, in deciding whether a pretest is necessary, is the question of how sensitive and reliable your outcome measure is. Building a good outcome measure is the single most difficult task in evaluative research. Your measure is likely to be somewhat low in reliability, may show considerable variability across subjects, and may be influenced by a number of extraneous factors other than exactly what you want to measure. If so, it will be hard for that measure to detect a difference even when one exists. When that is true, a pretest combined with a post-test can be more powerful statistically than a post-test only. This is so often true in evaluative research, that in previous publications I have simply recommended the pretest–program–post-test designs over the post-test-only designs. If you have a proven, good outcome measure and random assignment, use a post-test-only design. If you have any doubts, you'd better consider a pretest.

At this point, the matrix will indicate what kind of design you should use—the design that involves the most "yes" answers. Do, however, see the note on follow-up at the top of the matrix and read the section on follow-up later in this chapter.

If you had to answer "no" to Questions 2 or 4 on the matrix, you cannot use one of the best designs for the evaluation. Some researchers would feel that you should, therefore, do no evaluation, since the results could have alternative explanations. They are being far too rigid. Though you should be cautious about the findings and consider what might have influenced them, you can still learn a great deal that might help you make program decisions.

7. *Can you locate two similar groups, one of which will have (or already had) the program?* If so, you may have a natural experiment. You could apply the outcome measures to the groups and compare results, or you could find already existing information from before and after the program that would answer your questions. Of course, you have to use caution in interpreting the results, since they could be due to already existing differences between the groups before the program started.

8. *Can you give a pretest?* Or, alternatively, can you find already existing data that show what the group was like before the program started? The pretest is particularly valuable when you have not been able to use random assignment. It lets you know whether there were major differences in the groups before they started. It does not solve all your problems since without random assignment there may be other important differences related to outcome that the pretest did not measure, but it does improve the situation greatly. At least you know that the differences on your outcome measure were not already there before you started.

9. *Can you match samples?* Even if you cannot *assign* people to different groups, it may be possible to get a better comparison between the groups by matching samples of those groups after the fact. First, decide what characteristics might interact with the effect of the program. Would it be different as a result of sex, age, or college major, for example? Then identify those characteristics in the two groups, one getting the program and one not. Then, *before doing the final data analysis*, match subjects as closely as possible from the two groups so that the final subgroups that you are comparing are as similar as possible. Test the differences only between the matched samples. If your choices have been accurate, the comparison of the effect of the program on the groups will be much more precise than evaluating the total group.

*Note*: Think very carefully about what characteristics are truly important to match. If you miss one that is really important, you might have a difference between the two final samples because of that characteristic and not because of the program. But, if you list several characteristics that are not important, you will find it very difficult to actually match samples of the two groups and will gain nothing by matching the samples.

10. *Can you possibly find a comparison group?* Almost any kind of comparison group is preferable to not having one. If you don't have one, there are many different possibilities that could have led to the change outside of your program. It could be growth or maturation or the amount of time that passed. It could be just taking the pretest, or something random that happened (e.g., a riot, a campus speaker). Showing that a comparison group did not change during this period helps eliminate many of the alternative explanations for your results. That is why Question 10 of the matrix suggests looking for a comparison group.

11. *Can you establish a base line by giving more than one pretest?* If there is simply no possibility of a comparison group, some valuable data can still be obtained. Gathering base-line data becomes very important. If you can show that the outcome measure is relatively stable in the group before the program and then changed after the program, there are still alternative explanations that might have led to your results, but the chance that your program actually created the effect is better. Two, or even more, pretests help increase your confidence that the result was less likely to be due to maturing or simply giving the pretest. A follow-up can also help: see the discussion later in this chapter.

12. *Can you check on differential effects?* Only a very rare program would affect everyone in exactly the same way. Usually it is more effective for some and less for others. The above sections on blocking and matching samples show how you can balance two groups so that, if there are differential effects, they will average out across the two groups. This is an effective way to deal with the question if you are concerned about determining whether the program has an overall effect. When the treated group is large, you may be able to go beyond this. *Before analyzing the data*, sort out the group into separate subgroups with different characteristics that you expect would be related to the effect of the program and compare the effect across the subgroups. You may be able to find out not only whether the program works, but for whom it works best.

This approach may be particularly important if you do not have a comparison group. If you can predict ahead of time that the program will work well for some subgroups and not for others, and you can demonstrate those results, even without a comparison group you may feel some confidence that the program did work.

13. *You have only one group and only a post-test.* You cannot do a true evaluation of any kind, but you can still gather useful information. There are many practical questions that can be asked that could bear on whether you want to run the program again or how you might change it. Ask the participants how they felt about it, what they liked or disliked, how it changed them, and similar questions. Look for differences such as who liked the program and who did not. Check with staff on what responses they observed. Use program monitoring described below. Do not convince yourself that you have evaluated the program, but use the results to gain insights and ideas that will help you when you can later do a good evaluation.

**Table 2 A Decision Matrix for Selecting a Research Design for Program Evaluation**

**AFTER THE FIRST QUESTION, EVERY RESPONSE OF "YES" LEADS TO A BETTER DESIGN. *Note*: If possible, add a followup to the design.**

1. Are you testing a clearly defined program *and* are you concerned with either whether it works or how well it works?

   If NO, seek a consultant—this table is not appropriate.
   If YES, go on.

2. Is the program to be tested still in the future?

   If NO, go to Question7.
   If YES, go on.

3. Can a comparison group be found?

   If NO, go to Question 10.
   If YES, choose the type of comparison group by deciding which of the following questions you want answered:

   a. Does the program work?
      Use a waiting list or a no-treatment comparison group.
   b. Does it work better than the usual system (or better than another program)?
      Use your usual program or the other program as a comparison. (*Warning*: It is hard to show a difference between two fairly effective programs.)

c. Does the program work because of its content or just because *a* program was given?
Use a placebo program, one that has everything *but* what you feel are the effective program elements.

After choosing a comparison group, go on.

4. Can you use random assignment?

If NO, go to Question7.
If YES, go on.

5. Before assignment, can you sort people on characteristics that might relate to program impact (e.g., sex, age, socioeconomic status, ability, personality)?

If NO, blocking is not possible, go on.
If YES, use blocking; match people on important characteristics, and *randomly* assign one of each pair to your program and the other to the comparison group. Go on.

6. Do you have really good outcome measures, both reliable and valid?

If YES . . .
and blocking is possible, the design is:
Two groups, blocking–program–post-test only
and blocking is not possible, the design is:
Two groups, random assignment–program–post-test only

If NO . . .
and blocking is possible, the design is:
Two groups, blocking–pretest–program–post-test only (If a pretest is not possible, use a post-test only.)
and blocking is not possible, the design is:
Two groups, random assignment–pretest–program–post-test (If a pretest is not possible, use a post-test only.)

*Note:* Any of the above designs are *very* good. They can lead to results with few important alternative explanations.

7. Can you locate two *similar* groups, one of which will have (or already had) the program?

If NO, go to Question10.
If YES, go on.

8. Can you give a pretest?

Decide and go on.

9. Can you match samples, that is, match people in the two groups who have similar *important* characteristics?

If YES . . .

and a pretest is possible, the design is:
Two groups (matched sample), pretest–program–post-test

and a pretest is not possible, the design is:
Two groups (matched sample), program–post-test

If NO . . .

and a pretest is not possible, the design is:

Two groups (pre-formed), program–post-test
(*Note:* The above three designs are good. The results may be useful.)

and a pretest is not possible, the design is:

Two groups (pre-formed), program–post-test
*Treat results with caution:* the groups may have been different before the program started.

---

10. Below this line, you have only one group. Reconsider! Can you find a comparison group?

    If YES, return to Question 2.
    If NO, go on.

11. Can you establish a base line by giving more than one pretest?

    Decide and go on.

12. Can you check on differential effects (whether the program was more effective in one or more subgroups)?

    If YES, the design is:

    Predetermined subgroups) pretest–time lapse–second pretest–post-test
    or
    (Predetermined subgroups) pretest–program–post-test
    If NO, the design is:

    One group, pretest–time lapse–second pretest–program–post-test
    or
    One group, pretest–program–post-test
    (*Treat results with caution.*)

13. You have only one group and only a post-test.

    Ask useful questions.
    Use naturalistic observation.
    Do program monitoring.

---

## Follow-up

Almost every evaluative research plan would benefit from a follow-up test. In some cases, your program is meant to create a permanent change in the clients. A follow-up to check on whether they drift back to previous patterns is very valuable. For example, a frequent result of follow-up of counselor trainees is to find that they have returned to their earlier ways of doing things. On the other hand, we did a small study of attitude change in clients who had a very brief interview. There was more attitude change after 2 weeks than immediately. Thus a follow-up may show results that you could not find at the end of the program.

In other situations your program might be an environmental change that should directly influence people only as long as it continues. A follow-up can provide very valuable information. It may show that people adapt to the change and are no longer responding. If the environmental change is stopped, the follow-up may show a return to the earlier pattern.

The follow-up could be particularly important where you have only one group and an environmental change. For example, even if there is no comparison group, if you first established a base line, then changed things, got a change in your outcome measure, then changed them back and the outcome measure returned to the original value, the results would be very convincing.

## Step VII: PLAN THE PROGRAM

With the outcome measures ready and the research design selected, the next step is to get together with appropriate staff and administrators and work out the entire program plan. The plan includes all the elements of the program, how they will be run, and when and where evaluation data will be collected to fit the research design.

This is the step at which everyone working with the program must become fully knowledgeable about the evaluation and its importance. If the staff and administrators see evaluation as an integral and useful part of the whole program, it is more likely to actually work.

## Step VIII: MONITOR THE PROGRAM

Program monitoring is aimed at finding out whether your program plan was followed. It is usually not very expensive in either dollars or staff time, and it provides you with a lot of basic information about the program that is useful for future planning.

Monitoring is particularly valuable if you have not been able to use one of the better research designs. Even though you may not be able to tell whether the program had an actual impact on the clients, you can tell whether it is feasible, whether clients stay in it, what it costs, and whether the staff actually did what they planned to do. This information is sometimes more important in reaching a decision about whether to continue with a program than outcome results. Answer the following questions:

*Is the program being followed?* If the staff change the program or drift back into their previous way of functioning, make sure that you know what they did.

*Are clients participating as expected?* Check on attendance, dropout, and level of participation. Try to find out why people drop out or do not participate. You may have to compare high-participation and low-participation clients to learn more about why the program worked as it did.

*Is the program potent?* Are people just going through the motions? Are some parts still exciting and interesting and others passive and boring? Many evaluations fail because the program did not stay powerful and effective.

*Is the program maintained over time?* If the program is deteriorating part way through, you can go in and prop it up, but remember that when you describe the program you have to include monitoring and propping or it will fail when other people try it.

*Is the program meeting other goals?* Even though you planned it to meet one set of aims, sometimes you find out that it is doing something else, perhaps something valuable. You might have to change your outcome measures in midstream to measure what the program is really doing.

*Are research data being collected*? Since service staff often put research low on their priority list, unless you check, all too often the research procedures and data collection are neglected.

*Is anything happening that might distort the findings?* Check to make sure that nothing happens to the comparison group that doesn't also happen to the group getting the program. If you have only one group it is particularly important to be able to state with some assurance that nothing other than the program happened that should have led to the change that you found.

*What are the costs of the program?* Final decisions must always consider costs in both staff time and dollars. Gather information on costs while the program is running: they are always different from what you planned.

## Step IX: ANALYZE AND INTERPRET RESULTS

The statistical analysis, unless you are quite knowledgeable, may have to be placed in the hands of a consultant. Many of these designs, however, do not call for elaborate statistical techniques, and if you have some background and a good basic text, you should be able to carry through with no difficulty. Regardless of how the analyses are done or by whom, the responsibility for interpreting the results cannot be passed on to a consultant. The people who planned and did the evaluation have to make the decisions about what the results mean.

There will be two kinds of statistics to interpret: inferential statistics that indicate whether any differences are real, and descriptive statistics, for example; means and percentages, that describe what happened. Both are essential in helping you reach decisions.

The inferential statistics will provide you with probability statements. Traditionally, if the results are "significant beyond the .05 level" a real difference is assumed. If not, there is assumed to be no real difference. When you are doing a series of studies to find out why something happened and are testing an interlocking set of theories, this approach is very useful: any mistakes will be corrected in future studies.

Unfortunately, when you are doing evaluative research, you usually do not have a series of studies; you must reach decisions based on only this one. This means that you do not use statistical significance in the same way. When the results are "significant beyond the .20 level" it means only that there is one chance in five that you would get a difference that large by chance. You have to decide how that possibility will influence your decision. If a program were costly or difficult, and the results were this questionable, you might decide to try an alternative. If, on the other hand, the benefits from the program were very important and you had no solid alternatives to try, you might feel that the four in five chance that there was a real difference is worth taking.

Description statistics such as the size of the differences found, the variability, and even whether people moved from a negative side of a scale to a positive side are also important in reaching decisions. You might find, for example, that a change, even though statistically significant, was not worth the cost of the program.

When you consider the amount of change, how many people benefited, the chance that the change is real, and the costs, the critical question is what would be done with the assets if the program were not run. When you have only modest results and the alternative is a new program, it is tempting to rush into the new program. Remember, though, how enthusiastic you were about this one when you first started. When you actually evaluate the new program, it is likely to be much like this one—not quite what you dreamed. So, with caution, proceed to make the best judgment you can.

## Step X: PREPARE THE FINAL REPORT

The final report should not be a formal article with highly technical sections on results. It should be a clear, concise picture of what was done, why it was done, and what the results were. It should be aimed at a specific audience, the one that will have to make decisions about this program or similar ones. I have discussed such a report in considerable detail in previous articles (Oetting, 1976a; Oetting, 1976b).

## SUMMARY

The step-by-step procedure for planning evaluative research given above has three important elements that together will determine whether the research plan works. First, there must be a good outcome measure. Second, the experimental design should be as good as possible. Third, the program must be monitored to make sure that you are really testing what you hoped to test. With all three elements, excellent evaluative research can be produced.

Throughout, I have suggested involving staff, administrators, and representatives of the program recipients in every step. This is based on my conviction both that it will lead to better research and that it radically increases the chances that the results will actually be used. This whole process represents the ultimate in formal, solid evaluation.

There is, however, another type and another style of research. It is called naturalistic observation. It consists of observing with the unbiased eye, accurately describing what is seen, organizing those descriptions systematically, and developing a model or useful hypothesis about what is going on.

Evaluative research is the end product. The ideas that lead to it have to come from the much less formal process of naturalistic observation. It is the creative base. If you cannot fit your programs into this evaluative research model so that they can be tested, then turn back to the primary process. Observe, describe, think, and organize your thoughts. When your ideas are really clear, there *will* be a way to evaluate what you are doing. Then this chapter may help.

## REFERENCES

Boruch, R. F., A. J. McSweeney, and E. J. Soderstrom "Randomized field experiments for program development and evaluation: an illustrative bibliography." Cited in *Catalog of Selected Documents in Psychology*, Vol. 7. Washington, D.C.: American Psychological Association, 1977.

Buros, O. K. (Ed.) *The Seventh Mental Measurements Yearbook* (2 vols.). Highland Park, N.J.: Gryphon Press, 1972.

Campbell, D. T. and L. C. Stanley *Experimental and Quasi-Experimental Designs for Research*. Chicago: Rand McNally, 1966.

Campbell, J. P. *Managerial Behavior, Performance and Effectiveness*. New York: McGraw-Hill, 1970.

Cole, C. W. and E. R. Oetting *The Concept-specific Anxiety Scale*. Fort Collins, Colo.: Rocky Mountain Behavioral Science Institute, 1968.

Comrey, A. L., T. E. Backer, and E. M. Glaser *A Sourcebook of Mental Health Measures*. Los Angeles: Human Interaction Research Institute, 1973.

Hathaway, S. R. and J. C. McKinley *Booklet for the Minnesota Multiphasic Personality Inventory*. New York: The Psychological Corporation, 1943.

Hurst, J. C. and R. G. Weigel *Counseling Services Assessment Blank*, Fort Collins, Colo.: Rocky Mountain Behavioral Science Institute, 1968.

Oetting, E. R. Evaluative research and orthodox science: Part I. *Personnel and Guidance Journal*, 1976a, **55** (1), 11–15.

Oetting, E. R. Planning and reporting evaluative research: Part II. *Personnel and Guidance Journal*, 1976b, **55** (2), 60–64.

Oetting, E. R. and C. W. Cole Method, design, and instrument evaluation. *New Directions for Student Services*, **1** (Spring), 1978.

Robinson, J. P., R. Athanasiou, and K. B. Head *Measures of Occupational Attitudes and Occupational Characteristics*. Ann Arbor, Mich.: Institute for Social Research, The University of Michigan, 1969.

Robinson, J. P. and P. R. Shaver *Measures of Social Psychological Attitudes* (rev. ed.). Ann Arbor, Mich.: Institute for Social Research, The University of Michigan, 1973.

Thorton, G. C. and E. R. Oetting *Exercises in Psychological Testing*. New York: Harper and Row, 1980.

## REFERENCE NOTES

ERIC (Educational Resources Information Center)
Document Reproduction Service
P.O. Box 190
Arlington, VA 22210

PASAR (Psychological Abstracts Information Service)
American Psychological Association
1200 Seventeenth Street, N.W.
Washington, DC 20036

Smithsonian Science Information Exchange, Inc.
Room 300, 1730 M Street, N.W.
Washington, DC 20036

# III

# Student Affairs Intervention Programs

Part I introduced student development, environmental development, and the interaction between students and their environment as the three components which compose the foundation for student affairs work, (Figure 1, Chapter 1). Bodies of knowledge and skill necessary for the student affairs professional were identified as investigative, theoretical, and interventive (Figure 2, Chapter 1). The components of the conceptual framework were discussed in detail in Chapters 2, 3, and 4.

Part II described the three-dimensional intervention or "cube" model developed by Morrill, Oetting, and Hurst. The target, method, and purpose of interventions for human development were discussed in detail and the importance of basic and evaluative research explicated.

Part III builds on Parts I and II by examining the application to actual student affairs work of the material presented earlier.

Following is a two-dimensional chart designed to facilitate the application of the conceptual foundation described in Chapter 1. The left-hand margin contains the same conceptual foundation that is contained in Figure 2 of Chapter 1. The three major components are (1) the management of basic resources related to student needs, (2) the skills and knowledge necessary for students to make full utilization of the educational setting, and (3) the components of environmental development. The horizontal axis of the chart divides intervention activities into two categories: those programs that relate to specific needs occurring within the general student population and those intervention activities that

**STUDENT AFFAIRS INTERVENTION PROGRAMS**

| CONCEPTUAL FOUNDATIONS OF STUDENT AFFAIRS | Specific Programs for General Student Populations | | | | | | | | | | | | | | | | Unique Student Populations Receiving Programs | | | | | |
|---|---|---|---|---|---|---|---|---|---|---|---|---|---|---|---|---|---|---|---|---|---|---|
| | Counseling Center | Financial Aid | Housing and Food Services | Union Building | Recreational Sports | Health Center | Research and Evaluation | Student Activities | Discipline and Records | Career Development | Study Skills | Orientation | Environmental Design | Volunteer Services | Admission and Records | Student Resource Development | Ethnic Minorities | Women | Handicapped | Returning Students | International Students | Veterans |
| I. Management of Basic Resources | | | | | | | | | | | | | | | | | | | | | | |
| A. Food | | | x | x | | x | x | | | | | | | | | | | | | | | |
| B. Housing | | | x | | | x | x | | | | | | x | | | | | | x | | x | |
| C. Health | x | | | | x | x | x | | | | | | x | | | | | x | x | | x | |
| D. Finances | | x | | | | | x | | | | | | | | | | x | | | | | x |
| II. Student Development (Skills and Knowledge) | | | | | | | | | | | | | | | | | | | | | | |
| A. Intellectual | x | | | x | | | x | | | x | x | x | | | x | | x | | x | x | x | |
| B. Physical | | | | | x | x | x | | | | | | | | | | | | x | | | |
| C. Societal/citizenship | x | | x | x | | | x | x | x | | | | | x | | | | x | | | x | |
| D. Moral/ethical | x | | | | | | x | x | x | | | | | | | | | | | | | |
| E. Interpersonal | x | | | x | x | x | x | x | | x | | x | | x | | | x | | | x | x | x |
| F. Career | x | x | | | | | x | | | x | | x | | x | | | x | x | x | x | | x |
| G. Cultural | | | x | x | | | x | x | | | | | | | | | x | | | | x | |
| H. Intrapersonal | x | | | | x | x | x | | x | x | | | | | | | x | x | x | x | | |
| III. Environmental Development (Design and Modification) | | | | | | | | | | | | | | | | | | | | | | |
| A. Physical | | x | | | | x | x | | | | x | | x | | | | | | x | | | |
| B. Social | | x | | x | | | x | x | | | | | x | | | | x | x | x | x | | |
| C. Cultural | | | | x | | | x | | | | | | x | | | | x | | | | | |
| D. Academic | | | | | | | x | | x | x | x | | x | | x | | x | x | x | x | | |
| E. Administrative | | | | | | | x | x | | | | x | x | | x | | | | x | | | |

have emerged as a result of the recognition that there are distinct student subpopulations that require both general and unique intervention efforts.

The chart with its two dimensions can be useful in bridging the conceptual–applied gap in four ways. First, by listing the actual student affairs programs in existence in a specific institution, the management, student development, and environmental development activities may be plotted. The X's in the chart represent a hypothetical description of a division of student affairs and plots activities as they relate to the conceptual foundations of student affairs work. Through this plotting procedure it is possible to systematically describe the scope of activities of a division of student affairs. Second, and equally important, is the process of systematically identifying what does not exist. All too often student and environmental needs go unnoticed as a result of the lack of a systematic assessment or diagnosis. An assessment of student and environmental needs can lead to the determination of what is not being attended to. Once this diagnosis is complete, what is *not* included becomes intentional on the part of those determining what a division should include.

A third use of the two-dimensional chart follows from the description of what is and what is not contained in a program of services. Through the plotting process a division can make plans to deal with previously unattended student or environmental needs. This process can also provide the conceptual base for the reduction of programs during periods of financial cutbacks and subsequent retrenchment. Finally, the two dimensional scheme can be used to identify directions for staff development. This would include the selection of new staff who possess knowledge or skills that are absent in the present staff as well as provide direction for training of present staff.

Part III is intended as the applied section of this book. A group of authors describe the day-to-day functions of various agencies within student affairs and relate those functions to the what and how of student environmental development.

# 10
# Counseling

DONNA L. McKINLEY

The role of the counseling center in higher education is an evolving one. Although the history of each existing center is unique to the institution in which it resides, there are some common evolutionary patterns and influences. A review of some major historical forces will illustrate the breadth of roles currently undertaken by counseling centers.

Warnath (1971) traces the origin of many modern-day counseling centers to the guidance bureaus that were established by the Veterans Administration on college campuses after World War II. The function of the guidance bureau was to assist veterans in processing the necessary paperwork and to place veterans in educational programs and monitor their progress. Thus the individual educational–vocational guidance function for a counseling center was established early and has persisted as a central role for many centers.

As the number of veterans decreased, the Veterans Administration phased out its monetary support for the guidance bureaus. Many colleges and universities continued the service with internal funding and the counseling center typically became a part of a student personnel delivery system. The phasing out of the Veterans Administration control coincided with the development of counseling psychology as a specialty area within APA (Pepinsky, Hill-Frederick, and Epperson, 1978), and a typical pattern was for the psychology or guidance and counseling faculty to play a major role in the further evolution of the counseling center. College students were a convenient and relatively intact population with whom graduate students could practice their developing skills, and university administrators were happy to have cheap labor in a service they hardly understood. Although educational–vocational guidance continued to be offered, the adequate preparation of psychologists required that skills in personal–psychological counseling be developed also. Thus services to students were expanded to include that realm. The goal of the counseling, however, continued to be that of assisting the student to adjust to the available educational environment.

Hanfmann (1978) traces a somewhat different history that is more common to counseling centers on elite private liberal arts campuses. Based on a traditional psychotherapy model, the key to success for these centers involved separation from disciplinary functions, establishing the confidentiality of the counseling relationship, and maintaining an adequate staff-to-student ratio to permit all students who sought it to receive counseling for as long as they needed it. In the most responsive centers, such as the one at Brandeis which Hanfmann describes, the traditional psychotherapy model underwent a translation to take the environment into account. As she points out, "We started perceiving therapeutic opportunities in the features of college life which, to start with, we had viewed merely as obstructions . . . We also learned to pay close attention to the people and circumstances that are highly significant for the student because of their relevance to the development tasks of adolescence" (p. 8).

In the view of Hanfmann and others who established similar centers, the preferred role of the counseling center continued to be that of individual counseling with the enlightened goal of assisting the student to use environmental opportunities for personal growth. However, the student boom of the 1960s seriously threatened this and other centers' capacity to keep pace with the staff-to-student ratio required to deliver such service. Although Hanfmann lamented this assault on the center's fulfillment of its true potential to contribute to student development, others in the field began to propose alternative means to accomplish the same goal.

A major stimulus for change in the view of a counseling center's function came in the form of a proposal by Morrill, Ivey, and Oetting (1968) that the counseling center become a center for student development. Based on Oetting's (1967) developmental framework for the application of counseling psychology, the center for student development would incorporate three new directions: (1) movement out into the university community to create programs to prevent problems, (2) mobilizing community resources for mental health, and (3) redefining the counseling center's role within a developmental framework. Although traditionalists might agree, at least in part, with the definition of a mental health problem as "anything that interferes with or prevents the use of developmental tasks that are available in the environment for personal growth" (Morrill, Ivey, and Oetting, 1968, p. 142), a major role extension involved viewing the environment itself as a possible target for intervention. In other words, the focus of a counselor might be on making opportunities available in the environment rather than on counseling the individual to improve his/her capacity to make use of the existing environment. Additional implications of this model include a role for the counseling center in facilitating the development of all students, not just those with developmental deficiencies, and the active involvement of the counseling center staff as consultants to others who impact on students directly and as policy makers. The possibilities of impacting on larger numbers of students with the same resources seem obvious.

A national survey reported in 1970 (Oetting, Ivey, and Weigel) summarizes the evolution of counseling centers to that point and illustrates the diversity of roles and models. In this monograph eight prototypic counseling centers are described. In the *vocational guidance* model, testing and vocational choice counseling are the primary functions. Some short-term personal counseling on issues related to vocational choice may be provided; psychotherapy or developmental counseling are not. The *personnel services* model is found almost exclusively on the small college campus and incorporates many of the student affairs functions that would be found in specialized services on the larger campus, for example, financial aids, orientation, and freshman testing. Assistance with course selection, choosing a major, planning a program of study, and correcting probationary status are the functions of centers within the *academic affairs* model. *Psychotherapy* centers do just that; the emphasis is on the treatment of emotional problems of students with minimal attention to vocational or academic concerns. Typically a few students receive extensive service. The *training* model exists where the center is located in a department with a graduate training program. Graduate students provide most if not all of the service, and the functions are determined by the learning needs of the trainees rather than the service needs of the general student population. Relatively new (in 1970) efforts to focus on prevention and mobilization of university resources for mental health and student growth through consultation and training characterized the *consultation* model, and a center at which *research* was a primary function was also described. Finally, the *traditional counseling* model was described as providing vocational and personal–social counseling in a highly professional and essentially remedial manner with little involvement with other elements of the campus community.

Although the authors of the monograph did not include incidence data for the various models presented, it is my observation that the majority of well-established counseling centers of that time were of the traditional counseling variety. Based on a survey of outreach practices (defined as programmatic efforts to interact with administrators, faculty, and students to create changes in the educational process and environment that lead to maximal growth and development) of counseling centers, Morrill and Oetting (1970) speculated that as many as half of the existing services continued to operate in relative isolation from the rest of the institution. Although remedial counseling is a valued service, the authors warned that". . . there is a good chance that [these centers] are not changing along with the rest of the college environment and that they may find themselves outdated and irrelevant in the near future" (p. 52). On the other hand, 80 percent of the respondents (326 of the 397 surveyed) indicated significant involvement in outreach activities. Those activities included such things as studies of student characteristics, consultation with various groups on campus, and teaching personal development courses.

Recognizing the increased emphasis on outreach programming and the need for a clear theoretical rationale to guide these efforts, Morrill and Hurst (1971) proposed a comprehensive definition of the role of the counseling psychologist in the academic community. Based on the assumption that counseling center staff members are hired by an institution for the explicit purpose of assisting the institution to achieve its goals for students and that the goals of education encompass personal as well as intellectual development, the authors used information from the American Council on Education longitudinal research design (Creager, 1968) to generate a model. If the outcomes of a college education are a result of the student input variables, the college environment variables, and the interaction between the two, then the roles of the counseling center in assisting the institution to achieve its goals with students can be defined as follows: "(1) to contribute to, support, modify, and enhance the learning environment; (2) to facilitate maximum utilization of the learning environment by students; (3) to study the student, the learning environment and the interaction as a means of providing the necessary data base for the implementation of (1) and (2)" (p. 92). Although the bulk of activity in most counseling centers continues to relate to the role of facilitating maximum utilization of the learning environment by students, this comprehensive model guides much of the current thinking about total delivery of effective services.

In Chapter 1, Hurst and Morrill define three roles for student services in education: (1) understanding the student, the environment, and the outcomes of their interaction in order to identify potential mismatches and needed interventions, (2) teaching students the skills they need to take advantage of and profit from the learning environment, and

(3) environmental redesign or modification. Based on the above historical review of counseling centers, the first two of these three roles have deep roots in the formation and evolution of counseling centers. Although individual vocational and personal counseling continue to be a core service of most centers, the role of teaching students skills to use the environment has expanded, both in target—all students rather than just those who are sufficiently troubled to seek remedial assistance—and in method—adding media, self-help tools, structured groups, peer helpers, and other means to expand the capacity to reach large numbers of students.

The third role of environmental redesign or modification is an outgrowth of the expansion of the counselor's role to include a preventive and developmental focus. From the early days when the role of the counselor was to assist students to adjust to the college situation, counselor case notes have been a rich source of information on stresses arising from the developmental tasks of students and factors in the environment. Because of the narrow focus of the counselor on the individually troubled student, rarely was that information compiled, analyzed, and shared in such a way as to contribute to understanding the "normal" student and the characteristics of the environment that facilitated or inhibited growth and development. An expansion of the counselor's role inspired a new examination of the available data. Sometimes inept efforts to use new insights to change the environment and the people who inhabit it met with responses that varied from enthusiastic acceptance to rejection and resentment of the intrusion. The negative reactions have forced counseling center personnel to do more systematic and respectable research and to become more sophisticated and collaborative in the application of change agent and consultation skills.

Certainly not all counseling centers perform all three roles to an equal degree. This broad definition of roles, however, provides a conceptual base from which each center can determine how best to accomplish its mission within the institution which supports and profits from its presence. Examples of possible interventions within these broadly conceived roles are presented in the next section.

## INTERVENTIONS

The "cube" appeared in the literature in 1974 (Morrill, Oetting, and Hurst) and provided a conceptual scheme for organizing the expanded view of the role of counselors on a college campus. By specifying targets (individual, primary group, associational group, and institution or community), purposes (remedial, preventive, or developmental), and methods (direct, consultation and training, or media) of intervention for college counselors in a three-dimensional model, the authors offer a thirty-six cell stimulus for choosing intervention approaches. Though it is impossible to attribute direct causality, a review of four counseling-related publications since 1974 (*Personnel and Guidance Journal, Journal of College Student Personnel, Journal of Counseling Psychology,* and *The Counseling Psychologist*) suggest that the authors accomplished their goal of stimulating creative thinking about alternative interventions for counselors on college campuses.

In this section examples of interventions illustrating the cells of the cube are given. Material for the examples comes from the literature, known practice, and my own thoughts about possibilities of services. The list of examples is not intended to be an exhaustive review or an evaluation of efforts included or excluded. Rather, the goal is to illustrate possibilities and stimulate further creative thinking about the role and the means for a counseling center to contribute to the positive development of students. For ease of presentation, this section is organized by target of the intervention: individual, primary group, associational group, and institution or community.

## The Individual

Remedial services for the individual student delivered directly by the counselor have been and continue to be the primary service of counseling centers. In addition to traditional individual personal–social and educational–vocational counseling, group treatment is increasing. Many new groups using a skill-building and focused-issue format are being tried. Examples include stress reduction (Romano, 1978) and depression management (Ribner and Ginn, 1975) workshops.

The use of student paraprofessionals is a primary means by which consultation or training becomes the method for delivering remedial services. Treatment programs at Colorado State University for specific anxieties (math, test, public speaking) and study skills deficits employ paraprofessionals, and the Companion Program of American University is an example of using paraprofessionals in the treatment of social skill deficits. A relatively new focus for counseling centers is training of clients to make better use of therapy services. In a recent study, Corazzini and Heppner (1979) found that a written description of the termination process contributed to clients' expressed comfort, and they are testing the generalizability of this intervention to successful handling of other endings in clients' lives.

Self-help materials take a media approach to the remediation of problems. Decision-making manuals, video-taped study skills modules, and telephone-accessed tapes on a variety of topics are examples.

Preventive services aim to alleviate stresses in the environment and enhance skills of the individual or remedy problems before they reach crisis proportions. In an ideal form, students at risk are identified and offered services to increase their likelihood of success. Mass psychological testing, as reported at the University of California-Riverside (Magoon, 1977–1978), is one approach, and many centers are attempting to provide special services for culturally different and educationally disadvantaged students to ease the transition to college. Screening for learning disability is a new effort at Colorado State University. Group programs for new students (Knott and Daher, 1978) are used to impart knowledge and skills that will be needed for success.

A preventive consultation effort might involve training faculty and staff to recognize early signs of depression, stress, or alcohol abuse, for example, in order to intervene and refer. Work with student residence hall staff is particularly critical in this regard.

Many creative efforts are possible through media. Lowenstein (1978) reports radio broadcasts of biofeedback relaxation training in preparation for major exam periods. Mass mailings and timely articles in a student newspaper could also be used to alert students to potential stresses and coping strategies. Topics might be as varied as "what to expect from your parents the first time you go home" and "how to prepare for life after college."

Developmental approaches to individual students are based on theoretical conceptions about the developmental tasks of the college students and the assumption that growth can be enhanced by specific interventions. Chickering's (1969) seven vectors—achieving competence, managing emotions, becoming autonomous, establishing identity, freeing interpersonal relationships, clarifying purposes, and developing integrity—suggest a framework for counseling center developmental programming.

Career development groups (Davidshofer, Thomas, and Preble, 1966) and life direction seminars (Galassi and Lemmon, 1978) offer a direct approach to the developmental task of clarifying purposes; relationship skills training (Weissberg, Sofair-Fisch, and Fisher-McCanne, 1978) addresses the achievement of interpersonal competence.

Consultation with faculty to integrate developmental concepts with didactic material has potential for impact far beyond those students who would avail themselves of directly delivered programs. Although the humanities and social sciences seem obviously adaptable to this approach, the sciences also provide a good opportunity to address moral–ethical issues in the application of technology.

Strategically located computer terminals for career exploration, telephone-accessed tapes on developmental issues, and recommended reading lists are examples of media approaches.

## Primary Group

Primary groups are defined as "intimate, continuing personal associations on a face-to-face basis, determined by the degree of intimacy rather than by proximity" (Morrill, Oetting, and Hurst, 1974). The primary group is that unit of social organization which most influences the individual. Among students the primary group would include family, spouse or committed partner, and close friendship groups. Often, but not always, roommates have this degree of intimacy, and some religious groups take on the character of a primary group.

According to the 1977–1978 Counseling Centers' Data Bank (Magoon), counseling for marital, separation, and divorce problems is on the increase in many centers. With the growing number of older students on campuses, it is likely that centers will gear up to provide family therapy as well.

In general, student couples and families seem to be an underserved, sometimes ignored, population. There are a number of services a counseling center can provide, in addition to the remediation of problems after they have occurred.

Advocacy through consultation and education is one such service. If this is delivered for the benefit of an already troubled family, it is a remedial service; broader application contributes to the prevention of problems. Role shifts, poverty-level existence, one partner excluded from the stimulation of the educational environment to support the other, balancing two careers, and the extraordinary time demands of some educational programs (medicine is a prime example) are all stresses that many faculty may have experienced as students and gratefully put behind them. Assisting faculty to appreciate the ramifications of such stress on educational progress has the potential for improving the likelihood that couples will survive the experience.

Training campus police to intervene appropriately in instances of domestic disputes and assisting in the formation of neighborhood groups and child care collectives in family housing units are additional examples of preventive efforts using a consultation and training approach. Direct preventive approaches include a workshop for dual career couples to prepare for graduation and the future reported by Illinois State

University (Magoon, 1977–1978), communication skills workshops (Kahnweiler, Kahnweiler, and Woodard, 1978), and parent training. Campus radio and television broadcasts also offer potential. Useful topics would include predicting and planning for stressful times for your student spouse, conflict resolution strategies, and how to make the little time you have together count. Informational programs for children would also be possible.

Reported efforts directed to other primary groups include training in conflict management for roommates and resident assistants (Phelan and Heidke, 1977) and a workshop on how to help a friend (Duson, King, and Murphy, 1978). Chickering's (1969) developmental vector of freeing interpersonal relationships suggests efforts on topics such as maintaining personal identity within a close relationship and learning interdependence.

## Associational Groups

An associational group is an organized collection of individuals who share common interests or needs. Examples of associational groups are classes, residence units, student organizations, and athletic teams.

Remediation efforts with associational groups often involve resolving some conflict that has occurred. Counseling center personnel might be called in to mediate a dispute between majority and minority students in a residence unit or between the president and members of a student organization. Alternatively, the counseling center staff member may provide consultation to the residence hall staff member or faculty advisor for the same purpose. A conflict resolution manual for student leaders would constitute a media approach.

Other examples of consultation and training efforts include training food service workers at the University of Virginia to deal with disruptions in campus dining halls (Magoon, 1977–1978) and consultation with the staff of a high-rise dormitory which resulted in installing partitions in the communal dining hall to improve opportunities for social interaction (Holahan, 1977).

The death of a member of an associational group is an occasion for a preventive intervention. Timely teaching and facilitation of a grieving process will prevent destructiveness within or dissolution of the group, as well as benefiting the individual members.

In a less crisis-oriented vein, the counseling center might assist an academic department to conduct an environmental assessment related to majors. The results could be used to develop policies and practices that support cooperation rather than competition within the group of majors. Similarly, helping a resident assistant to assess the interests of unit members and plan activities accordingly may prevent conflict and lack of commitment to the group.

Some of the developmental issues of an associational group are establishing norms and goals, balancing individual and group desires, organizing to accomplish task, and maintaining effective communication. Training resident assistants in group process is one approach to encouraging the development of associational groups in a residence unit (Winston and Smith, 1978). The Residence Environment Adaptation Program (Daher, Corazzini, and McKinnon, 1977) is another. In this program, counseling center staff serve as consultants to the residents of a dormitory floor or Greek house to assess discrepancy between real and ideal environment and plan change strategies. Media approaches are also possible, ranging from video-taped introduction to group process for a class using small group discussion to goal setting manuals for student organization officers.

**Institution or Community**

Interventions targeted for the institution constitute the greatest departure from the traditional counseling center role and represent a change in philosophy from fitting the student to the environment to impacting the environment so that it is more facilitative for students. A different perspective as well as an expanded knowledge base and set of skills are required in order to intervene effectively. It is, therefore, not surprising that relatively few institutional interventions are reported in the literature.

A necessary precursor to functioning as a campus change advocate (Conyne, 1977) or institutional intervenor is credibility. Although linkages and personal power help, within a campus community research data are particularly potent. For that reason environmental assessment has become an important tool of counseling centers. Whether gathered by paraprofessionals as described by Conyne (1975), telephone interviews, or more traditional survey techniques, the information can guide the counselor's actions as well as provide concrete input to those who have the power to change institutional policy and practices. The purposes for collecting and disseminating environmental assessment information may be remedial, preventive, or developmental. The definition of the purpose depends on whether a problem has already been identified (e.g., low retention rate of academically qualified minority students), some stress-producing event is predicted (e.g., the institution has made a commitment to recruit more disabled students), or potential for positive development is posited (e.g., opportunities for interaction between faculty and students on important issues contribute to campus cohesiveness).

Concrete examples of institutional interventions include an experiential workshop on attitudes toward the handicapped (Fix and Rohrbacher, 1977), training minority paraprofessionals to assist in the classroom (Thomas and Yates, 1974), and using environmental assessment data to accomplish a change in examination schedules (Conyne, 1977).

## CONCLUSION

The role of the counseling center in relation to student development clearly can encompass the three elements of (1) understanding the student, the environment, and the interaction, (2) teaching students skills to use the environment, and (3) modifying the environment. The possibilities for services in fulfillment of these roles are almost limitless. What has not been addressed is the efficacy of the roles and the services. The question of efficacy has both empirical and situational components. Obviously, each intervention must be evaluated both for its effectiveness in producing desired results and its comparative effectiveness and efficiency in relation to other approaches. To date, creative social science research is lagging behind creativity in intervention strategies, and that suggests an additional research function of counseling center personnel.

The situational component addresses the appropriateness of roles and strategies for a particular setting. Although the temptation is to suggest that any quality center would function in the manner described in this chapter, to do so would be irresponsible. Factors that must be considered include institutional goals, the center's mandate, coordination with other components of the institution, readiness of the institution to respond, and expertise available. In the final analysis, each counseling center must make a careful assessment of the campus environment in order to adopt the roles and provide the services that are most likely to contribute to student development.

## REFERENCES

Chickering, A. W. *Education and Identity*. San Francisco: Jossey-Bass, 1969.

Conyne, R. K. Environmental assessment: Mapping for counselor action. *Personnel and Guidance Journal*, 1975, **54** (3), 151–154.

Conyne, R. K. The campus change advocate. *Journal of College Student Personnel,* 1977, **18** (4), 312–316.

Corazzini, J. G. and P. P. Heppner Effect of preparing clients to terminate from group therapy. Unpublished manuscript, Colorado State University, 1979.

Creager, J. A. Use of research results in matching students and college. *Journal of College Student Personnel,* 1968, **9**, 312–319.

Daher, D. M., J. G. Corazzini, and R. D. McKinnon An environmental redesign program for residence halls. *Journal of College Student Personnel,* 1977, **18** (1), 11–15.

Davidshofer, C. O., L. E. Thomas, and M. G. Preble Career Development Groups: A program description. *Journal of College Student Personnel,* 1976, **17** (5), 413–416.

Duson, B. M., M. R. King, and B. Murphy Building blocks for a campus helping network. *Journal of College Student Personnel,* 1978, **19** (1), 76.

Fix, C. and J. Rohrbacher What is a handicap?: The impact of attitudes. *Personnel and Guidance Journal,* 1977, **56** (3), 176–178.

Galassi, M. D. and S. M. Lemmon Life direction seminars: Facilitating human development at a women's college. *Personnel and Guidance Journal,* 1978, **57** (3), 172–175.

Hanfmann, E. *Effective Therapy for College Students.* San Francisco: Jossey-Bass, 1978.

Holahan, C. J. Consultation in environmental psychology: A case study of a new counseling role. *Journal of Counseling Psychology,* 1977, **24** (3), 251–254.

Kahnweiler, W. M., J. B. Kahnweiler, and W. Woodard A workshop in communication skills for couples. *Journal of College Student Personnel,* 1978, **19** (1), 77.

Knott, J. E. and D. M. Daher A structured group program for new students. *Journal of College Student Personnel,* 1978, **19** (5), 456–461.

Lowenstein, T. J. Biofeedback relaxation training via radio. *Journal of College Student Personnel,* 1978, **19** (4), 372–373.

Magoon, T. M. College and University Counseling Centers' Annual Data Bank. College Park, Md.; University of Maryland, 1977–1978.

Morrill, W. H. and J. C. Hurst A preventative and developmental role for the college counselor. *The Counseling Psychologist,* 1971, **2** (4), 90–95.

Morrill, W. H., A. E. Ivey, and E. R. Oetting The College counseling center: A center for student development. In J. C. Heston and W. B. Frick (Eds.), *Counseling for the Liberal Arts Campus.* Yellow Springs, Ohio: Antioch Press, 1968.

Morrill, W. H. and E. R. Oetting Outreach programs in college counseling. *Journal of College Student Personnel,* 1970, **11** (1), 50–53.

Morrill, W. H., E. R. Oetting, and J. C. Hurst Dimensions of counselor functioning. *Personnel and Guidance Journal,* 1974, **52** (6), 354–359.

Oetting, E. R. Developmental definition of counseling psychology. *Journal of Counseling Psychology,* 1967, **14** (4), 382–385.

Oetting, E. R., A. E. Ivey, and R. G. Weigel *The College and University Counseling Center.* Student Personnel Series No. 11, American College Personnel Association, 1970.

Pepinsky, H. B., K. Hill-Frederick, and D. L. Epperson *The Journal of Counseling Psychology* as a matter of policies. *Journal of Counseling Psychology,* 1978, **25** (6), 483–498.

Phelan, D. J. and J. D. Heidke Conflict management in residence halls: An organizational development approach. *Journal of College Student Personnel,* 1977, **18** (6), 523–524.

Ribner, N. and R. Ginn Overcoming and managing depression. *Personnel and Guidance Journal,* 1975, **54** (4), 222–224.

Romano, J. L. A stress reduction workshop. *Journal of College Student Personnel,* 1978, **19** (4), 374.

Thomas, L. E. and R. I. Yates Paraprofessionals in minority programs. *Personnel and Guidance Journal,* 1974, **53** (4), 285–288.

Warnath, C. F. *New myths and old realities.* San Francisco: Jossey-Bass, 1971.

Weissberg, M., T. Sofair-Fisch, and L. Fisher-McCanne A relationship skills training program for college students. *Personnel and Guidance Journal,* 1978, **57** (4), 220–223.

Winston, R. B., Jr. and K. D. Smith, III Intentional group development in residence halls. *Journal of College Student Personnel,* 1978, **19** (6), 571–572.

# 11
# Housing

JOHN H. SCHUH

The purpose of this chapter is to discuss student housing in the context of the two models presented in this work: the environmental model (Morrill and Hurst, 1971), and the three-dimensional model of counselor functioning (Morrill, Oetting, and Hurst, 1974). As a result, the chapter's specific focus is on the environment created by and for students in the residential setting. It is not meant to be a complete discussion of all aspects of student housing. In fact, little or no attention is paid to the following functional areas of student housing: finance, food service, judicial affairs, maintenance, operations, staff selection, training and supervision, and student government.

As a caveat to the reader, these areas should not be ignored in developing a housing operation, for they form significant parts of what might be termed a total residential living program. For example, a poorly financed residence hall system will be unable to deliver basic services which in turn will create student dissatisfaction. Or, if student government does not play an active role in policy-making decisions affecting residential students, students will take little ownership in their residential environment. Therefore, the reader should pay careful attention to these critical areas.

The two models around which this discussion is built present an interesting framework for student housing. The environmental model places heavy emphasis on the impact of and interaction between the environment and students. The other, the three-dimensional model, provides a format for specific interventions within that environment. Placed in this context, student housing has tremendous potential for influencing student growth and development. The major issue this chapter addresses is how to develop an environment that will maximize student growth.

This chapter attempts to provide a format by which a growth-producing environment can be created. The first part discusses methods by which the environment within a residence hall can be assessed. Moving from assessment tools, the chapter then presents a discussion of how to maximize the physical environment and then develop the programmatic environment. Finally, since the models place great emphasis on output, the chapter concludes with a discussion of the impact of residential living on students.

The author's intention is to give the reader a variety of means by which to create a growth-producing environment for students. There is no attempt to prescribe what might be appropriate for any specific situation. Rather, it is hoped that the reader can select from a variety of options, ranging widely in their degree of sophistication, which will assist in the development of the living environment on any particular campus. Individual housing officers are best able to judge what is most appropriate for their specific campuses, and it is their responsibility to determine what is the best means of creating the optimum environment in the residential setting.

## ASSESSING THE RESIDENTIAL ENVIRONMENT

Morrill and Hurst (1971) place a strong emphasis on studying the student, the environment, and the interaction between the two. Such study is particularly important in the case of residence halls. Without careful study of the student environment, residence halls can become places where students neither grow nor develop. Moreover, for the business manager, the ramifications of residence halls not meeting students' needs can be disastrous, since residence halls usually are supported entirely by the revenues collected from students, and when students are dissatisfied with residence halls, they move out. Toward the latter part of the 1960s and the early part of the 1970s students became very dissatisfied with the in loco parentis position that many colleges and universities took regarding the living environment, and their resulting action was a mass exodus to off-campus living accommodations. A number of colleges and universities around the country found themselves with large residence halls that either were filled partially or were empty altogether. The financial results created severe hardships for the institutions, and even as we head into the 1980s some of the institutions still have not solved the critical financial problems created by underutilization of residence hall space. Therefore, careful assessment of the student environment serves two purposes: to create a living environment where students can thrive, and to provide a living environment that satisfactorily meets students' living needs, thereby ensuring a reasonable occupancy level.

There are a number of methods that can be used to assess the student living environment in residence halls, and since an entire chapter of this work has been devoted to environmental assessment, this discussion attempts to outline a number of ways that student environment can be assessed specifically in the residence hall setting. The discussion does not focus particularly on methodology, but rather on simple applications of environmental assessment techniques that residence hall staff and students might utilize in the actual living situation.

The initial decision that must be made relative to environmental assessment in the residential setting is to define the scope of the project. This scope can range from assessing the environment of students in a particular living unit, such as a floor or house, to an entire residence hall system. Such factors as time, resources, and expertise will influence the decision. A particularly effective program for assessing the needs of students in the small living unit has been described by Daher, Corazzini, and McKinnon (1977) at Colorado State University. Their program, called REAP (Resident Environment Adaptation Program), was developed jointly by the counseling service and housing department with the purpose of modifying small unit living environments. They developed a five-stage process that provided consultation to individual living units that were attempting to assess and redesign their living environments. Although the researchers identified several difficulties in developing the project, they found that the model did provide a strong foundation upon which to change the student environment, thereby doing a better job of meeting student needs.

Larger-scale needs assessment projects have been undertaken at the University of Arizona, Arizona State University, and Indiana University. These projects undertook to study the needs of students across an entire residential system. Reports of these studies (Schuh and Allan, 1978; Schuh, 1978; and Elliott, 1977) indicate that major modifications of an entire residential system can be effected after careful research of the system. In the case of these three projects, the ecosystem model for environmental assessment was employed. The training manual for implementing the ecosystem model (Aulepp and Delworth, 1976) provides an easy, step-by-step process by which the model can be applied on a given campus. The size of residential systems involved in the model applications described above ranged from 4500 students to more than 12,000. In each case major modifications were implemented in the student environment, thereby yielding evidence that it is possible to apply environmental assessment and redesign strategies to large student populations in a short period of time.

Not all environmental assessment projects need be massive, or heavily steeped in research methods. Several rather simple methods for assessing the student environment have been developed which require little technical expertise. One often overlooked device that can be used to measure the student environment is the telephone. Telephone polls, using checklists or highly structured questionnaires, can provide immediate feedback to those trying to assess the student environment. In a hypothetical situation let us suppose that students are trying to develop a recreational sports program for a residence unit. One means of trying to determine which activities students would like to participate in would be to place a questionnaire in each mailbox, with instructions indicating that the completed questionnaires be returned to a student government office. Students tend to be disinterested in completing paper and pencil instruments since they often perceive themselves as being the subject of too many such questionnaires. Those taking this survey on recreational activities would be lucky to generate a response of 50 percent of those polled. With that low a response rate, it is questionable if a solid data base could be developed upon which to plan the program. The alternative to this process is to use the telephone. Since student telephone numbers are readily available, and in most situations all students have telephones in their rooms, those conducting the survey can call each of the intended respondents and, using a checklist technique, can find out which activities might interest the students. Telephones are underutilized by those seeking data concerning student needs in the halls.

Another very simple technique is the use of interest matching. Whether one uses large sign-up sheets, interest surveys, or other simple, information-gathering devices, interest matching is a very effective way of providing a means by which students who have common interests can interact with one another. This technique can be as simple as providing sign-up sheets in common areas for those students who have common interest, such as playing tennis, backpacking, or cooking oriental foods. The possibilities for this type of interest matching are limited only by the creativity and imagination of those planning the projects.

On the other hand, there are a number of sophisticated methods of assessing student needs and interests, such as the student interest survey. As with other "homemade" assessment techniques, this type of survey can be used on either a micro (living unit) or macro (residence hall or system) basis. Also, it can be as simple or sophisticated as those conducting the survey would like. Basically, this approach to needs assessment provides students an opportunity to indicate (on a checklist) the activities in which they would like to participate throughout an academic year. Typical areas that might be included on the checklist include arts and crafts, lectures, seminars and workshops, athletics, student government committees and projects, literary activities, drama and film productions, musical productions, or academics. In preparing the survey, lists of activities are generated in the various subject areas, and students then indicate their interest in participating in the activity on a Likert-type of scale. This kind of assessment is very helpful to planners as they make determinations as to the types of programs that the residential unit will provide. And, used in its purest form, students from student government can use the survey to provide direction for their efforts over the course of the academic year.

For those who are interested in using standardized tests for the purpose of assessing student needs, there are several instruments that can fulfill this need. These include the College and University Environment Scales (CUES), the College Student Questionnaire (CSQ), and the University Residence Environment Scale (URES).

The CUES instrument is designed to measure student perceptions of the atmosphere at the given campus. The items describe possible characteristics of the collegiate environment, and students are supposed to indicate whether they perceive the items to be true or false for their campus. There are 160 items in the instrument, and it takes about 30 minutes to complete. A later edition of the CUES provides several items that can be used at the discretion of the local campus. These local option items can provide additional useful information for those conducting the survey.

The CSQ consists of two parts. The first part deals with information for entering students, and the second part is designed for students who have had at least 1 year of experience at the given institution. Though somewhat lengthy, this instrument also can provide useful information about the student environment.

The URES is designed specifically for assessing the social climate of living situations. The instrument contains three major dimensions, and generates a number of subscales that have utility for those assessing student environments.

Regardless of what process is utilized by those responsible for assessing the student environment, the critical factor is that some form of assessment takes place on a regular basis. Such assessment will yield a residence hall program that will meet the needs of residence hall students, thereby providing for an opportunity to maximize their growth and development, and provide an attractive, enjoyable place for them to live, which should maintain an occupancy level that will keep the campus business manager smiling.

## MAXIMIZING THE PHYSICAL ENVIRONMENT

After completing an assessment project, the next step that should be taken by those responsible for the residential environment is to maximize that environment, in both a physical and programmatic sense. This discussion will focus on maximizing the physical environment, and it will be followed by a discussion that will outline possible methods for developing the programmatic environment.

The model discussed by Morrill and Hurst (1971) placed heavy emphasis on facilitating maximum utilization of the total learning environment by students. Placed in the context of Maslow's hierarchy of needs, the physical environment in a residence center can have a dramatic impact on the development of students. DeCoster and Mable (1974) pointed out that, unless students perceive their physical environment as satisfactory in a physical sense, they will be unlikely to move on to developmental activities. Placed in a practical context, it is unlikely that a student will be interested in attending an interpersonal communications skills workshop if, for example, that student's bathroom sink continuously stops up. Hence real concern must be placed on the physical environment in which students live.

Miller and Prince (1976) pointed out that people need to have control over their personal property, their "life space," and their functioning within that space. By having control over their personal space, people can determine the level of security, order, and freedom that they choose to have around themselves. In short, they are able to develop territoriality. Heilweil (1973) developed the concept of territoriality by indicating that a lack of control over personal space can result in student dissatisfaction brought on by an absence of privacy and opportunities for solitude, inability to control personal space, roommate conflicts, enforced sociability, and the absence of a opportunity to change the institutional atmosphere through a process of personalization.

Jackson and Schroeder (1977) took the concept of territoriality a step further when they indicated that residence educators must provide residents with an opportunity for a variety of accessible, novel, intense, complex, and ambiguous stimuli. They argued that such will enhance the natural development of students.

According to Grant (1974), there are four basic human needs that are necessary for human development. These needs include security, stimulation, freedom, and order. It is clear that in many ways these needs tend to be the antithesis of one another. For example, security, which in the residential setting might be translated into privacy, is difficult to provide while simultaneously providing stimulation or interaction. Moreover, it is difficult to provide order and freedom simultaneously. By providing for greater freedom in the residential setting, universities and colleges often limit the amount of order in the residence halls. In working with students to structure the environment, it is clear that careful planning and milieu management must be undertaken to provide for each of these needs.

Grant (1974) suggested two methods for keeping human needs in balance. He recommended that students be a part of an identifiable group and that they have some control over their personal space. In short, he called for devoting greater attention to the concept of territoriality. By recommending that students have considerable impact over their personal space, Grant believed that such would contribute to humanizing human experiences.

Building on the philsophical foundation created by Grant, Miller, Prince, and others, Schroeder (1978–1979) developed a conceptual framework for territoriality. This framework included four basic strategies for application of territoriality. These strategies included personalization of space, defensible space, social interaction and group stability, and privacy regulation. He believed that each of these strategies would enhance the residential experience.

Some of the specific aspects of personalization of space that Schroeder suggested included changing the atmosphere of rooms, hallways, and common areas such as lounges or activity rooms. In the area of creating defensible space he recommended that students mark secondary territory such as hallways with distinctive painting, that houses and corridors be locked to restrict access to these areas by nonresidents, and that damages be assessed collectively to students who live in common areas. Social interaction and stability can be created, according to Schroeder, by converting public areas into socialization space, changing individual resident rooms into group rooms for common use, and having staff spend more time in helping students with their development of territorial behaviors. Finally, in the area of privacy regulation, he suggested that offering more private rooms is one means of enhancing the privacy students seek in the residential environment. Although these concepts are not necessarily novel, they provide a means by which students can develop ownership of their environment. Within the student room, students can be given the freedom to paint their walls, build lofts, place posters on the walls, and build furniture, including such items as bunk beds, special desks, and clothes containers. By working on the environment of their room, students can personalize their space, take pride in what they have done, and frequently they will return to that space over the years they are enrolled in the institution.

In hallways, the use of dramatic color patterns can break up the institutional look that is fostered by long corridors painted with drab colors. Students not only should be able to undertake the painting of these walls, they should be encouraged to develop their own designs and logos for their floors. In lounge areas, decoration of the walls as well as building furniture can support the concept of ownership. A particularly helpful monograph on the development of personalizing the residence hall space was written by Anchors, Schroeder, and Jackson (1978). Their detailed work described the process by which space can be personalized.

One other concept worth examining in relation to the development of the physical environment is the concept of behavioral zoning, as described by Jackson and Schroeder (1977). Their concept is that when students lack a variety of stimulation in the residential environment, they create their own. This can include such activities as water fights, shaving cream fights, and damage to physical facilities. To combat this behavior, they advocated developing zones where students can get the necessary stimulation that will reduce unproductive behavior. One means of developing such a zone is the development of a recreation complex, which might include such items as workout facilities, weights, exercise machines, and the like. They concluded that such behavioral zones will contribute greatly to the reduction of damages and the enhancement of student growth and development.

By encouraging students to shape their residential environment, student development educators can greatly promote student growth and development. When the physical environment provides the necessary stimulation for students in a positive sense, opportunities are created for educationally related experiences. In a sense, when perceived positively, the physical environment provides a stage for greater academically related development. However, when the physical environment detracts from student satisfaction, it can be a powerful force which will inhibit student growth. Through the methods listed above, and others that may be unique to a particular campus situation, those responsible for residential life can make significant contributions to the physical environment which will enhance student growth and development.

## DEVELOPING THE PROGRAMMATIC ENVIRONMENT

The model discussed by Morrill and Hurst (1971) placed heavy emphasis on developing an environment that will facilitate maximum utilization in a learning sense by students. The development of the physical environment by students has been discussed already, and the other part of the learning environment, that which contributes to student growth in a programmatic sense, must be addressed. The role of operations and assignment staff is critical in this aspect of environmental development, since by carefully assigning students to living units, the stage can be set for a variety of programmatic interventions. Those interventions are congruent with the targets and purposes of intervention, as described by Morrill, Oetting, and Hurst (1974).

Brown (1972) suggested that student development staff need to move into the curricular world to legitimize programs and experiences now available to students. This move can be accomplished nicely in the residential setting. There are a number of methods discussed below which can be employed to bring the curricular offerings of the institution of higher education directly into the residential setting.

Miller and Prince (1976) indicated that there must be a purposeful relationship between formal learning and the student's growth outside the classroom. They suggested that by developing an environment that encourages and rewards academic inquiry, academic success is more likely. Thus the residential environment must be constructed so as to support academic endeavors.

Brown (1974) discussed five methods by which residence halls can become a part of academic life. These methods included having faculty members hold discussions in residence halls; having regular classes taught in the halls; establishing living–learning environments; establishing coeducational residence halls; and merging academic and student development goals.

The living–learning environment is a particularly effective method for creating an academic environment in residence halls. Adams (1974) called the integration of the academic sector with the residence hall experience one of the most profound changes taking place on college and university campuses. And well it should be, for the living–learning center provides a superb environment in which students can learn and develop.

Rowe (1979) has developed a model for the development of living–learning centers. At the outset, it should be noted that living–learning centers are not created merely by offering classes in residence halls. Tollefson (1975) has pointed out that when students are not intentionally placed in an atmosphere where they share similar values, such assignments inhibit rather than facilitate the growth process that causes a group of students to mold into a community. Thus merely offering classes in the residence halls is not enough.

Rowe's model for living–learning centers incorporates five key elements. The first of the elements is that goals and philosophy of the living–learning center must be stated clearly. Without such, she warns, the living–learning center will flounder. These goals must be established to fit the needs of the institution and should be written by faculty, staff, and students.

The second key element is that some sort of application/selection process should be developed. Besides the selection process, the center must present some rather clear expectations for involvement from students. Without this process students tend to lose interest and do not contribute to the center program.

The third element is that the center should have major student involvement in governance. This involvement should include design, administration, and implementation of center programs.

The fourth element is that academic and faculty support are critical. Although verbal support may be easy to secure, financial backing can be more difficult to obtain. In many ways, the living–learning program must be promoted to the faculty. However, once a good job of representing the center to faculty is accomplished, faculty can become powerful allies of the program.

Finally, the program should not be so large as to inhibit a sense of closeness among students. When programs become too large, individual students tend to lose interest in their program because the amount of personal attention they receive is reduced. Hence there is an optimal size beyond which the program can become too large.

The actual programmatic content of living–learning centers can vary widely from campus to campus, but some of the aspects might include the following: regular university courses, experimental seminars, and colloquia; noncredit courses; social and cultural activities including artists-in-residence and literary magazines; and faculty discussions and receptions. Facilities utilized to accomplish such programs can include classrooms, a library, a coffeehouse, a computer terminal, and a cooperative store. Funding for the living–learning center may be underwritten by the liberal arts college, student housing fees, and special fees paid by each of the residents.

Obviously, the program listed above can be modified greatly and still fit the definition of the living–learning center. The most important ingredient is that it does marry the academic side of the institution with the residential. In doing so, the living–learning center provides a unique environment for students in which they can learn and enhance their growth.

Not all students are well suited for living–learning programs. In fact, such programs are probably inappropriate for many students. However, there are other means of shaping the programmatic environment for students who have specific academic interests, but are not interested in the type of environment that a living–learning center can create. For these students, thematic housing is a viable alternative.

Thematic housing has been utilized at a number of colleges and universities with excellent results. There are two principal means by which thematic housing can be arranged. One method is to assign students to living units based on common extracurricular interests, such as an interest in backpacking, playing bridge, or camping. The other method is to develop themes around special academic interests. This type of housing lends itself particularly to foreign languages, although some institutions have developed engineering houses or astronomy houses, for example. Thus the environment promotes programming built on the interests of the students, and provides excellent format for group interaction.

For other students, interested in neither living–learning centers nor thematic housing, there are special assignment possibilities that can facilitate their opportunities for growth. These assignment techniques include matching roommates who have the same majors, matching students who are enrolled in the same courses, assigning students to the same living area with the same majors, assigning high-ability students in the same living area, and assigning students on the basis of academic classifications, that is, upperclassmen with upperclassmen and underclass students with their peers. These methods of assignment can have some positive effects on academic performance, as Williams and Reilley (1974) have concluded, and they also provide for potential programmatic interventions to individuals and small groups. Feldman and Newcomb (1970) cite numerous studies that disagree with this conclusion, however, so the academic advantages of these types of assignments are unclear. In any event, they offer additional alternatives for students to select from in choosing their housing option.

One other variable in the assignment of students to residential communities must be addressed, and that is the matter of coeducational housing. For the purpose of this discussion, coeducational housing is defined as any situation where men and women live under the same roof. It does not mean that they share rooms, but perhaps live in alternate wings, or alternate floors of a building. Adjacent living, such as men and women living in buildings next to one another and sharing common dining and activity facilities, is not defined as coeducational living.

Most students can profit from coeducational living arrangements. Duncan (1974) advocated coeducational living as a vital component of residential living. He has outlined a number of advantages of coeducational living, including the following:

1 The student living situation is more natural and closer to "real life."
2 Students tend to exhibit more mature behavior in a variety of situations.
3 Educational and recreational programming are accomplished more easily.
4 Damage decreases.
5 Students plan and participate more in cultural activities.
6 Females tend to be more secure.

The coeducational living style, however, has not been embraced by all students. Toupin and Luria (1975) found that black females generally do not choose the coeducational living situation. They could not identify why black women chose single sex halls, but it is interesting to note, particularly in light of the fact that if more and more nonblack women choose coeducational living, the result could be segregated, single sex residence halls.

In reviewing the types of living options that will maximize the programmatic environment, the choices range from living–learning centers to coeducational living. Thematic housing and special assignment centers also provide mechanisms for special living environments. These special types of living create a means for programmatic interventions, where the targets can be individuals, such as in a coeducational hall; primary groups typified by those in thematic assignment centers; or an associational group, such as all the members of a living–learning center.

Programs can be built around the special environments created by the special living arrangements. Only the imagination of the students and staff within the living environment limits the programmatic offerings available to residents. There is no question that the programs resulting from this type of environment enhance the growth and development of resident students.

## THE IMPACT OF RESIDENTIAL LIVING ON STUDENTS

The final aspect of this discussion on student housing deals with impact of residential living on students. Although the results of studies concerning the impact of residential living are not completely definitive, it is clear that many support the contention that residential living does tend to foster student growth and development. Put in the context of the environmental model (Morrill and Hurst, 1971) students are the output of the residential experience. Their growth and development are a result of their interaction with one another, and the impact of the residential environment on them.

According to Astin (1978), the most critical environmental factor dealing with persistence is whether or not a student lives in a residence hall during the freshman year. He pointed out that after controlling for entering characteristics and environmental factors, students who live in residence halls have a 12 percent better chance of finishing college than those who live with their parents. He indicated that this positive effect of residential living applies to both men and women, as well as to students of differing abilities.

Students who live in residence halls tend to have more contact with faculty, do better academically, and are more satisfied with their undergraduate experience than commuters (Astin, 1973, 1975; Chickering, 1974). Obviously, opportunities created for student interaction with faculty and one another are enhanced by their being located on campus, as Welty (1976) has pointed out. When students commute to the campus, they spend a more limited amount of their time in the university environment and as a result have fewer opportunities for such interaction.

Bowen (1978), on the other hand, indicated that one study (Bradshaw, 1974) may have generated data which suggest that campus residential living is not necessarily preferable to off-campus living away from parents in apartments or rooms. Bowen reported that Bradshaw found that living on campus did not produce as great gains from the freshman to senior years as were generated by living off campus, away from parents.

Astin (1978) summarized the impact of living on campus on achievement and career development of students. He indicated that living on campus tends to increase the student's chances of aspiring to graduate or professional degrees. Moreover, he found that residents are more likely to achieve in extracurricular areas, such as leadership and athletics. And among men, residents often achieve higher grade point averages. Although residents are more likely to implement careers in business, they command lower salaries than commuters in nursing and social work. Finally, Astin concluded that residents express more satisfaction with their undergraduate experience than commuters.

Perhaps the strongest support for the residential experience has been expressed by Chickering (1974) in an exhaustive study of residential and commuter students. He concluded that the learning and personal development of students who live in college dormitories exceeds what would be predicted when ability, prior educational and extracurricular activities, and community and family backgrounds are controlled. He also indicated for several different large samples, students who live at home, in comparison with those who live in college dormitories, are less fully involved in academic activities, in extracurricular activities, and in social activities with other students. He also reported that the aspirations of students who live at home diminish and they become less committed to school and to a variety of long-range goals. They are less involved in activities and report lowered self-ratings of competence, abilities, and desirable personal characteristics. In addition, their satisfaction with college decreases, and they become less likely to return.

Chickering's findings indicated that not only do commuters and residents begin their college careers with an unequal start that strongly favors the residents, but the gap between them grows. Residents are forced to encounter diverse experiences and persons, whereas this happens much less for commuters. Thus Chickering indicates that the major consequence of American higher education as it currently functions for commuters and residents is to increase the distance between them.

In the development of the three-dimensional model (Morrill, Oetting and Hurst, 1974) four targets of intervention were identified: individuals, primary groups, associational groups, and institutions or communities. In the residential community, the individual student is the individual target of intervention. In this context, it is clear from the research cited above that individuals tend to grow and develop in a variety of ways as a result of their residential experience. Studies generally do support the notion that students grow and develop more fully as a result of the residential experience than those who live at home with their parents. Rather than concluding that residential experiences facilitate growth, one might surmise that living with parents tends to inhibit such growth. Reasons for such are obvious. Students do not have the freedom to make individual choices while living at home. They are restricted and structured into a family schedule much like they were subject to prior to entering the college or university. They are not forced to be as self-reliant as they might be if they lived away from parents. For these reasons and others, the residential experience helps foster student growth.

While living at home, students are faced with a much more difficult task relative to building primary groups. When living in a residence hall, Greek letter house, or away from home in a room or apartment, students reside with their peers. They interact with their peers and develop close friendships that can arise only from close, personal contact over a protracted length of time. Hence primary groups develop within which the student functions. Such is much less likely to take place at home, since there the primary group is the family. Families provide different types of support for students than do a group of peers. Hence development is slowed, and the resulting college experience is perceived less positively than if the student had lived away from home.

Associational groups, such as clubs or student government, are strongly supported by residential groups of students. As has been pointed out in the literature, residential students are much more likely to become involved with associational groups. The reason for this involvement is obvious. Students who live on campus have a much greater opportunity for such involvement, and can see more direct impact on themselves than can those who live at home. The mere act of commuting from home reduces the opportunity for involvement in associational groups.

The final target of intervention, the community, also reflects a marked impact on the residential student. Residential students tend to be more satisfied with their undergraduate experience than are commuters. They have greater involvement in nearly all aspects of the university community, and report much greater satisfaction with their experience as a result of that involvement.

If one perceives the purpose of intervention (Morrill, Oetting, and Hurst, 1974) in a hierarchical fashion, students who live on campus tend to respond more to the highest level of intervention, development, than do commuters. Although there is a clear and obvious role at the levels of remediation and prevention, students who live on campus tend to develop in ways very different than those who live at home. Chickering's research and conclusions clearly point to the gap in development that takes place between residential students and commuters. He suggested that the differences between commuters and residential students when the two groups begin their college experiences are exacerbated by the residential experience. Students who live on campus simply grow at a faster rate than those who live at home.

The implications of the impact of residential living of students for the student development worker are severalfold. First, there is much work to be done by those who work with commuter students to bridge the developmental gap between commuters and residential students. Because of the exigencies of the living situation, it is doubtful that the gap can be bridged entirely, but students who are commuters should be brought into the life on campus so as to encourage their growth and development.

Second, it is clear that a marvelous opportunity exists for students who live on campus. Hence methods of intervention by student development workers must fully exploit this superb learning situation. In a sense, residential students are a captive audience, and their situation should be developed more fully.

Third, the issue of consultation and training can be developed more fully. Students who live on campus should be utilized more extensively to provide services to their fellow students. Such involvement will provide greater growth-producing experiences for them, and will provide needed services for their fellow students. The use of peer counselors has just begun to develop this area, and obviously through the use of peer counselors (resident assistants) in the residence halls, an ideal format for such involvement is created.

In the future the residential situation will continue to provide excellent learning opportunities for students. The challenge will be to develop the residential situation more fully and to provide even greater opportunities for student development.

## REFERENCES

Adams, D. V. Residential learning opportunities. In D. DeCoster and P. Mable (Eds.), *Student Development and Education in College Residence Halls*, Washington, D.C.: American College Personnel Association, 1974.

Anchors, S., C. E. Schroeder, and S. Jackson *Making Yourself at Home*. American College Personnel Association Commission III, 1978.

Astin, A. W. Impact of dormitory living on students. *Educational Record*, 1973, **54**, 204–210.

Astin, A. W. *Preventing Students from Dropping Out*. San Francisco: Jossey-Bass, 1975.

Astin, A. W. *Four Critical Years*. San Francisco: Jossey-Bass, 1978.

Aulepp, L. and U. Delworth *Training Manual for an Ecosystem Model*. Boulder, Colo.: Western Interstate Commission for Higher Education, 1976.

Bowen, H. R. *Investment in learning*. San Francisco: Jossey-Bass, 1978.

Bradshaw, T. K. *The impact of education on leisure socialization in college*. Unpublished doctoral dissertation, Berkeley, Calif.: University of California, 1974.

Brown, R. D. Student development in tomorrow's higher education—a return to the academy. *Student Personnel Series No. 16.* American College Personnel Association, 1972.

Brown, R. D. Student development and residence education: should it be social engineering? In D. A. DeCoster and P. Mable (Eds.), *Student Development and Education in College Residence Halls.* Washington, D.C.: American College Personnel Association, 1974.

Chickering, A. W. *Commuting versus Resident Students.* San Francisco: Jossey-Bass, 1974.

Daher, D. M., J. D. Corazzini, and R. D. McKinnon An environmental redesign program for residence halls. *Journal of College Student Personnel*, 1977, **18** (1), 11–15.

DeCoster, D. A. and P. Mable Residence education: purpose and process. In D. A. DeCoster and P. Mable (Eds.), *Student Development and Education in College Residence Halls.* Washington, D.C.: American College Personnel Association, 1974.

Duncan, J. P. Emphasis on the education in coeducational living. In D. A. DeCoster and P. Mable (Eds), *Student Development and Education in College Residence Halls.* Washington, D.C.: American College Personnel Association, 1974.

Elliott, O. V. Assessing student needs. In J. Schuh (Ed.), *Programming and Activities in College and University Residence Halls.* Association of College and University Housing Officers, 1977.

Feldman, K. A. and T. M. Newcomb *The Impact of College on Students* (Vol. 1). San Francisco: Jossey-Bass, 1970.

Grant, W. H. Humanizing the residence hall environment. In D. A. DeCoster and P. Mable (Eds.), *Student Development and Education in College Residence Halls.* Washington, D.C.: American College Personnel Association, 1974.

Heilweil, M. The influence of dormitory architecture on resident behavior. *Environment and Behavior*, 1973, **5**, 377–411.

Jackson, G. S. and C. Schroeder Behavioral zoning for stimulation seekers. *The Journal of College and University Student Housing*, 1977, **7** (1), 7–10.

Miller, T. K. and J. S. Prince *The Future of Student Affairs.* San Francisco: Jossey-Bass, 1976.

Morrill, W. H. and J. C. Hurst A preventative and developmental role for the college counselor. *The Counseling Psychologist*, 1971, **2** (4), 90–95.

Morrill W. H., E. R. Oetting, and J. C. Hurst Dimensions of counselor functioning. *The Personnel and Guidance Journal*, 1974, **52** (6), 354–359.

Rowe, L. P. *Living Learning Centers.* American College Personnel Association Commission III, 1979.

Schroeder, C. C. Territoriality: conceptual and methodological issues for residence educators. *The Journal of College and University Student Housing*, 1978–79, **8** (2), 9–15.

Schuh, J. H. Implementing the ecosystem model: Phase II. *The Journal of College and University Student Housing*, 1978–79, **8** (2), 6–8.

Schuh, J. H. and M. R. Allan Implementing the ecosystem model. *Journal of College Student Personnel*, 1978, **19** (2), 119–122.

Tollefson, A. L. *New Approaches to College Student Development.* New York: Human Sciences Press, 1975.

Toupin, E. A. and Z. Luria Coed housing: a conflict for black parents. *Journal of College Student Personnel*, 1975, **16** (5), 395–399.

Welty, J. D. Resident and commuter students: Is it only the living situation? *Journal of College Student Personnel*, 1976, **17** (6), 465–468.

Williams, D. E. and R. R. Reilley The impact of residence halls on students. *Journal of College Student Personnel*, 1972, **13** (5), 402–410.

Williams, D. E. and R. R. Reilley The impact of residence halls on students: the research. In D. A. DeCoster and P. Mable (Eds.), *Student Development and Education in College Residence Halls*. Washington, D.C.: American College Personnel Association, 1974.

# 12
# Orientation

SHARON H. JUSTICE AND
MARGARET J. BARR

Entering a new university is in many ways similar to moving to a foreign country. The new student must negotiate an environment that contains a plethora of new customs, terminology, interaction patterns, and regulations. These factors create a need for information about expectations, resources, and support systems in the new culture. Most institutions recognize the demands of this enculturation process and have designed specific programs to assist. Although these programs may be labeled in a variety of ways, they all provide a method to orient students to the new culture.

Orientation is a function of a vast majority of universities. Van Eaton (1972) reported that 89 percent of the 4-year colleges with enrollments under 10,000, 85 percent of the junior colleges and 80 percent of the larger institutions have implemented some type of orientation program. Butts (1971) confirms the universality of orientation procedures, indicating that they have the following common goals: completion of the registration process, dissemination of information, building awareness of educational opportunities, exposure to career resources, and relationship building. Institutional differences, however, require that specific orientation programs be developed to fit the situational context. An ideal orientation program thus will attend to management of basic resources, student development, and environmental development. This can be accomplished through the organization of an integrated program of activities and services. Later in this chapter specific applications of this theoretical framework are discussed within the context of orientation.

Two elements, however, affect the orientation process: the mission of the university and the conceptual foundation of the student affairs division. The first element, the primary mission of the institution, has an effect on all the programs and activities within it. A community college, for example, serves diverse needs including the part-time learner in the surrounding community. An urban university, on the other hand, must develop services and programs to accommodate the needs of commuting students. A multipurpose institution must not only meet undergraduate needs, but must balance research and graduate education activities. Thus the mission of the institution affects the characteristics of the student population. It also may define the role and scope of services offered to students. To illustrate, in a small liberal arts college, orientation may be delegated to faculty members as part of their regular duties and responsibilities. In a large multi-university, orientation may be a separate administrative unit with diverse resources available to meet the needs of the client population.

The second element, the conceptual foundation, will also mold the role and scope of student services units. Orientation, as a student services function, can be affected by the underlying philosophy of the division. For example, if the student affairs division is based on an efficient management/administrative philosophy, the orientation program might concentrate only on registration and other enrollment procedures. If, however, the conceptual framework is one of student development, activities and programs might be expanded to include exposure to all facets of the university and systematically teach students how to negotiate and profit from their exposure to the university environment. Hurst points out in Figure 1 of Chapter 1 of this text that the three foundations that support any student affairs operation, including orientation, are student development, environmental resource development and managerial/administrative skills.

Staff members who are responsible for program development must not only understand these conceptual foundations but most also possess appropriate implementation skills. Orientation is a prime example of a student services program which involves diverse elements within the academic community in the delivery of direct student services. A void in any one of the three foundations could result in orientation activities which are not directed to the underlying purposes of the institution and the student affairs division.

For example, concern with managerial and administrative details to the exclusion of personal development of the student will result in a mechanical approach to students. It is easy to fall into the trap of offering the same services, such as advanced placement tests, every year without evaluating the impact of those services on the new student. In addition to scheduling advanced placement tests the orientation staff must invest time and energy to provide opportunities for students to make responsible decisions regarding their academic options based on their test results. If the orientation program staff views their function in isolation, the institution is also shortchanged. In the example cited above, failure to identify problems with the advanced testing program and communicate them to those responsible creates problems. Information about new students, their reaction, and these problems must be transmitted to the institution's decision-making apparatus.

The question then becomes how student affairs practitioners in orientation can effectively integrate the diverse elements in Hurst's conceptual framework as they plan and deliver orientation activities.

## STAFF DIMENSIONS

The foundation of all program development includes investigation skills, theoretical knowledge, and knowledge and skill in intervention procedures. This is particularly true in orientation. It is essential that the orientation staff member have a strong foundation in student development theory. This includes knowledge of developmental patterns of late adolescence, as well as understanding the problems facing the adult learner. Our student populations are changing and the wise practitioner must keep abreast of new theoretical developments in order to translate them into services that are responsive to the changing needs of students.

Although a practitioner may have a solid theoretical background in organizational development theory, this is not enough. Useful applications of these theoretical constructs must be operationalized in the design and implementation of orientation activities. Change theory (Bennis, Benne, and Cline, 1962) conflict management (Filley, 1975), systems theory (Katz and Kahn, 1966), and bureaucratic theory (Blau and Meyers, 1956) all have implications for orientation program personnel. The realities of managing an orientation program require the student affairs professional on an annual basis to modify existing procedures, negotiate resolution of interagency conflicts, provide services that are useful and productive to the environment, and interrelate with the bureaucratic structure of the institution. Organizational theory, then, can be a practical tool in the development and management of orientation programs.

It is also important that the orientation personnel understand the interrelationship between the orientation program and the larger institutional organization. No program stands alone and it is essential that orientation staff members understand the impact of their activities on the institutional environment. By systematically identifying problems encountered by new students orientation practitioners are in an ideal position to locate student–environment mismatches which would interfere with the students' success and the institution's goals. At the very least, familiarity with environmental assessment theory (Banning and Kaiser, 1974; Barker, 1968; Fawcett, Huebner, and Banning, 1978) can become a practical powerful tool for the practitioner.

Management theory has often been overlooked as a resource for student affairs workers. In an era of fiscal restraint and accountability, a foundation in such theory becomes even more critical. As an example, MBO (Deegan and Fritz, 1975) is used in many institutions as a resource allocation tool. Understanding and application of this decision-making process is essential, particularly when resources are scarce. Although student personnel workers may feel that it is difficult to translate their activities into specific objectives, it must be done. State legislators, governing boards, and institutional fiscal officers work from a philosophy based on sound fiscal management. We must learn to speak their language and prepare information in a form which they can understand. In addition, we have also been reluctant to use the technologies available to us in managing data and student records. Too often we have relied on a computer specialist to assist us in using these new technologies. As data processing systems become more universal, student affairs personnel must not only rely on the specialist but also understand the processes involved in data management. If we do not fully utilize the technology available to us our job is much more difficult. Student need assessment and program evaluation are two examples of ongoing activities which could require less staff time if data processing and evaluation techniques were fully understood by the practitioners.

## FOUNDATION OF INVESTIGATIVE SKILLS AND KNOWLEDGE

On the whole, investigation is the weakest of all our skill foundations. Too often in orientation we collect data in such a form that it is unusable for other agencies in the academic community. For example, in many institutions, attendance at orientation is the best predictor of ultimate student enrollment. However, if the data are held in isolation and not shared with those agencies who could benefit the most from this information the entire institution will suffer. The responsible orientation program staff should, therefore, design their data collection systems not only for their internal use but for the potential application of such data throughout the institution. This often will require consultation with computer and data processing specialists in other agencies and may take more time. The eventual outcome, however, can have a positive impact on the university community.

Evaluation, unfortunately, is often talked about but seldom practiced. Although the need for evaluation is usually agreed upon, the function becomes a low priority item for most program developers (Barr, Yancey, and Justice, in press). This is a mistake! How can we systematically improve our service programs if we don't evaluate them? In addition, how can we profess validity for our programs if we do not have data to support that assumption? The argument that program evaluation takes too much time, energy, and expertise is shortsighted. If the student affairs professional possesses a background in evaluation theory, at a minimum, a rudimentary evaluation instrument can be internally designed. If such knowledge is not available within the staff team, the consultants from academic departments and other agencies can often be employed. Evaluation for evaluation's sake is not useful. At the University of Texas at Austin the orientation program, with assistance from the Research and Evaluation unit, has designed an evaluation process that provides immediate feedback on staff performance and program impact. You must know what you want to evaluate, why you want to evaluate it, and what use you will make of the results. Thus understanding of the theory is not sufficient: integration must be made with the ongoing processes of the orientation program (Brown, 1978).

## FOUNDATION OF THEORY

Theory building and intentional theory application are often the last things the orientation practitioner considers. Both uses of theory must be considered and can prove to be powerful tools for the development of successful orientation programs and activities. Too often we notice behaviors or identify trends, but do not try to determine the underlying cause. A foundation in learning, developmental, and organizational theory can assist with this process. Orientation provides a rich environment in which to extend theories through hypothesis testing with specific subpopulations or groups. Durkheim's (1950) work provides an excellent example of the extension, development, and refinement of theory which is applicable to orientation. If Durkheim had merely acknowledged the difference in suicide rates between Catholics and Protestants, little would have been contributed to our understanding of human behavior. In orientation, merely acknowledging that students in the social and behavioral sciences are more likely to express interest in becoming paraprofessionals with the orientation program leaves many questions unanswered. Application of relevant theories to this observation through hypothesis testing can serve to extend the theory and make it more applicable for other practitioners. Since the function of theory is to explain or predict (Hoy and Miskel, 1978). more attention to theory extension, building, and testing would assist the practitioner in understanding current events and predicting future trends that affect the orientation program.

Intentional theory application is also often overlooked by many orientation practitioners. Successful program development is usually based on accepted theories of learning and human interaction. However, many times programmers do not attend to theory application in the program development stage. Instead they base current program development on past experience and expertise. This is certainly valid and should continue to be a mainstay for the successful program developer, but the added dimension of theory application could enrich past program efforts and make them more substantial.

Theory thus can be a powerful foundation for successful program development and should be a skill area that is nourished and encouraged for practitioners.

## FOUNDATION OF INTERVENTION STRATEGIES

Hurst outlines six skill and knowledge areas for the design of successful intervention. All are applicable to the development of successful orientation programs. Administrative skills are clearly an expectation for most student affairs professionals. Scheduling, budgeting, supervision, and long-range planning are integral parts of an orientation program. Very often the lack of these skills creates a negative impression of the practitioner and the program.

A second implicit expectation for student affairs professionals is program development. The concept, although talked about a great deal, is often fuzzy. For some, a program is a one-time activity which is offered to students and then disbanded. It may or may not be offered again. To others, a program is a distinct administrative entity and is organized to provide long-term services to students. Both definitions are applicable in orientation. The nature of the orientation program requires that a variety of distinct activities be offered while a permanent administrative organization is maintained (Justice and Ragle, 1979). More often than not, the methodologies are not clearly defined and are learned through trial and error on the job. Orientation particularly needs staff members who can conceptualize organizations and manage a wide variety of programs simultaneously. In order to do this, program development skills must be systematically used in all aspects of orientation activities.

Although the prime mission of orientation is not counseling, orientation staff members must be able to detect potential problems and facilitate referrals to appropriate resources. Ignorance in this area is not bliss. Staff members in student affairs, whatever their area of responsibility, should possess elementary helping skills (Ivey, 1971). This is particularly true in orientation when students feel stress and anxiety when entering the new environment.

During the past few years there has been an enormous increase in the utilization of paraprofessionals to extend services in student affairs (Delworth and Aulepp, 1976). The orientation staff members who are employing paraprofessionals must be able to design and implement a training program which meets their specific programmatic needs. Familiarity with diverse training approaches is essential for this task. It would behoove staff members to experiment with a variety of models and to keep abreast of new developments in training. Also, the orientation program can serve a training function for the new student by assisting them in acquiring the requisite skills and knowledge to successfully complete their academic experience.

Television, radio, film, and programmed self-paced modules are examples of media interventions that have contributed to the learning patterns of modern-day students. Information presented in an audio-visual approach may be more easily understood than a lecture or straight printed material. Orientation planners must know the most effective ways to capitalize on this tendency of new students. Lack of technical expertise should not be a barrier for the use of media. Most institutions have audio-visual resource centers which can help staff develop the requisite skills. Full utilization of the potential of media as a method of transmitting orientation information has yet to be realized.

Orientation programs, as we indicated earlier, must interrelate with most facets of the university community. Too often when confronted with a problem in another agency, we assume that their present practices cannot be changed. A fresh perspective is often all that is needed to solve the problem. This requires that staff members demonstrate a high level of consultation skills in their interactions with other agencies (Hamilton and Meade, 1979). Orientation must be open to requests from other facets of the institution for assistance. Often a request for a direct service can escalate to an ongoing consultative arrangement which will not only solve the immediate program, but enhance future decisions affecting students.

Although the previous discussion has focused on these base-line skills and knowledge in the orientation program, staff members also have an institutional commitment. It is shortsighted to assume that mere attention to development of the orientation program is enough. Our professional responsibilities extend beyond our program responsibilities. The student affairs professional should be able to apply these base-line skills and knowledge within a variety of institutional settings. Serving on committees is often time-consuming and may appear to have few tangible rewards. The presence of orientation staff members on key university committees, however, has a potential to influence university policies and procedures which affect all students. Sometimes committee assignments may appear to be tangential to the orientation program, but relationships are often present. The calendar committee provides one example. If the university calendar is structured with insufficient time for necessary enrollment and orientation procedures, the student suffers. Orientation staff members can provide valuable data to avert this possibility.

Too often high-level administrators are accused of being unaware of student needs and interests. Their position in the hierarchy often contributes to the feeling of isolation. Orientation staff members, on the other hand, are in constant contact with new students and student employees. The information they gather about student concerns should be transmitted to their administrative superiors. In addition to formal interactions, orientation staff members often have the opportunity to engage in informal conversations and social acitivities with students. Impressionistic data from these sources often provides valuable insights for those at the top. Thus the orientation staff member is in a unique position in the university hierarchy and should capitalize on it for the good of the institution.

## INTERVENTION APPLICATIONS IN ORIENTATION

An orientation program, because of its diversity, has multiple targets of intervention. The application of the cube model (Morrill, Oetting, and Hurst, 1974) to the program planning effort can assist orientation staff in identifying prime target populations. In addition, delineation can be made of why we need to intervene and what methods would be most appropriate.

Orientation programs have both first- and second-level target populations including individual students, primary groups such as parents and family, the associational group of paraprofessional advisers, and the institution. The purposes of orientation also stretch across prevention, development, and remediation. Methods of service delivery vary, but must be directly related to the target population and the purpose of the intervention.

As an example, many orientation programs provide individual academic advising services for new students. The purpose of such one-to-one interventions is to prevent problems and to assist the new students with acquiring the requisite skills and knowledge as an advisee to negotiate the academic environment. As a direct service function, such advisement procedures are expensive and time-consuming. When combined with media interventions that provide information on scheduling procedures, understanding the catalogs, and negotiating the registration process, the cost effectiveness can be enhanced.

Often consideration is not given to primary groups such as parents in the design of orientation delivery systems. Parents have needs, too, and if these needs are not addressed, problems may arise for student services agencies within the institution. The prime purpose of such activities with parents should be to prevent problems with the institution and their children, to provide a support system, and to assist them in understanding the predictable problems which arise with college-age students. Depending upon institutional circumstances, a variety of methods can be employed. One option might be an on-site campus program which provides the opportunity for parents to become familiar with the campus and personally interact with significant staff and faculty members. Many institutions have also provided a parents' handbook. Such a document can be distributed to all parents and should contain answers to questions most frequently asked. If your student profile suggests that significant numbers of parents may be non-English speaking, consideration should be given to translating material into their native language. Outreach programs with parents are also feasible. Slide–tape shows that can easily be transported to churches, civic organizations, and alumni(ae) groups can provide information to prospective parents at relatively low costs and investment of staff time. The advent of public television provides yet another approach. At a major university, orientation staff members with the technical assistance of the radio, television, and film department produced a 30-minute video tape and made it available to public broadcasting stations across the state. Creative application of Morrill, Oetting, and Hurst's model (1974) to parent needs can generate multiple intervention strategies that are appropriate to the target population.

Orientation programs have employed student advisers over a long period to extend service delivery impact. Such paraprofessional staff groups often develop strong interpersonal bonds and can be classified as second-level associational target population. Orientation paraprofessionals are the vehicle for providing direct service to new students but also due to their unique role can be viewed as a target population in and of themselves. After the orientation program is completed these trained paraprofessionals often serve in leadership and service roles throughout the campus community. Thus training and supervision of paraprofessionals focusing on personal development, information dissemination, remediation in skill areas, and prevention of potential problems can have benefits beyond the orientation program.

Direct service, consultation, training, and media are all appropriate methods to use in paraprofessional development and supervision. Often in a supervisory intervention, the target becomes the individual adviser and direct service is offered through training and supervisory consultations to improve skills and competencies. Training interventions, however, focus on the entire second-level associational group. As goals for the training program are defined, a variety of methods can be employed to extend resources and provide quality educational experiences. Self-paced instructional modules are particularly effective for disseminating factual information (Barr, 1978). Media interventions such as the slide–tape presentation developed at the University of Texas at Austin may also be used. "As a primary or adjunct training tool, video tape can add excitement, clarity and interest to most training programs" (Barr, 1978). Applications include presentation of information, skill-modeling, and individualized feedback on the trainee's performance. Use of video tape and self-paced instructional modules extends program staff resources and frees the staff to intervene directly when problems are identified in the training process.

Working in close proximity and in an intense environment such as an orientation program often causes conflicts to develop in the staff team. The student affairs staff members working with the paraprofessionals must design ways to deal effectively with staff problems during actual program implementation. Two choices must be considered: individual intervention with a staff adviser experiencing difficulties or consultation with the entire associational group. The decision as to which strategy to employ depends upon the circumstances at the time. Continued use of individual intervention can be counterproductive and time-consuming.

Making the associational group the target of the intervention can change the purpose of the intervention from remediation to development. Consultation and training appear to be the most effective ways to accomplish this goal.

The institution as a target should not be ignored by orientation planners. Problems of individual students consume a great deal of staff time and energy in the orientation program. If, however, the staff merely continues to solve each individual concern similar problems will emerge every year. Focus on the institution as the target of the intervention can prevent needless duplication and repetition of such efforts. Many times policies and procedure that affect students are not under the direct control of the orientation staff and too often we tend to make the assumption that there is nothing we can do to change the policies of external agencies. This is a mistake! Interdependence with these other agencies provides an opportunity to make suggestions regarding procedural changes. A master plan for the ultimate desired change should be developed and through cooperative problem solving, incremental steps toward the final solution can be made.

As an illustration, in many institutions registration procedures appear to be difficult if not impossible to change. The procedures are complex, involve many institutional departments, and are embedded in the traditions of the institution. If current practices do not allow summer orientation students to receive the benefits of preregistration for fall courses, change is needed. A careful plan mutually developed with the registration staff can provide for installation of such services over a period of time. One way to approach such a problem is to develop a plan involving equal investments of staff time from both agencies in the early stages of procedural change. Eventually, as procedures are refined and policies are developed, the prime responsibility for preregistration of new students can revert to the legitimate domain of the registrar's office.

Orientation programs often deal primarily with information dissemination. When the content and presentation are under the control of orientation planners, adjustments are easy to make. Problems arise when other agencies are not clearly communicating their message to the new students. This requires action on the part of the orientation staff. By allowing confusing and contradictory information to go to new students, staff members compound the difficulties faced by students in their transition to the university environment. As such problems emerge, orientation staff members have an obligation to provide feedback to other agencies and to offer assistance in redesigning information dissemination procedures. Again time is involved, but the results can prevent unnecessary confusion for students.

At times, orientation programs will design information programs to meet the unique needs of incoming students. These approaches should be carefully examined to see if enrolled students could also benefit from the activity. At the orientation program at the University of Texas at Austin, new students expressed a need for more specific information about course content and requirements. Student staff members and orientees both felt that there was not enough data for the new students to make careful decisions about course options. To deal with this problem, the orientation staff compiled a reference notebook of course descriptions written by faculty members for use in academic pre-advising. This intervention was so successful that requests for copies of this information came from academic deans and others engaged in the advising process. Thus an institutional need emerged. Over the years, the reference notebook has been expanded to include a majority of undergraduate courses and is published and distributed in the campus newspaper just prior to spring preregistration. This publication, called *Of Course,* is now used by new, returning, and prospective students, as well as academic advisers throughout the campus.

The institution also becomes a target of intervention when problems emerge for specific subpopulations. Rules and regulations are often designed for the traditionally aged student. Older adults returning to college may find some of these regulations to be superfluous and actually interfere with their educational endeavors. Two options are available to approach such a problem: individual interventions with the student involved, or advocacy for an institutional change in regulations. Both have merit and can occur simultaneously. While direct service is provided to older students encountering difficulty within the academic environment, data can be collected to advocate change. The purpose of such an institutional intervention is remediation of an existing difficulty. Often such rigidity in regulations emerges from a lack of understanding regarding the unique problems faced by older students. A carefully designed training program for campus academic advisers can by itself introduce flexibility in the application of regulations. If this is not enough, orientation staff members should be prepared to be advocates for the returning student population. Through data collection, design of alternative solutions to the problem, and frequent interactions with decision makers, change can occur within the system. As an example, rigid adherence to a 12-hour course load as a minimal standard for enrollment can produce insurmountable problems for the older returning student. Initially, staff members may decide to intervene only when an older student asks for assistance. This direct troubleshooting service is certainly appropriate; however, little institutional change will result. By concurrently collecting data and presenting the problem to those who enforce the regulations, staff members can demonstrate a need for a change in course load expectations. Such changes do not come easily and persistence is needed to assure that older students are not forgotten in the development of rules and regulations.

A last institutional intervention which is often overlooked is the development of service delivery systems for specific subpopulations. Graduate, international, and handicapped students all have unique needs which are not addressed in the traditional orientation program model. Merely extending an invitation to join ongoing activities usually is not enough. Modification of program activities is needed and may involve other offices and agencies on the campus. The governmental mandate for equal educational opportunities for the handicapped cannot effectively be met by isolated program responses. Because orientation programs often are the first point of entry to the institution, problem identification regarding access for the handicapped is relatively easy to accomplish. When such problems as architectural barriers, access to certain academic programs, and assumptions about the ability of handicapped students to pursue higher education emerge, something must be done. Thus the orientation staff must refer and follow up on such problems with appropriate offices and agencies on campus.

The orientation program itself may offer specialized assistance and services. Examples might include readers for the blind, temporary wheelchair attendants, and modified campus tours. At the same time, attention must be given to problems that exist elsewhere on the campus. If the student must interact with other agencies in the enrollment procedure, the orientation staff should pave the way.

Until a systematic approach is developed for registration and academic advising of handicapped students, it may be necessary to invest disproportionate amounts of orientation staff time in this endeavor. The goal should be, though, to develop a registration and advising system which is flexible enough to meet the needs of all unique student populations. Through cooperative use of consultants familiar with the problems faced by handicapped students, multiple agencies can work in concert to eliminate problems before they start.

Thus the orientation staff should constantly review their internal policies and procedures and assess their effect on emerging student populations. If there are problems in the orientation procedures, usually this is an indication that blocks may exist elsewhere in the institution.

After such an obstacle is identified in orientation, additional action must be taken. It is not enough to change just the orientation procedure. Interdependence among service units requires that when procedural change occurs in orientation other elements in the system are also affected. These problem areas must be identified. Then the orientation staff should take the initiative to pull all affected agencies together and find a solution to the entire procedural difficulty. In such problem-solving endeavors, the institution is the target of the intervention. The specified method used to accomplish such a systems change will vary from institution to institution. Good judgment is needed to determine the best method of intervention when staff members are faced with campus-wide concerns. The cube provides a way to examine multiple solutions to such concerns.

## AREAS OF CONCERN

Throughout this chapter we have attempted to show practical applications of these theoretical constructs in the day-by-day activities of student affairs staff members. Often, however, it is hard to relate abstract concepts to ongoing operations. By examining the theoretical foundations of our work, we may discover needed skills and competencies that would strengthen and enrich our programmatic efforts. Discovery of these voids in staff preparation then requires investment in staff development to remediate the problems. At times this is not enough and orientation planners must augment their own skills and competencies through employment of external and internal resources. Theory then provides a method of problem diagnosis and enriches your repertoire of possible solutions to program ills. In addition, theory application may open new vistas of program involvement.

For the practitioner unfamiliar with the cube model of interventions of student development, it may appear too confusing and complex. Many times student affairs workers assume that institutional interventions are better than individual approaches. Both are equally important and value judgments should be made carefully. It is a mistake to always assume one is better than the other—situational factors must be considered. The strength of the cube is in providing a method to develop simultaneous solutions to the same problem area. Individual interventions using direct service methods for purposes of remediation can be compatible with an institutional intervention targeted at prevention or development using media as a vehicle. Orientation provides a particularly rich environment to address problems in the many dimensions of the cube. Target populations can be individual, primary, associational groups, or institutional. Purposes range from remediation of an individual's presenting problem to development of the student's full potential. The diversity of an orientation program permits many methods to be used to meet program goals. Again, direct service can be offered to the new student while consultation is provided to other agencies. Each choice of method should relate to the overall program design and reliance on a few favorite approaches can limit the impact of the program. The exercise of applying the cube is in itself a fruitful endeavor. Orientation staff members are then able to articulate who they serve, why they serve them, and how they accomplish the mission of the program.

## REFERENCES

Banning, J. H. and L. Kaiser An ecological perspective and model for campus design. *Personnel and Guidance Journal,* February, 1974.

Barker, R. G. *Ecological Psychology.* Stanford, Calif.: Stanford University Press, 1968.

Barr, M. J. Self-paced and video taped training innovations. In U. Delworth (Ed.), *Training Competent Staff, New Directions for Student Services.* San Francisco: Jossey-Bass, 1978.

Barr, M. J., B. A., Yancey, and S. H. Justice Evaluation issues in orientation. In G. Kuh (Ed.), *Evaluation in Student Services.* Washington, D.C.: American College Personnel Association, in press 25 Fall, 1979

Bennis, G, K. D. Benne, and R. Cline *The Planning of Change.* New York: Holt, Rinehart and Winston, 1962.

Blau, P. M. and M. W. Meyers *Bureaucracy in Modern Society.* New York: Random House, 1956.

Brown, R. How evaluation can make a difference. *Evaluating Program Effectiveness, New Directions for Student Services.* San Francisco: Jossey-Bass, 1978.

Butts, T. T. New practices in student orientation. *Personnel Services Review.* Ann Arbor, Mich.: Counseling and Personnel Services Information Center, 1971.

Deegan, A. X. and R. J. Fritz *M.B.O. Goes to College.* Boulder, Colo.: Center for Management and Technical Programs, 1975.

Delworth, U. and L. Aulepp *Paraprofessional and Allied Professional Programs.* Boulder, Colo.: Western Interstate Commission for Higher Education, 1976.

Durkheim, E. *Le suicide* (translated by Spalding). Glenview, Ill.: Free Press, 1950.

Fawcett, G. L. Huebner, and J. H. Banning Campus ecology: implementing the design process. *Campus Ecology: a Perspective for Student Affairs.* Cincinnati: NASPA Journal monograph, 1978.

Filley, A. C. *Interpersonal Conflict Resolution.* Glenview, Ill.: Scott, Foresmont Co., 1975.

Hamilton, M. K. and C. J. Meade (Ed.). *Consulting on Campus, New Directions for Student Services,* Number 5. San Francisco: Jossey-Bass, 1979.

Hoy, W. K. and C. G. Miskel *Educational Administration: Theory, Research and Practice.* New York: Random House, 1978.

Ivey, E. *Micro-counseling: Innovations in Interview Training.* Springfield, Ill.: Charles C. Thomas, 1971.

Justice, S. H. and S. H. Ragle Once you've got it, how do you keep it? *Establishing Successful Student Services Programs, New Directions for Student Services.* San Francisco: Jossey-Bass, 1979.

Katz, D. and R. L. Kahn *The Social Psychology of Organizations.* New York: John Wiley and Sons, 1966.

Morrill, W. H., E. R. Oetting, and J. C. Hurst Dimensions of counselor functioning. *Personnel and Guidance Journal,* February, 1974.

Van Eaton, E. W. National study of trends in orientation. *The National Orientation Bulletin.* Stillwater, Okla.: Oklahoma State University, 1972.

# 13
# The College Union

SHIRLEY BIRD PERRY

College unions are essential components of academic institutions. This chapter on college unions includes a series of basic assumptions, a review of fundamental philosophies and goals, a summary of some relevant conceptual foundations and research, a view of the college union's impact on the campus environment, elaborations on ways the college union fulfills primary goals, and a brief outline of some key issues confronting college unions.

## BASIC ASSUMPTIONS

When described in succinct and somewhat simplistic terms, the college union is most frequently characterized as the *community center* of an academic institution. It may be labeled a college or university "center," a "student union," a "house," or a "hall." Although enormous diversity exists from campus to campus, and college unions clearly differ in philosophy, nature, priorities, and programs, the following basic assumptions are outlined for the focus on college unions included in this publication.

1 The academic institution is committed to a liberal or comprehensive education, that is, to maximum growth and development of multifaceted individuals. Regardless of its size, setting, structure, or objectives, the institution is dedicated to the provision of numerous and varied learning opportunities and experiences which impact on the cognitive and affective development of people.
2 The college union is an essential and fundamental part of the

college's basic educational mission. It is designed as a major contributor to the total educational process and serves the institution's multiple constituencies, including students, faculty, administrators, and staff, as well as others related to the college, such as trustees, alumni(ae), guests, and specified members of the external community. Therefore, the college union is *not* considered to be ancillary to the principal goals of the college, nor is it solely for students.

3 Although a college union "role statement" (Association of College Unions, 1956) has long been available and widely shared, a single college union is designed, organized, and operated in relation to the unique institution it serves. The institution's history, purposes, and directions influence the specifics of an individual college union. Because a college union reflects the distinctive nature of the parent institution, no two college unions are completely alike.

4 The college union's thrust encompasses *facilities*, *services*, and *programs*. The three form vital parts of a whole and are inextricably intertwined, even if they are administered by individuals in different reporting channels, or if certain units are operated via a contract with a corporate entity. (*Note*: In some instances, food services, retail areas, or other units are operated via special contracts between institutions and commercial agencies.

5 The college union functions *in collaboration with* the various departments, agencies, and divisions of the institution, including academic disciplines, business affairs, student service agencies, alumni(ae) and development offices, and other components of the college. Therefore, as the institution engages in research, goal development, evaluation, or other general activities, the college union is a part of the effort. Concurrently, college union personnel are committed to a *collaborative* model as opposed to a *competitive* one.

Though it is clear that the foregoing assumptions are not applicable for all institutions, they are germane for the discussion to follow.

## COLLEGE UNION PHILOSOPHY AND GOALS

Since the first college unions grew out of debating societies at Oxford and Cambridge in the early 1800s, their development, philosophies, goals, and activities have been chronicled in a myriad of publications. Some relevant samples include those by the Association Of College Unions–International (1956), Self-Study Commission (1975); Berry

(1960, 1964, 1966, 1971); Blackburn (1968); Butts (1949, 1962, 1964, 1971); Harper (1963); and Perry (1972, 1976).

A review of college union literature reveals a consistent emphasis on the college union's significant role in the areas of human development and services. In essence, the college union is viewed as having a substantial impact on the total environment of the college and as contributing substantially to the physical, social, cultural, and intellectual development of persons in the academic community. Statements of college union philosophy have historically addressed the elements of the schematic representation found in a "Conceptual Foundation For Student Affairs" as developed by Hurst (1980). For example, the college union has long been concerned with the diverse dimensions of student development, including responsible, effective management and administration, the importance of an institution's total environment, and those areas which Hurst outlines under the categories of "investigation," "theoretical," and "intervention."

Further, the two-dimensional table developed by Hurst and Duncan (1980) entitled "Student Affairs Intervention Programs" can be utilized to broaden and sharpen one's understanding of the comprehensive and complex mission of the college union. For instance, college unions typically facilitate the management of basic resources by offering food, recreational activities, and numerous programs that contribute to physical and mental health, as well as low-cost meals, programs, and services that assist with financial concerns. College unions have potential impact on all the components included under the segments relating to student and environmental development. The following summary of fundamental goals of the college union amplifies the applicability of the Hurst–Duncan table for the college union.

1 The college union responds to numerous *physical and tangible needs* of individuals (examples: food, recreation, supply services, meeting spaces).
2 The college union facilitates a *sense of identity with the institution*, contributing to a feeling of community or connectedness among members of the college (examples: special institutional events, from orientation to commencement; programs involving students in issues affecting the college).
3 The college union extends and enhances the *intellectual or cognitive learning* which may have its genesis in the classroom, the library, or the laboratory (examples: lectures, seminars, student–faculty discussions, conferences).

4 The college union impacts on the *cultural and aesthetic growth* of people, expanding cultural consciousness and establishing lifelong patterns of appreciation and enjoyment (examples: Concerts, exhibits, poetry readings, colloquiums to enhance cultural awareness).

5 The college union provides avenues for *creativity and innovation*, processes for experimenting with alternative possibilities for self-expression (examples: arts and crafts workshops, dramatic productions, noncredit classes).

6 The college union assists with meeting the *social needs of the college's population* via both formal and informal methods (examples: films, musical entertainment, dances, conversations in campus taverns).

7 The college union plays a valuable role in aiding individuals as they *explore, identify, review, and evaluate their beliefs and values. (examples: debates, interaction, and confrontation with individuals with diverse viewpoints and life-styles).*

In summary, the college union is designed to contribute to the *individual's quest for identity*, for a sense of self which encompasses autonomy and independence in concert with the *development of interpersonal competencies and meaningful relationships.*

## CONCEPTUAL FOUNDATIONS AND RESEARCH

Stated goals of college unions are well served by continuous and careful scrutiny by those within and outside the field. Espousing philosophies is a relatively painless endeavor; *supporting* them often becomes complex and problematic.

Human development theories and research are the underpinnings of college union concepts. Basic goals have been influenced and sustained by the work of theorists such as Erikson (1950, 1959, 1965, 1975). His conclusions relating to those persons forming the traditional collegiate population are of special importance; his research and views encompassing the full range of life stages become increasingly relevant as post-secondary institutions and college unions serve persons of all ages.

In a focus on youth, Erikson (1965) summarizes numerous characteristics of the development of the late-adolescent or young adult, including various physical changes, energy which seeks multiple outlets, cognitive development, alternating patterns of conformity and deviance, rejection of parents and other authorities, new historical and cultural perspectives, the need to "make a series of ever-narrowing selections of personal, occupation, sexual, and ideological commitments" (Erikson, 1959, p. 13). He focuses on "identity confusion" and the search for a sense of identity, what he terms becoming "a special kind." Erikson (1975, p. 165) provides this succinct comment regarding adolescence:

> Adolescence has always been seen as a state of transition from an alternating invigorating and enslaving sense of an over-defined past to a future as yet to be identified—and to be identified with. It seems to serve the function and the comprehensive ideals of a viable or developing civilization.

When adolescents are also college students, the college union can assist the individual as he or she struggles with this important state of transition. Through multiple avenues, the union can enhance the institution's response to the developmental needs of youth as described by Erikson.

College union philosophies and activities should be further reviewed in relation to research and writing which concentrate more specifically on human development in higher education settings. Among the pertinent studies are those reported by Astin (1977), Chickering (1969, 1972), and Feldman and Newcomb (1969).

Of major importance is Astin's (1977) longitudinal study of college impact. Spanning more than a decade and involving more than 200,000 students at over 300 diverse institutions, Astin's conclusions constitute a powerful affirmation of college union philosophies and goals. His findings analyze the effects of college on knowledge, beliefs, and attitudes—key factors in the student's development. Astin's conclusions emphasize a resounding theme: *involvement.* He notes that the student's association with the campus community, with other students, and with the faculty significantly impacts on affective development, patterns of behavior, competence and achievement, and overall satisfaction with the undergraduate experience. Since participation is at the axis of college union philosophy, Astin's research does much to support long-standing beliefs, theories, and philosophies that have been shared via a variety of college union-related writings. For example, the widely quoted "Role Of The College Union" (Association Of College Unions–International, 1956) underscores the importance of "informal association outside the classroom," of the college union as a "laboratory of citizenship, training students in social responsibility and for leadership in our democracy," and of the provision of "a cultural, social, and recreational program." The role statement, framed and displayed in countless college unions, includes this summary relating to involvement:

"In all its processes, it [the college union] encourages self-directed activity, giving maximum opportunity for self-realization and for growth in individual social competency and group effectiveness."

Numerous studies have been completed which involve college unions at multiple institutions. Much of the research has been conducted or approved by the Association Of College Unions–International, the intercollegiate educational organization dedicated to the development and enhancement of college unions and student activities programs. Multi-institutional studies of particular note are the in-depth analyses of the operation and administration of college unions by Bell (1965) and Jenkins and McQueen (1973). The report of the ACU-I's self-study (Self-Study Commission, 1975) provides an overview of college union characteristics and a listing of widely accepted philosophies and assertions. Another example is a study (Association Of College Unions–International, 1979) that focuses on the relationship between college union program functions and the general coordination of student activities on the campus. Of special importance is the Association's "Data Bank," a continuing, computerized research system which entails the collection, storage, and analysis of a large quantity of information regarding college unions and student activities programs. The central data bank seeks and stores data regarding institutional demographics, size and nature of college union facilities, budgets, services, staffs, structures, and programs, as well as a qualitative profile of programs and activities. Reports and interpretations emanating from the data bank form invaluable sources of information and are published on a regular basis (e.g., Association Of College Unions–International, 1978a, 1978b, 1978c, 1978d, 1978e, 1979,.

Any accurate view of the note and impact of the college union requires exploration of basic human development concepts and research, reviews of fundamental goals of education and the research illustrating the impact of the total collegiate environment on learning and development, and the research findings which focus on the college union in more specific terms. Such a view is essential if one is to understand the collage that is the college union.

## THE COLLEGE UNION AND THE CAMPUS ENVIRONMENT

### The Campus Community

If asked to describe the components of an exciting, satisfying college environment, many would mention intellectual stimulation, a varied social life, the sharing of friendships, frequent student–faculty interaction, chances to pursue special interests, and opportunities relating to career development. To underscore a previous point, Astin (1977, p. 186) reports that "the student's ratings of the undergraduate college experience and environment are strongly influenced by various kinds of involvement."

When the college union functions as a community center and provides a wide assortment of involvement opportunities, its impact on the total environment can be a powerful one. As a community center, it can include the many individuals who compose the college "family." A strong case can be made for a "college union" as opposed to a "student union," especially when the "student" connotation infers that others are excluded. An "off-limits" perception excuses the faculty from informal contact with students, impedes the administration's continuous discussion of concerns facing the college, and prevents alumni(ae) from retaining valuable bonds and serving as positive role models for current students. A "student" union catering only to students diminishes everyone, most of all the student!

Erikson (1965, p. 23) observes:

> Adolescent development comprises a new set of identification processes, both with significant persons and with ideological forces, which give importance to individual life by relating it to a living community and to ongoing history, and by counterpointing the newly won individual identity with some communal solidarity.

Through multiple strategies, the college union can enhance "the living community" formed by the college. Association with faculty, staff, alumni(ae), and guests can provide the "ongoing history" and many of the "significant persons" noted in Erikson's statements. The union can assist by cutting through age or status boundaries and by breaking through the rigidity of specific disciplines. In collaboration with individuals and agencies, it can work to create, redesign, or sustain a campus environment which supports growing, evolving people.

One is often asked, "What difference would it make if the college union didn't exist?" Gone would be a "unifying force," an important service agency, a program abundant with interaction potential, a "laboratory for citizenship," a social and cultural center. The campus atmosphere would be diminished immeasurably.

## Students Impacted by the Union

Any analysis of the potential impact of the college union on the campus environment and student development suggests a broad clustering of the students related to the union. Three general categories follow.

***Student Participants or Users.*** Among the most identifiable students influenced by the union are those who utilize the union's services and facilities and participate in its programs. These are the students who use the snack bar, receive information at the reception desk, play backgammon in the recreation center, or attend seminars, lectures, concerts, films, and other programs.

***The Student Leaders.*** Although the label is perhaps too inclusive or misleading, these are the students who are actively engaged in the planning, production, and evaluation of campus activities and programs. Student leaders include those serving with the college union's various boards and committees—both on policy-making bodies and on program committees. In addition, the category includes those who hold membership in general student organizations, student government, and interest groups. Recent research (Association Of College Unions–International, 1979) reveals that a large number of college union administrators also serve as general coordinators of student activities. (Of the 428 institutional representatives responding to a random sampling questionnaire, approximately 75 percent have responsibility for both the college union and general campus activities.) Thus it can be concluded that the college union has direct or potential influence on much of the campus life and therefore the student leaders.

***Part-Time Student Employees.*** With few exceptions, college unions consider students to be an integral part of the labor force. Opportunities for employment vary—from graduate interns to weekend managers, from bellhops to bartenders, from desk attendants to delicatessen managers, from noncredit class instructors to poster-makers, from theater directors to short-order cooks. Although the number of student employees and the nature of the jobs vary in relation to the specific institution, this category of student has unique opportunities for learning and development. Of direct relevance are Astin's comments (1977) on the possibilities of expanding part-time student employment opportunities as a means of getting more students involved in campus life.

In most institutions, of course, there are those *uninvolved students* who seldom or never utilize the union or participate in its activities. Clearly, this is a concern for those who are responsible for the union's leadership and development. This cluster constitutes the "untapped market" and is often the target for problem-solving sessions and special research, including assessments of student needs and interests.

## ELABORATION ON COLLEGE UNION FUNCTIONS

Although some basic assumptions have been stated, a list of college union goals have been shared, some conceptual foundations and research have been outlined, and a focus on the campus environment has been included, it is important to provide some details regarding ways the college union attempts to fulfill its responsibilities to the community and individuals.

### The College Union as a Place

What are college unions like? The response is both complex and revealing. Research completed by the ACU-I (1978a) reveals expected diversity in the *size of facilities* (i.e., from less than 10,000 square feet to more than 300,000 square feet) and the *nature of facilities*. A list of union-operated facilities and services includes banks and bakeries, guest rooms and gymnasiums, libraries and discos, bookstores and barber shops, taverns and theaters, boathouses and faculty clubs, ski slopes and swimming pools. Most frequently, the college union facility includes food service areas, meeting and multipurpose rooms, art galleries, information centers, music practice and listening areas, recreation centers, television lounges, conference rooms, general lounges, administrative offices, and headquarters for college union boards and committees, student government, and student organizations. Also among the more predictable college union facilities are copy centers, crafts facilities, ticket sales areas, photographic darkrooms, outing centers, outdoor patios and terraces for programming, and video-tape services.

College unions need not be elaborate or luxurious, although some of them are. The essential element is a special kind of *feeling*, a climate or ambience that welcomes people. The spaces differ—from areas where a large number can gather for a program, to places where three or four people can have quiet conversation, to sheltered retreats where a person can simply sit alone and *be*. As a community center, the college union meets specific physical needs, as well as those needs that are intangible but equally important.

### The College Union as a Synthesis for the Curriculum

An effective college union can provide countless opportunities for students and faculty to interact and grow intellectually. College union programs can and should serve as extraordinary extensions of the formal academic curriculum, which is often related to the official degree plan or the traditional classroom kind of learning. Programs such as lectures, seminars, discussions, noncredit courses, films, conferences, drama productions, readings, and exhibits can contribute substantially to the college's total environment for learning and, in turn, the cognitive and affective development of its constituents.

Appropriately, the first college unions sprang from debating societies. The college union has a responsibility for perpetuating this salient legacy by facilitating the discussion of *all sides* of timely and timeless topics, ensuring that individuals interact in an open, honest, civilized manner. The union should be the setting where free discussion is nurtured. When the campus community confronts a crisis which focuses on a volatile issue, the model for positive interaction has been established and can form the natural vehicle for ventilation and healthy debate.

A fine college union program is, in essence, an interdisciplinary curriculum. A review of programs offered by college unions is a special adventure. Sturgell's (1974) comments on college union programs tend to make believers of the most jaded cynics! Particularly impressive are the seminars (or "theme" programs) which stress involvement by students and faculty from multiple disciplines, plus consultants or resource persons, and members of the community. Sturgell observes the mixes which can result, noting: "Possibly some unlikely academic bed partners now find themselves embracing, figuratively speaking, to provide a high level of excitement and intellectual challenge. . . ." Interdisciplinary noncredit seminar topics included "Urban America: Processes, Problems, And Projects," "Sports In American Society: Literature, Culture, And Philosophy," and "Chemocology: Integrated View Of Chemical And Ecological Concepts."

Clearly, program planning and development corresponds to Astin's (1977) finding regarding the importance of student–faculty interaction and involvement in the activities of the institution. Since the early days of college unions, the student has been in a key decision-making role, in collaboration with college union staff and faculty members. The students involved in the planning process learn on two fronts: via *content* and via the program *process*. As with other union programs, the interdisciplinary noncredit seminar may trigger the involvement of the shy, usually uninvolved student, or it may bring to the front the student who is generally unmotivated to participate. The student may work side-by-side with a professor who might have thought him/herself "too busy," but who experiences a new dimension of teaching and renewal. The college union can serve as the catalyst, providing the skills and expertise of its staff and ongoing student leaders, its fiscal and physical resources, and its reputation for quality. The potential for this kind of programming—and related programs—is limitless; they may move individuals toward commitments to lifelong curiosity, analysis, and study.

**The College Union and the Socialization Process**

Although it is recognized that all of what impacts on a college student relates to the "socialization process" in the broadest sense, the college union can contribute rather specifically to the student's social needs. As emphasized in earlier sections, one of the college union's prime roles relates to bringing people together and helping them interact with each other. Directly related is the college union's role in assisting students deal with the stress of the college experience, in providing productive outlets for energy, and in helping the individual have "fun" and develop that ever-important sense of humor.

Among the more predictable or traditional social activities offered by the union are dances, entertainment films, recreational programs (e.g., bowling, billiards, card games), and informal concerts. In recent years, many college unions have responded to students' increasing interest in the outdoors and physical fitness, giving rise to exercise facilities, outing centers, and increased programming activities such as hiking, backpacking, bicycling, water sports, and wilderness adventures. Ironically, as outdoor enthusiasts have combined physical fitness with socialization, the incidence of coin-operated amusement machines has also risen, creating a population devoted to interaction with man-made machines!

Programs designed "strictly for fun" are currently enjoying a major revival in college unions. In contrast to the students of the late 1960s and early 1970s, today's students rather unabashedly show up for programs in zany costumes. The programs may be movie "fun clubs" which feature "high camp" cartoons and films, bubble gum, and paper airplanes, or "Las Vegas Nights" with simulated casinos and "play" money, or "trivia bowls." Enjoying much popularity is an "all-nighter," a program which usually extends from approximately 7:00 P.M. until 3:00 or 4:00 in the morning. The union is teeming with activity, including dances, concerts, drama productions, films, food and drink specials, and other featured attractions such as fingerpainting, fortune-telling, sing-alongs, clown acts, and puppet shows. The program usually concludes with a special breakfast.

The union's social program can encompass more subtle activities which facilitate interaction by those who might not otherwise meet. For example, the union can work with faculty members, encouraging them to hold an informal class meeting in the union. Many unions offer complimentary or low-cost food and/or drink in an effort to encourage such sessions. In the same vein, the union may work with residence hall staff members and student leaders to encourage social gatherings for the residents of multiple dormitories. The union can also work with the student–faculty councils from departments as diverse as music and microbiology, encouraging them to meet in the union and get to know those they may stereotype by academic major. By serving as the "go-between" organizer, the college union can create and legitimize informal social programs which have far-reaching implications.

For understandable reasons, college unions have traditionally fought images as "fun houses" or "pleasure palaces." When such labels occur, the multifaceted role of the union is diminished and the union is easily written off by many members of the community. However, the college union indeed has a significant role in the campus's social life. The key element in fulfilling its broader role is *balance* in programming activity.

## The College Union's Role in Cultural and Aesthetic Growth

Just as the college union has continuous concern for the general socialization process, it is also part of the ongoing culturalization process. Again, it is appropriate that a narrower view be taken in order to focus on the union's potential impact on the individual's awareness and appreciation of the aesthetic, artistic, and literary aspects of the broader culture.

Much has been written about the stratagems that have been employed to encourage students to come to appreciate and enjoy the visual and performing arts which are not necessarily in the "popular" category. In addition to more formalized "audience development" plans, the college union usually adheres to the time-proven "art by accident" strategy. The student may walk through the union's lobby and encounter a sculptor; his curiosity may pique a long-term interest. A student may meet a friend for a post-class beer, and discover a string ensemble can make beautiful tavern music. Or a student may wander by the college union terrace, hear a poet reading his work, and decide to listen while having a sandwich in the sun. A participant in a seminar on world issues may really *talk* with international students and gain an understanding and appreciation of their cultures.

The college union's place in helping students understand other cultures includes other *American* cultures. Minority students on many campuses have found the union eager to assist them in sharing their culture with others. Concurrently, minority students have become more involved with nonminorities and with the campus as a whole. The college union's resistance to separatist centers for blacks, chicanos, native Americans, and others has been important. Despite compromises that allow for identification needs, efforts have been made to combine spaces with programs that focus on the art, music, drama, film, and poetry of the minority culture.

If the college union is to play a part in expanding the cultural and aesthetic horizons of students, it must work closely with other organizations and agencies. Good rapport with departments such as art, drama, music, anthropology, international studies, and American studies is essential. Close cooperation with advisors to international, black, chicano, native American, and other minority groups is also essential. Community art groups, state boards on arts and humanities, and any number of other agencies share common goals and may wish to pool resources in order to broaden the perspectives and sensitivities of the college population. As one college union program director noted, "All our graduates may not earn the 'Renaissance' crest—but it won't be because we didn't try!"

### The College Union as a Provider of Opportunities for Creativity and Innovation

Although this is closely aligned with other college union goals, it warrants emphasis. The college union has a special obligation to provide students with opportunities for experimentation, for trying things which are—for them—new and different. The union can provide conditions that permit certain low-risk expressions of creativity and innovation.

The college union can encourage the student to examine and experience that which has little or nothing to do with his/her academic major. Here the math major can make a film, the accountant can "throw a pot," the musician debates politics, the biologist plays a guitar, the artist takes an informal course in investments. Perhaps a student's eye is drawn to a session on aerobic dancing, and expressive dance becomes a lifelong avocation. And it is possible that a student may join a union committee and learn the creative joy that can be derived from service as a volunteer.

Creativity is an overused word which is too frequently associated only with the arts. In the college union, individuals can learn the exhilaration that can come from a group problem-solving session, a communications breakthrough, or a meeting that was "right on." Training programs relating to creativity may be, in themselves, creative experiences.

The point is simple, yet important: the college union can provide the climate, the resources, and the opportunities for individuals to experience and utilize the creativity that is theirs.

## The Role of the College Union in Shaping Belief and Value Systems

Almost without exception, human development specialists concur that the college experience has great impact on the individual's development of a system of beliefs and values. Erikson (1965) focuses on youth's interest in what others "stand for" and the quest for what is "truth" and "right." Research by Astin (1977), Chickering (1969, 1972), and Feldman and Newcomb (1969) underscore the impact of college on attitudes, beliefs, and values.

The college union's potential role in the development of beliefs and values has been noted in other sections. The extension of the curriculum via discussion and debate stresses the importance of carefully examining different philosophies and viewpoints. Flowing from such experiences is the evolvement of what one believes. Social interaction may force a student to relate to those with widely divergent life-styles, behaviors, and values; the by-product may be a sorting out of what one wishes to adopt, reject, or adapt. Experimenting with new behaviors or appearances may help the student come to recognize what "fits." Broadening cultural or aesthetic horizons may court the kinds of changes in value systems that will enrich one's life. In concert with other areas of the campus, the college union can assist the student with this important dimension of development.

The college union may be involved with efforts that will *influence* or *alter* attitudes or behaviors that are self-destructive. A single example will be utilized to make the point. It is generally agreed that alcohol abuse is a serious problem among college students (Ingalls, 1978). College unions are increasingly involved with the sale and service of alcoholic beverages (Association of College Unions–International, 1978a) and thus have special responsibilities for ensuring that they are utilized in a mature, responsible manner. Therefore, the college union must be involved in proactive plans and programs designed to prevent or reduce alcohol abuse. The strategy may include continuous efforts to create an ambience which stresses good conversation and fun and discourages the drink-to-get-drunk syndrome. The tavern program may be of such diversity and quality, the student is more attracted to the stage than the sauce! Concurrently, college union personnel are major partners in all-campus alcohol awareness/education programs, sponsoring seminars, displaying posters, including information on closed-circuit public information monitors, and providing other avenues for impactful emphasis on a serious problem.

A discussion of the college union's possible influence on value systems and behaviors would be incomplete without a mention of its contribution to learning via role models. Through its programs, its advising systems, and its avenues for interaction, the college union can place students in touch with positive role models, persons who exemplify the multifaceted and vital elements of a fully functioning individual.

### Identity and Interpersonal Relationships

Erikson (1965, p. 13) provides an important summary statement when he notes: "Identity is a term used in our day with faddish ease; at this point, I can only indicate how very complicated the real article is." Despite recognized complexities, it is widely accepted that an individual's ever-evolving sense of identity is influenced by his/her total milieu. In the collegiate setting, the college union has potential impact on the individual's quest for identity through the provision of services, the integration of cognitive learning outside the classroom, the opportunities for cultural awareness and appreciation, social relationships and interaction, the development of value systems, and creativity and experimentation. All are a part of the total process and the college union is one of the agencies that can assist the individual to explore and move toward a sense of identity, a sense of self, which encompasses autonomy and independence. Concurrently, the individual is engaged in the development of meaningful interpersonal relationships and competencies, including the capacity for intimacy. In essence, this is a restatement of a basic mission of education.

## KEY ISSUES CONFRONTING COLLEGE UNIONS

The central issues confronting college unions predictably vary in relation to the times, to institutions, and to individuals. Following are some brief descriptions of emerging and enduring areas of concern.

***Effective Articulation of College Union Values and Philosophies*** If the college union is to fulfill its potential as a unique force in the college's environment, it must have the support of those individuals and agencies which have influence. It is not unusual to observe dramatic shifts in the nature and impact of a college union based on the perceptions of one or more key persons. Persistent and forceful articulation of college union philosophies and possibilities is essential. At no time can that critical process be ignored or deemphasized.

***An Ongoing Research and Evaluation Program.*** No unit within the institution has a greater need for a continuous research and evaluation program than does the college union. The well-managed college union makes assessment and review a part of its regular agenda. Few institutional evaluations or efforts to cut budgets threaten the very existence of the math department; the college union, however, is easy prey for uninformed or misguided proponents of "no frills" education. By doing its "homework," the college union can scrutinize its impact and can make appropriate changes. The studies may range from formal, statistically sound comprehensive endeavors (i.e., professionally designed instruments completed by random samples with findings analyzed by recognized experts) to informal surveys, questionnaires, and interviews. The research may include student need assessments, traffic counts, program participation profiles, facility usage reviews, inventory tabulations, visits by consultation teams, product evaluation, and accounting summaries. The numerical data may be supplemented by the comments of those who are unable to quantify the educational value of their involvement with the college union.

***The College Union Staff*** The overall effectiveness of the college union is directly related to the strength, competence, skills, and commitment of its staff. If college unions are to fulfill their goals, institutions must place a high priority on the recruitment, selection, training, supervision, and evaluation of its staff. A continuous concern is the ability to *attract* and *retain* high-quality staff. It is amusing, although tragic, to scan announcements seeking applicants for key college union positions—institutions seem to want an educator, a corporate executive, an arbitrator, a tireless worker, and a wealth of experience, all for 12,000 dollars for 12 months! When institutions fail to recognize the importance of its investment in competent staff, there is limited hope that the college can fulfill its goals.

***Quality Student Leadership.*** At the cornerstone of college union philosophy is high-quality involvement by students at many levels. A major challenge is the attraction of students who will respond to training and support and provide the necessary leadership. When the quality of student leadership sags, specific strategies must be devised to alter the trend and restore or develop a body of effective student leaders.

***An Emphasis on Training.*** Inasmuch as there is no specific academic discipline designed to prepare college union professionals, continuous, first-rate training is essential. The training must include the chief administrator, professional and supervisory personnel, support and non-professional staff, part-time student employees, volunteer members of advisory and policy-making boards, and student leaders. The training program may be formal and informal and may employ a variety of approaches; it should be a *given*, an expectation recognized by all persons related to the organization. An ongoing concern in the college union field is the development and maintenance of relevant training programs specifically designed to increase the odds of goal fulfillment.

***Collaboration.*** Although the importance of the college union's cooperation with other departments and agencies both on and off the campus has been noted earlier, it bears mention again in this section. No fully functioning college union can operate in isolation or with territorial postures. Strategies for collaboration are essential.

## SUMMARY

The foregoing chapter on the college union suggests in the main that Astin (1977, p. 115) is accurate when he makes the following observation:

> For many undergraduates, extracurricular activities provide some of the most significant consequences of college attendance. In certain respects, these activities offer an opportunity to develop skills that are more relevant to later life than the knowledge and cognitive skills acquired in the classroom. Undergraduate extracurricular activities may be the forerunner of adult achievement in a variety of fields. . . .

This focus on the college union has emphasized its role as a primary force in human development in the post-secondary institution. The college union has been viewed as multifaceted, designed to serve the entire institution. Thus the college union, including its programs, services, and facilities, can respond to various physical and tangible needs, facilitate a sense of community among the college's diverse constituencies, enhance and expand intellectual and cultural growth, appreciation, and awareness, encourage healthy creativity and innovation, assist with socialization processes, and contribute to the development of belief and value systems. In essence, the college union has been described as having potentially significant impact on the individual's discovery of a sense of self or identity and on the ways individuals develop and maintain satisfying, productive interpersonal skills and relationships. Although concerns have been noted, the basic theme is a positive, optimistic one: the college union *can* be a powerful force in the institution and can assist individuals as they move toward becoming people they *know* and *respect*.

## REFERENCES


Association of College Unions–International. The role of the college union. *Proceedings of the 33rd Annual Conference of the Association of College Unions–International.* Ithaca, N.Y. 1956.

Association of College Unions–International. Data bank activated; findings summarized; use outlined. *Bulletin of the Association of College Unions–International*, 1978a, **46** (1), 1, 14–23.

Association of College Unions–International. Branch unions respond to data bank. *Bulletin of the Association of College Unions–International*, 1978b, **46** (3), 2.

Association of College Unions–International. Data bank fiscal analysis begins with fees. *Bulletin of the Association of Unions–International*, 1978c, **46** (4), 1.

Association of College Unions–International. Data bank shows sources of income for unions. *Bulletin of the Association of College Unions–International*, 1978d, **46** (5), 10–14.

Association of College Unions–International. Data bank examines union income and expenditures. *Bulletin of the Association of College Unions–International*, 1978e, **46** (6), 10–11.

Association of College Unions–International. Union salaries up some. *Bulletin of the Association of College Unions–International*, 1979, **47** (1), 1, 10–11.

Astin, A. W. *Four Critical Years.* San Francisco: Jossey-Bass, 1977.

Bell, B. C. *Administration and Operation of the College Union.* Ithaca, N.Y.: Association of College Unions–International, Cornell University, 1965.

Berry, C. A. *Planning a College Union Building.* New York: New York Bureau of Publications. Teachers College, Columbia University, 1960.

Berry, C. A. The next fifty years. *College Unions—1964.* Ithaca, N.Y.: Association of College Unions–International, Cornell University, 1964, pp. 48–57.

Berry, C. A. *College Unions—Year Fifty.* Ithaca, N.Y.: Association of College Unions–International, Cornell University, 1966.

Berry, C. A. The union and the two cultures. *College Unions—1971.* Stanford, Calif.: Association of College Unions–International, 1971, pp. 1–1, 1–11.

Blackburn, R. D. The people processors. *Proceedings of the 45th Annual Conference of the Association of College Unions–International.* Association of College Unions–International, Stanford, Calif., 1968.

Butts, P. State of the union in 1949. *College Unions—1949.* Ithaca, N.Y.: Association of College Unions–International, Cornell University, 1949, pp. 15–30.

Butts, P. Goals of the college union—historical background, current trends. *Wisconsin Summer Course—1962.* Madison, Wis.: Wisconsin Union, 1962.

Butts, P. *The College Union Story.* Ithaca, N.Y.: Association of College Unions–International, Cornell University, March 1964, pp. 1–8. (Reprinted from the *Journal of the American Institute of Architects.*)

Butts, P. *The College Union Idea.* Stanford, Calif.: Association of College Unions–International. 1971.

Chickering, A. W. *Education and Identity.* San Francisco: Jossey-Bass, 1972.

Erikson, E. *Identity and Life Cycle.* New York: International Universities Press, 1959.

Erikson, E. *Childhood and Society.* Norton, New York, 1950 (2nd ed. 1963).

Erikson, E. Youth: fidelity and diversity. In E. Erikson, (Ed.), *The Challenge Of Youth*, Garden City, N.Y.: Anchor Books, Doubleday, 1965, pp. 1–28.

Erikson, E. *Life History and the Historical Moment.* New York: Norton, 1975.

Feldman, K. A. and T. M. Newcomb. *The Impact of College on Students*, Vols. I and II. San Francisco: Jossey-Bass, 1969.

Harper, E. E. *A union credo.* Ithaca, N.Y.: Association of College Unions–International, Cornell University, 1963.

Hurst, J.C. The emergence of student/environmental development as the conceptual foundation for student affairs and some implications for large universities. *Current Issues in Student Development.* American College Personnel Association Monograph, 1980.

Ingalls, Z. On campus, the biggest drug problem is alcohol. *The Chronicle of Higher Education*, 1978, **17** (7), pp. 3–5.

Jenkins, J. and S. McQueen *Administration and Operation of the College Union.* Stanford, Calif.: Association of College Unions–International. 1973.

Ketter, J. The study of campus activities administration. *Bulletin of the Association of College Unions–International*, 1979, **47** (2), pp. 14–19.

Perry, S. B. Presidential remarks. *Proceedings of the 49th Annual Conference of the Association of College Unions–International.* Stanford, Calif.: Association of College Unions–International, 1972, pp. 6–10.

Perry, S. B. The big assessment: do we feel guilty when we don't know? *Proceedings of the 56th Annual Conference of the Association of College Unions–International.* Stanford, Calif.: Association of College Unions–International, 1976, pp. 1–5.

Self-Study Commission of the Association of College Unions–International, ACU-I: priorities for effectiveness. *Final Report of the Self-Study Commission of the Association of Unions–International.* Stanford, Calif.: Association of College Unions–International, 1975.

Sturgell, J. S. *An Uncommon Guide to College Union Programming.* Stanford, Calif.: Association of College Unions–International, 1974.

# 14

# Discipline As A Developmental Intervention

DAVID McCLINTOCK

Among the many functions associated with student affairs in colleges and universities, the most traditional and consistent task has been discipline. Many, if not most, student personnel professionals deliberately try to dispel the stereotypical presumption often made by laymen and academic colleagues alike that the "dean" is responsible for controlling the behavior of students. Although the student personnel administrator fully realizes the impossibility of controlling behavior, nevertheless parents, governing board members, and chief administrative officers, among others, attach much importance to the disciplinary function. Indeed, any young professional with aspirations of becoming a chief student personnel officer must consider what training, skills, and experiences would be useful in preparing for successful performance of the discipline responsibility.

## ANTECEDENTS TO DISCIPLINE AS DEVELOPMENT

Many levels of student affairs staff, in addition to the chief student personnel officer, become involved in some aspect of discipline either in the role of administrator or in the classroom teaching role should the staff member also have a teaching assignment. Advisers to student activities and organizations, union program staff, and residence hall staff members are frequently required to engage in a disciplinary interaction with students. Even though discipline has had an important and lengthy history within student affairs, and even though the responsibility has involved many staff members, the basic conceptualization of the task and philosophy of discipline has remained relatively static until the latter part of the 1960s (Fley, 1964). The discipline officer's approach to student conduct and university regulations began to shift in the 1960s as a result of several factors. The opinion in the case of *Dixon* v. *Alabama State Board of Education* in 1961 introduced the requirement for according students due process and thereby suggested not only that students had constitutional rights, but that colleges and universities must also observe those rights. The discipline function itself and the premises upon which it was based were questioned extensively by students who began to assert their rights during the period of activism in the latter half of the 1960s. As a result of the court rulings, student activism, and the assertion of students' rights, the legal concept of in loco parentis began to erode as a basis for discipline. Bakken (1967) expressed concern in 1967 about a shift from the principle of in loco parentis and concluded that discipline might become a punitive action rather than an educational experience.

Under the doctrine of in loco parentis, institutions often placed emphasis on controlling behavior. Even though the student personnel literature emphasized that discipline should be educative, the regulatory nature of discipline remained a central feature of the discipline program in most institutions. When the courts began to articulate procedural requirements for colleges and universities to follow in administering discipline, many discipline procedures became so legalistic that the regulatory aspects of discipline were severely challenged by students and attorneys who looked for errors of technicality. A further result of the trend to highly legalized procedures was that the educative purposes of discipline efforts were hampered. Students no longer spent much energy reflecting upon their conduct, or misconduct, but rather spent much effort preparing a defense for a hearing.

With the demise of in loco parentis as a basis for discipline, the rationale for and practice of discipline have been influenced significantly by the emergence in the late 1960s and the 1970s of the concept that student personnel workers should engage in student development rather than merely student services. The work of Chickering (1969) in describing the seven vectors of growth and development for the college-age youth and the emergence of the concepts of student development as articulated by Miller and Prince in *The Future of Student Affairs* (1976) have suggested new ways to think about the rationale and purpose for discipline. Greenleaf (1978) and Caruso (1978) have both written about the impact of student development theories on the practice of discipline.

At about the same time that student development philosophies were being expounded in the literature, the counseling literature also began to include observations that environmental factors played an important role in the development of students. Thus both student and environmental development were proposed as appropriate concerns for the work of the counselor (Morrill and Hurst, 1971; Oetting, 1967). Although student development and environmental development each provides new ways of defining the task of student personnel work, the combination of both student and environmental development provides a more comprehensive framework for postulating a philosophy, rationale, and methods for "doing" student personnel work, including the discipline function.

## THE ROLE AND MISSION OF DEVELOPMENTAL DISCIPLINE

For many years student personnel professionals have emphasized the need to adopt educative methods of discipline. Personnel officers have disparaged a punitive and legalistic approach to discipline (Fley, 1964). The 40-year-old "personnel point of view" emphasized the need to develop fully each student to his or her individual potential, including the troubled and/or troubling student who might be involved in a disciplinary interaction (Greenleaf, 1978). Developmental and educational concerns have long been part of the discussion about discipline. Nonetheless, most discipline programs in collegiate institutions have heretofore been primarily remedial rather than preventive or developmental.

A typical sequence for discipline interactions, for example, would involve the following events: (1) an accusation that a student has violated institutional standards of conduct; (2) an "investigation" by the discipline officer to determine the validity of the charges; (3) an administrative or judicial hearing that assures that due process rights are accorded the student; (4) an assessment of penalty should the student be found guilty; and (5) an attempt to "educate" the student through informal counseling or through referral to the counseling agencies on the campus. (Enthusiastic discipline officers often proceed to step 5 even if the student is found not guilty!) The exercise of these steps in the process have usually been carried out by dedicated professionals who have a sincere respect for the student and who strongly desire to assist the student in adopting acceptable patterns of conduct. The informal, anecdotal "histories" of deans of students attest to many "successes" that have occurred through the years among students who have been disciplined. The procedure does, however, have the characteristic of being reactive and remedial rather than proactive or preventive.

The basic tasks of enforcing institutional regulations and of following proper procedures with students who are accused of misconduct remain necessary features of every institution's discipline program. The scope of the discipline function varies from campus to campus, depending on the nature of the campus and the particular historical development of its organizational structure. Some student personnel staff members have responsibilities for all conduct regulations, including academic misconduct. Some institutions delegate responsibility for scholastic dishonesty to the academic departments. The characteristic cases also vary from one type of institution to another. No matter what the structure and history may have been at any given institution, the emerging concepts of student development and environmental development are not likely to alter radically the goals and purposes of the discipline program. The concepts do, however, offer stimulating prospects for enlarging our conceptualization of the task of discipline. The development literature also provides a basis for stating goals in concepts more explicit than the broad notions of being "educative" or of attempting to "develop fully" each student to his or her potential. Those student affairs staff members with specific duties involving discipine should possess expertise in all aspects of discipline: legal, procedural, developmental, and educational.

Three roles for student services have been described in Chapter 1 of this book. The roles—understanding the student and the environment, teaching students skills, and modifying the environment—provide a framework for thinking about the role of the discipline officer.

## Understanding the Student and the Environment

The first role for the student affairs professional is to understand the student, the environment, and the interaction between the two. Understanding may be based on evaluations and studies that are conducted within the institution, on the vast literature concerning development and environmental factors that impact on that development, and on interactions with students themselves. The effectiveness of the discipline officer can be enhanced significantly by continually expanding his or her understanding of students and the environment.

***Institutional Studies*** Many institutions conduct studies of the characteristics or needs of their student population. The information may be compiled by staff in an office of institutional studies, by student affairs staff members, by faculty in relevant disciplines, or by graduate students involved in educational and other behavioral fields of study. The data available through such sources can provide the discipline specialist with such information as a general assessment about the types of students that attend the institution, the background of students, pressures that students experience, and attitudes of students. The primary value of such data for the discipline officer is to "map" the human environment in which he or she will perform the discipline functions. Institutions and the persons within institutional communities have distinctive "corporate personalities" and characteristics. The more general knowledge an administrator has about the characteristics of the institution and its students, the better able the administrator is to judge the impact of decisions and actions which he or she must make. An enhanced ability to assess the impact of alternative courses of action increases the likelihood that the administrator will pursue the most desirable and effective alternative.

***Development Literature*** Perhaps the most important resource for the discipline officer's increased understanding of students is the expanding literature on the characteristics of students' development through the young adult years. The most prominent work on this subject has been that of Chickering (1969). In his book, *Education and Identity*, he identified seven vectors of student development, most of which have relevance to disciplinary concerns. The vectors along which students develop in young adulthood are establishing identity, achieving competence, managing emotions, developing autonomy, freeing interpersonal relationships, developing purpose, and developing integrity. Caruso (1978) has suggested that many discipline problems are symptomatic of the student's difficulty in mastering one or more of these developmental tasks. He cites such examples as academic cheating being a possible indicator of deficiency in developing integrity, or dormitory fighting being related to difficulty in managing emotions. The developmental tasks can also represent specific goals that the discipline officer can incorporate into his or her disciplinary interactions with students. For example, a primary goal of any disciplinary interaction is to encourage the student to accept responsibility for the consequences of his or her behavior rather than placing the blame on other persons or on external factors. The characteristic of accepting responsibility for oneself can relate to several of the developmental tasks identified by Chickering: developing autonomy, establishing identity, and developing integrity.

Kohlberg (1971) has also provided useful conceptualizations about the theory of moral development. He identified six stages of moral development that describe the manner in which a person decides how to resolve a moral dilemma. The literature in the area of moral, ethical, and personal development, especially that by Kohlberg, Erikson (1964, 1968) and Perry (1970), provides an important theoretical background for the understanding of young adults in the typical college-going years.

***Environmental Considerations*** An understanding of the environmental factors that impact on student development can be increased through a variety of activities and efforts on the part of the discipline specialist. Environmental assessment in relationship to the discipline function is more diffuse than the tasks of studying theories of student development or reviewing studies of student characteristics. Further, each campus constitutes its own distinctive and different environment within which the student lives, studies, works, and socializes. Each student also brings a completely individual environmental background from family and community. In spite of the complexity of the task, several environmental factors that interrelate with concerns for students' behavior can be listed. (1) The discipline officer should be familiar with the various legal considerations that apply to students in the specific jurisdiction within which the institution is located. The official not only should study the law concerning contitutional rights, but also should have some basic information about applicable criminal laws. (2) The officer should be familiar with all institutional regulations, including residence hall rules and academic dishonesty rules. (3) The discipline specialist should have extensive knowledge of supportive services available to students such as counseling, medical, academic, and financial services. Services may be available within the institution although many communities also provide a variety of services for students. (4) He or she should be familiar with the academic calendar so that the administrator can anticipate those "stress periods" which increase the incidence of deviant behavior. (5) Efforts should be made to understand the function and role of the faculty, and the organizational structure of the academic departments. A knowledge of the academic environment is especially necessary for those discipline officials who have a role in cases of scholastic dishonesty.

***Interaction with Students*** The thoughtful discipline administrator should continually seek to be aware of particular environmental factors that have relevant impact on student misconduct. One of the important ways that the administrator can enhance his or her sensitivity to individual student developmental needs and to environmental factors is regularly to seek opportunities for interaction with students outside of a disciplinary procedure. If possible, the administrator should teach a course periodically. In addition, work with student organizations, student government groups, and residence hall groups provides opportunities to gather information about student needs and characteristics. Interactions with students provide opportunities for informally "testing" impressions that may have formed about environmental stresses or student concerns.

## Teaching Students Skills

A second role for student services in higher education suggested by Morrill and Hurst (1971) is that of teaching students the skills that are necessary to take full advantage of the learning environment. The teaching of skills, behavioral skills in particular, is a lifelong process that must be shared with parents, with peers, and with educators at every level. Student affairs administrators in general and discipline officers in particular have limited time and circumstances in which to guide students toward acquiring appropriate skills. These limitations create the necessity for the administrator to be creative and to use time effectively. Student affairs administrators must also work cooperatively with colleagues to enhance and encourage student learning.

The administrator of discipline has several ways in which to foster skill development and personal development for students. The activity in which the discipline officer has the broadest impact is the development of conduct codes and behavioral expectations. A clear and meaningful statement of conduct regulations allows students to assess community expectations and to adapt behavior accordingly. Emile Durkheim has described morality as adhering to norms which society establishes for the purpose of enhancing the well-being of the society (1973). Within the context of community standards and expectations, the student can grow along several of the developmental vectors described by Chickering (1969). Developing integrity, for instance, involves establishing a coherent and consistent value system and reconceptualizing rules in terms of the social purposes which the rules were designed to serve. If institutional behavior codes are actually consistent with community expectations, the regulations can also provide a basis upon which a student can increase his or her ability to manage emotions and to integrate emotion and behavior. Interpersonal relationships are affected by a student's conduct and behavior in relationship to others. Although the administrator's work in developing conduct codes constitutes an indirect teaching activity, the results of the effort can have an effect throughout the student population.

A significant amount of direct teaching can occur in disciplinary interactions with individual students. Depending on the specific circumstances of each case, including the nature of the misconduct and the background of the student, the discipline administrator may discover and identify developmental deficiencies in the misbehaving student. The opportunity to teach behavioral skills often occurs in the counseling aspects of the disciplinary process, although students with serious maladjustments may require referral to mental health agencies on the campus or in the community.

Part of the teaching aspect of discipline actually takes place through the demeanor, attitude, and manner with which the discipline administrator interacts with students. Honest, straightforward responses to questions and concerns can serve as model behavior for students who are dishonest or devious in their dealings with others. Students who are suspicious or even paranoid may have a surprising reponse to the administrator who speaks to students genuinely, respectfully, and with concern. A student who is antiestablishment may be quite amazed to encounter a discipline administrator who looks out for the student's constitutional rights. Students who are manipulative can sometimes learn alternative behaviors from an administrator who refuses to use manipulation with the student. The vexatious student may relax and cease to use intimidating strategies when the discipline officer remains unruffled and does not reward the effort to intimidate.

In practice, of course, it is not possible for the administrator always to maintain an even temperament, nor will every student who is the object of disciplinary counseling interactions respond to the best efforts of the educator/administrator. Consequently, discipline penalties themselves can be useful in "teaching" recalcitrant students. To the extent that a student may not exercise sufficient internal control over his or her behavior, discipline penalties may serve as an external motivation for the student to control behavior and thus avoid unpleasant consequences. For example, a student in a residence hall may engage continuously in behavior that is disruptive to neighbors and that disregards the rights of others for privacy and quiet study times. The unwillingness to exercise control—rare is the absence of self-control because of inability—may change if the student is confronted with the prospect that continued infractions may lead to dismissal from the institution. In addition to the more traditional penalties such as probation, restitution, suspension, and expulsion, a number of institutions provide for creative penalties that may require some constructive task to be performed by the penalized student. Some institutions have also found success with the use of behavioral contracts wherein a student agrees to conform to certain conduct expectations that have been agreed upon in writing by the administrator and the student. Although the use of penalities may not be considered direct teaching, the appropriate use of penalties can establish parameters within which students can develop and practice more acceptable modes of conduct.

The activity of teaching has many components, of course, and many different methods of teaching may be employed. The discipline administrator has numerous opportunities to guide and encourage students to develop new skills in improving interpersonal relationships, in managing emotions, and in developing integrity. The administrator's teaching methods may not be traditionally didactic. To the extent, however, that a student may learn new or modified behaviors as a result of the discipline officer's efforts, the administrator may appropriately be considered a teacher.

## Modifying the Environment

The third role that Morrill and Hurst have identified as an appropriate activity for student affairs staff is redesigning or modifying the environment based upon an assessment and evaluation of the interaction between student needs and environmental impacts.

The previous discussion relating to the first two roles—understanding the student and the environment and teaching student skills—provides the background for considering appropriate environmental modifications. Each institution and each administrator offer differing needs and opportunities for enhancing or modifying the environment. The methods for effecting the desired changes also vary according to the nature of the task and the characteristics of the institution. Examples of targets for environmental modification, however, can serve to demonstrate possible activities that the discipline officer may undertake in carrying out the third role.

The discipline officer should constantly provide leadership to assess the effectiveness and appropriateness of conduct regulations and discipline procedures. As noted above, codes of behavioral expectations constitute a substantial part of the student environment. The conduct of most students is such that the code remains an unobtrusive part of the environmental background. Nevertheless, if students cannot understand the regulations or if they do not perceive the relevance of the rules to their own student experience, the code probably does not serve effectively the purpose for which it was designed. The activity of modifying and improving regulations may apply either to campus-wide codes or to regulations in residence halls or union buildings.

The student affairs administrator who specializes in discipline can provide important consultation services to several components of the institution, with an anticipated result of enhancing the environment, specifically the classroom environment, for the students. The discipline official can encourage improved effectiveness among faculty members in confronting academic dishonesty through consultation with deans, department chairpersons, and individual faculty members. Not only might regulations and procedures be reviewed, but the individual skills of faculty members in confronting students with allegations of dishonesty might be improved.

Misbehavior by students quite often is a consequence of alcohol abuse or drug abuse. The discipline officer can work with established agencies such as health centers and counseling centers to provide programs designed to combat the problems associated with alcohol and drugs. Consulting with and cooperating with residence hall advisers, union staff members, and student organization advisers concerning alcohol and drug problems can increase the overall institutional capability of coping with problems of this nature.

As the student affairs specialist becomes better informed about the issues of student and environmental development, the types of appropriate and helpful environmental modifications will undoubtedly become more apparent. The most important factors affecting the administrator's role in environmental modification are development of a heightened awareness of students and the environment and adopting an attitude of willingness to seek continued improvement in the institutional environment.

## INTERVENTION STRATEGIES FOR DISCIPLINE

If discipline programs at institutions of higher education are to achieve excellence in the task of student development, the discipline administrator must remain alert for opportunities to encourage needed environmental changes. Part II of this book describes a model that may be used by student affairs administrators in developing intervention strategies. The discipline task involves numerous activities and potential interventions that illustrate the "cube" model (Morrill, Oetting, and Hurst, 1974).

The cube provides a three-dimensional analysis by which an administrator or counselor may classify and describe possible interventions within the institutional setting. The first dimension is identified as the "*target* of the intervention," and includes four possible targets: the individual, the individual's primary group, the individual's associational groups, and the institution or community. The second dimension, the "*purpose* of the intervention," includes remediation, prevention, and development. The "*method* of intervention," the third dimension, includes three possibilities: direct service, consultation and training, and use of the media.

The target of most discipline activities, by definition, is the individual. Though it is possible, of course, for an organization (primary or associational group) to violate institutional regulations, most such instances would involve procedural breaches rather than behavioral misconduct. In instances of misconduct, the group activity is, of course, the composite of individual violations.

When considering the purpose for potential interventions by the discipline administrator, it is possible to identify activities in all three categories of purpose. In fact, each referral for an individual discipline case involves remedial, preventive, and developmental considerations. The institutional interest is to stop the misbehavior, to discourage further violations, and to assist the student in adopting new, more useful behavioral skills and attitudes. Nonetheless, the process of responding to individual cases of violations is by definition remedial since the misconduct has already occurred.

Interventions by the discipline administrator for prevention purposes might include efforts to reduce abuse of alcohol, to encourage better skills among faculty in designing evaluation methods that discourage dishonesty, or to adopt more meaningful and impactful penalties for misconduct. Prevention may occur by training academic counselors or residence hall counselors to be alert to students who may be experiencing unusual amounts of stress. A developmental purpose might be served by establishing effective cooperative relationships between the discipline office and the mental health services so that students who need counseling can be assisted. The counseling activity by discipline staff members can also serve a developmental function by assisting a student in such activities as evaluating and adopting standards of conduct or in accepting responsibility for the consequences of one's own behavior.

The methods of intervention can also be quite varied for the discipline administrator. Direct interventions with individual students are all too familiar to discipline officers. In student/administrator interactions, both administrative and counseling activities are likely to occur. Preventive or developmental interventions by discipline officers are, however, more likely to involve activities such as consultation or training. The discipline specialist should be involved significantly in consulting activities with appropriate staff and faculty throughout the institution. The discipline specialist may consult with individual faculty members who are confronting a student or students suspected of cheating. The administrator may consult with the academic deans about policies, procedures, and other broader concerns about dishonesty. Regular communication should occur between the discipline officer and the security or police department administrators. Consultation and communication should also occur with residence hall staff about policies, procedures, and individual problem cases.

Training interventions regularly occur with residence hall assistants or with judicial board members. In the long range, training sessions for graduate students who have teaching assistantships and who anticipate academic careers can have significant impact. Training through consultation with faculty members, department chairpersons, and academic advisers can improve an institution's ability to confront scholastic dishonesty. Training of colleagues may include not only review of regulations and procedures, but also rudimentary skills in confrontation, counseling and referrals, and suggestions on ways to minimize cheating opportunities.

The use of media as a method of intervention would certainly involve the traditional efforts to publicize institutional regulations and procedures. The media might also be used in the various training sessions that involve discipline. Printed training materials and video-taped examples of confrontation and counseling skills may significantly augment more traditional approaches to training.

The cube model provides a useful tool in postulating innovative approaches to the complex task of administering and coordinating a discipline program. By analyzing the types of activities in which the administrator engages, he or she can establish priorities for those tasks that involve prevention or development. The administrator can also increase efforts to enhance the skills of colleagues in dealing with misconduct or dishonesty.

Many student personnel administrators express discomfort with the task and role of discipline in higher education. The concepts of student and environmental development have, however, called attention to the significant role that the discipline function can play in the personal growth and development of individual students. That task, fostering individual student development, is an essential part of the institution's educational mission.

## REFERENCES

Bakken, C. J. *The Journal of College Student Personnel*, 1967, **8**, 234.

Caruso, R. G. In E. H. Hammond and R. H. Shaffer, (Eds.), *The Legal Foundations of Student Personnel Services in Higher Education*, Washington, D.C.: The American College Personnel Association, 1978, 116.

Chickering, A. W. *Education and Identity*, San Francisco: Jossey-Bass, 1969.

Durkheim, E. *Moral Education: a Study in the Theory and Application of the Sociology of Education*, New York: Free Press, 1973.

Erikson, E. H. *Insight and Responsibility*, New York: Norton, 1964.

Erikson, E. H. *Identity: Youth and Crisis*, New York: Norton, 1968.

Fley, J. A. *Journal of the National Association of Women Deans and Counselors*, 1964, **27**, 105.

Greenleaf, E. A. In E. H. Hammond and R. H. Shaffer, (Eds.), *The Legal Foundations of Student Personnel Services in Higher Education*, Washington, D.C.: The American College Personnel Association, 1978, p. 34.

Kohlberg, L. In C. M. Beck, B. S. Crittenden, and E. V. Sullivan, (Eds.), *Moral Education*, Toronto: University of Toronto Press, 1971.

Miller, T. K. and J. S. Prince, *The Future of Student Affairs*, San Francisco: Jossey-Bass, 1976.

Morrill, W. H. and J. C. Hurst, *The Counseling Psychologist*, 1971, **2**, 90.

Morrill, W. H., E. R. Oetting, and J. C. Hurst, *Personnel and Guidance Journal*, 1974, **52**, 354.

Oetting, E. R. *Journal of Counseling Psychology*, 1967, **14**, 382.

Perry. W. G., Jr. *Forms of Intellectual and Ethical Development in the College Years*, New York: Holt, Rinehart and Winston, 1970.

# 15
# Student Organizations and Activities

JAN M. CARLSON

Under the heading of "student organizations and activities" is incorporated a wide range of programming which effects the students' out-of-class lives. Some activities have a base in the curricular offerings of an institution and may supplement the academic environment. Others may seem to be serving the sole purpose of providing distractions for the students. Between these extremes are a variety of other activities in which the students become involved as part of their collegiate experience.

It is recognized that many significant activities of students occur through small friendship-based groups outside the institutional milieu; however, this chapter does not attempt to deal with these. It is the intent rather, to examine those student activities and organizations that operate within the institutional setting and with which there is an interaction of students and staff. Even with this limitation, there is great diversity of organizations and activities in which students become involved. The extracurricular life of students, with its diversity, is a reflection of their varied interests. Associational groups that are formed serve to meet the needs and interests of the students. The rise and decline of student organizations and activities provide a barometer of student interests and concerns. The student personnel professional must be sensitive to changes in the student extracurricular life in order to work effectively with student groups.

It is not possible to outline a standard pattern for the administration of all student activity programs. The variations from campus to campus are too numerous to present every type of administrative system that has been implemented. The areas of student activities examined in this section are those of student organizations, student government, the fraternity–sorority systems, and campus entertainment.

The models used for this examination of student organizations and activities have been Hurst's Conceptual Foundation for Student Affairs, the Hurst and Duncan model for "Student Affairs Intervention Programs" (1980), and the Morrill, Oetting, and Hurst 1974 model for counselor intervention. From these models have come the style of intervention to be used in this chapter. These are program development, consultation, administration, and training, although other interventions may be appropriate from time to time.

Figure 1 illustrates the areas described and the type of intervention that may be utilized.

## STUDENT ORGANIZATIONS

Student organizations on campuses reflect a broad spectrum of student interests and concerns. Larger institutions may have hundreds of student groups, each with its own specific objectives and constituencies. Group size varies also as widely as do the interests reflected by student groups. Small groups vie with organizations of 100 or more members for space, resources, and membership. Students may form organizations which rise to preeminence rapidly, attract large numbers of students for short periods, and then pass from the campus scene just as swiftly as they came. Other organizations, founded years ago, have persevered

| | Program development | Consultation | Administration | Training |
|---|---|---|---|---|
| Student organizations | X | X | X | X |
| Student government | X | X | X | X |
| Fraternities and sororities | X | X | X | X |

**Figure 1** Interventions in student activities.

and remained stable. Groups may undergo a continuing ebb and flow of both membership and activity, depending to a large degree upon their leadership and the relevance of the group's objectives to the student constituency. Variations may be seen from the perspective of effective continuing leadership within the group. A strong group probably has

Figure 1 illustrates the areas described and the type of intervention

## Types of Student Organizations

There are some broad categories that may be utilized to describe the types of student organizations that exist on most campuses:

**1** Honorary and recognition societies.
**2** Recreational–sports clubs.
**3** Religious organizations.
**4** International groups.
**5** Departmental organizations.
**6** Political groups.
**7** Special interest organizations.

Not all student organizations fit neatly into one of the above categories. A particular group may have purposes that transcend these categories and could therefore be placed under more than one heading. Also, the purpose cited by a group may differ from those reflected in the group's activities and a group may change its purposes over time. The significance of the activities of students through their organizational life is that they can provide valuable insights into the change of student interests and concerns.

Each category of student activity groups has certain characteristics and functions that are important to recognize. Honorary and recognition societies are some of the earliest student groups to be active on campus. The attraction of these groups is twofold. They serve a social function in which students can interact with other students with common interests and abilities. Membership in honoraries, and to a lesser degree, affiliation with recognition societies, provides a valued notation on resumes. Some honorary and recognition societies also present educational programs for members and service projects for the campus which also serve to attract members.

The rapid growth in the popularity of recreational and sports clubs is a recent development in student activities, although many such groups have long traditions on campus. Since the earliest days of higher education, students have engaged in sports and recreational activities, but popularity of these activities in recent years has brought expansion in the type of activities in this area, as well as the number of students involved. Sports clubs differ from recreational organizations in that the sports clubs have a program that stresses the competitive aspects of a sport, especially at the intercollegiate level. The recreational groups tend to be more oriented to the noncompetitive activities. Both types of groups may place a heavy emphasis on skill building for new members. An example of this dual role may be a ski club which offers opportunities for both recreational and competitive skiing.

Student religious organizations have very different roles on college campuses depending on the type of institution—private denominational or state supported. The student religious group in a private denominational institution may be a welcomed adjunct to the purposes of the institution. In the public institution, the place of the religious group becomes more complex, depending on the institution's interpretation of the separation of church and state doctrine. In some state institutions, student religious groups are granted the same status as any other campus group, whereas other institutions severely limit the access of religious groups to facilities on the campus. Another difference that is notable within the religious group area is the differential between the church related groups and those that have a nondenominational thrust. On many campuses, the denominational groups have student centers that house the activities of the group. The nondenominational groups are those too small to support a separate facility are the groups most frequently found requesting the use of on-campus facilities.

Student organizations that are becoming increasingly more visible on campus are those groups that are internationally oriented. When the number of international students on campus was relatively small, most of the student organizational activity was oriented toward the promotion of international understanding with students from the United States. Groups were formed to bring U.S. students into contact with international students in order to provide social and educational benefits for all. All international students tended to be grouped together with little concern as to their national origin. Recently, the influx of international students has resulted in there being sufficient numbers of students from one nation or area of the world to form national identity groups. This process has tended to cluster groups of international students by their national origin, thereby breaking down objectives that spoke to the interchange of national cultures. In addition, a large number of students from one nation or area of the world has brought to the American campus a microcosm of the problems that take place back in the student's native land. This work with international student groups poses a number of unique and exciting challenges for student activities.

One of the most stable areas of the student extracurricular life comes from those groups designated as academic departmentally sponsored organizations. These groups frequently have a high level of faculty involvement in their programs. This involvement provides a stability and continuity for the group's objectives and programs.

The popularity of political groups has waxed and waned over the past years. Organizations representing the major political parties become very active during state and federal elections, but may be dormant at other times. Some groups represent the spectrum of political thinking whereas others serve as vehicles for the promotion of specific issues. These latter groups may stimulate a great deal of activity for a brief period and then decline rapidly depending on the strength of the leadership, the group's purposes, and its ability to attract attention to itself and carry out its programs. The political sphere has not retained the prominence that it had during the late 1960s and early 1970s, but it could revive if issues of compelling student interest were to surface once again.

The category of special interest groups is a general one, encompassing a wide variety of student interests. These organizations are founded to serve the special needs of groups of students. These groups are often small and transitory, although some have large memberships and a long, proud tradition on campus. Often the student leadership component plays a critical role in the continuing viability of these groups.

## Purposes of Student Organizations

Student organizations serve a number of purposes for the student on a campus. They serve to promote student concerns and interests through an organizational setting. They provide students with a valuable opportunity to experience leadership through involvement in the tasks necessary for the maintenance and development of the organization, and they promote skill building. Student groups also serve as identity groups for students on campus and provide a vital social function, wherein students can interact with one another in an informal atmosphere.

The work of the student activities professional with student groups has tended toward an administrative model of record keeping and policy interpretation, although recently there has been an increasing emphasis placed on developmental programming (Williamson, 1961). The record-keeping function has entailed the establishment of methods whereby the records of the organizations (officers, constitutions, faculty advisors) are kept current. In addition, a responsibility of a student activities office has been to work with newly established groups in the gaining of official institutional recognition. These administrative functions provide a tremendous opportunity to meet with both new and established groups to discuss their goals, plans, and problems. These contacts also provide the staff member with an opportunity to share with the students the services that are available through student activities. It is important for the student activities staff member to recognize that regular contacts of this nature need not be just routine, but can serve as an opportunity to develop ongoing contacts with the student groups.

The function of interpreting institutional regulations also provides developmental opportunities in the staff's contact with students. It is not sufficient for the staff to know the institution's policies and regulations, but also to interpret them to students. The staff member should be prepared to explore alternatives should a group's activity fall outside institutional guidelines. The student activities staff must be aware of the purposes of any organization and be prepared to work with the group members in exploring program options available to the group. Often, the staff member can serve as a resource to students when, following an interpretation of a policy, they are able to discuss what other alternatives will meet the needs of a group but not conflict with the institutional policy. Thus the administrative component of student activities can serve to promote program development and consultation activities.

## Staff Involvement with Student Organizations

The use of administrative functions is a creative way to establish contacts with groups and become active in an organization's program planning. Another way of achieving the same result is to schedule meetings with the officers and faculty advisors of student groups throughout the year. In doing this, the staff members should plan the agenda to be discussed. This agenda should cover such items as the group's program plans, purposes and problems, as well as covering the services provided through student activities. These meetings should be structured in a way that will allow for the students and faculty advisors a maximum of input. Meetings of this type can be instrumental in the establishment of contacts between the students and the staff. Another way to gain knowledge and familiarity with campus groups is to ask to attend a meeting of the organization. This provides an opportunity to observe the group in action while providing visibility for the staff. These meetings can also be used to facilitate future contacts with the groups. By attending group meetings, the staff member moves from the confines of the student activities office into the places where the students are, and a professional in student activities should not become trapped into the routine of an 8:00 a.m. to 5:00 p.m. day spent in the office (Wise, 1978).

If involvement in student activities is to be one in which learning takes place, it is incumbent upon the student activities staff to work with students in making this learning as meaningful as possible. One way this can be accomplished is by the use of a consultation model in the planning process of student groups. In program planning, the student activities specialist may be involved as a resource or facilitator to the group. The student activities professional, following observation of a group's functioning, may determine that either process or content interventions would be most effective. A content intervention is one in which the staff member proposes ideas that can be considered and discussed with the others already put forth. In this manner, the staff member joins the group members in proposing alternatives to be considered. The staff member must be cognizant of the fact that his or her content interventions may hold implicit authority and therefore could inhibit, as well as facilitate, the student decision-making process. In process intervention, the staff member and students examine the manner in which the group functions and how the members interact. In many cases, a process intervention can help a group to achieve excellent outcomes in program planning through assessing how the group functions.

Serving as a resource for student groups is an important role played by staff members. Students can become frustrated in their planning if they are unable to acquire necessary information. The staff member may have the needed information or may have knowledge of where the students can obtain the information. The staff member can be a helpful resource for student groups, but should not deprive the students of the opportunity to seek out information on their own.

Training is another part of the work with students in a learning environment. Training may utilize a number of formats from individualized training with officers of specific group to working with several organizations at the same time. Different groups have very different needs and a training approach can be utilized to meet the need of one group or a number of groups with similar needs. Information on the student organizational needs for training can be gathered by attending the meetings of student organizations, by consulting with officers of the groups, or by instituting surveys of student groups to ascertain their needs. Training may be viewed as skill building and information dissemination, and both can be very useful for student groups. Some areas in which training can be used for large groups are as follows:

1 **Goal setting:** Examining organizational goals and objectives to assist in the development of programs that are consistent with the purpose of the group.
2 **Leadership:** The training of students in the various aspects of leadership and examining the dynamics of groups, leadership styles, and skills of a leader.
3 **Communication:** Examination of verbal, nonverbal, and written communication, listening and feedback, and ways in which communication can be enhanced.
4 **Personal Growth:** Oriented toward heightening personal self-awareness and enhancing interpersonal relationships.

These topics cover some broad areas that can be presented for individual students or groups. In addition, there are a number of workshop topics that are more specific and would appeal to certain individuals or organizations:

1 Publicity
2 Financial Planning
3 Time management
4 Conducting meetings
5 Parlimentary procedure
6 Faculty advisement of student groups
7 Program evaluation

Workshops on these and other topics of interest to students can be organized by the student activities staff. The decisions about the topics for workshops should be based on assessments of student needs. Although the student activities staff may organize the workshops for student organizations, it is not necessary that the staff have the responsibility of conducting these workshops. It would be unusual for a staff to have sufficient expertise in all areas to be able to facilitate every type of workshop. The student activities staff member does need to be aware of available campus resources. A survey of the student affairs staff and faculty will point out the individuals with the skills needed to conduct various types of workshops for student groups.

The process used in student activities work with student organizations, whether it be administrative, consultation, program development, or training, should maintain the position that the student's growth and development are central to every aspect of student activities. Administrative requirements must facilitate rather than impede student organizational development. The process of administering a student activities program offers an opportunity for the staff to have contact with the student groups. Consultation and program development with student groups are central to all activities programming. Although not all programs necessarily must be initiated by the students, the work with organizations should reflect the group's purposes, not those of the staff. Skill building in the training of student leaders is another important intervention that the student activities professional can develop with students in response to their needs.

One other aspect of student activities work is the relationship that can be developed with the faculty. The recognition and use of faculty resources is an important aspect of student activities. In some instances the faculty can be utilized through the application of their skills toward a training program for student groups. Faculty serving as organizational advisors may need support, recognition, and information about institutional expectations and their responsibilities. Faculty members have traditionally played a vital role in the students' extracurricular lives and continue to be an important source of assistance to student activities.

## STUDENT GOVERNMENT

It is tempting to consider student government as just one of the many organizations of students. Certainly, the need for administrative intervention, consultation, program development, and training is as important in working with student government as it is with other student groups. Student government does, however, have a unique position vis-à-vis other student organizations. The advising responsibilities are, on many campuses, delegated to staff of the office of student activities. Student governments have wide ranging responsibilities in the allocation of student fees. On some campuses, they may have no responsibility for student fee allocation whereas on others, student government has a strong voice in determining how the student fee money is spent. Student government may also be visible on campus as the representative of student concerns and positions on issues.

Student government has experienced periods of great influence and great decline over the years. Initially formed as a laboratory for students in the policital arts, student governments have grown strong on some campuses through continued vital leadership, whereas at other institutions, student governments have become weak and ineffectual.

Working with student government should involve an awareness of the political environment of the students. It can also stimulate the recognition of student government's need for a publicity approach in order to promote the visibility of student government services. The staff member assigned to student government must be aware of campus politics and the use of publicity in order to assist the student government leaders in gaining needed visibility.

Owing to the elective nature of the student government executives and respresentatives, it is necessary to develop and implement training programs which aid in the continuity from one administration to another (Carlson, 1980). These training programs should be a joint project of staff and the student leadership. Training programs can consist of a formal workshop approach and informal sessions with new executive officers to include information related to the following:

1 The structure of the institution.
2 The role of student government.
3 The structure of student government.
4 The institution's fiscal policies.
5 Basic leadership training.
6 Goal setting.
7 Parlimentary procedure.
8 Writing bills.
9 Publicity.
10 Surveying a constituency.
11 Program evaluation.

Student governments differ widely from institution to institution and these differences influence the staff's style of interaction with the student government leaders. The most generally utilized approach would be that of consultation with specific instances calling for administrative, program development, and training approaches. The most effective approaches are those that encourage student government members to recognize their potential as vital components in the institution's decision-making process and allow for the student "voice" to be heard in the most effective manner.

An important yet frequently ignored component of student government is those students serving on institutional committees (Stroup, 1965). The call for "student power" of the 1960s opened up opportunities for students to serve on many faculty and administrative committees. Too often, the students selected for those bodies found the work unrewarding and tedious rather than exciting and meaningful. This disillusionment may be reflective of the lack of preparation the students received prior to their appointment and lack of support received following their selection. The staff member working with student government should be alert to the problems confronted by committee appointees and encourage student government offices to train student appointees before appointments and to continue the training process after the appointees are selected.

The process of working with student government requires all the skills necessary for working with any student group, plus sensitivity to political issues and an awareness of the potential student government has to be positive force on campus. The organization of student government affords tremendous opportunities for significant training and program development with students.

## THE FRATERNITY AND SORORITY SYSTEM

Recently there has been a trend in student affairs to eliminate the offices of dean of men and women and to shift the responsibilities of these areas elsewhere. It is not uncommon to find Greek activities organized under an office of student activities. This change has given new dimensions to the student activities area. The work with fraternities and sororities demands a certain amount of administrative work in institutions where the Greek system is a living option.

The work of the student activities staff with the Greek system involves administration, program development, consultation, and training. The administration component is relatively heavy in working with Greek groups. As a living option for students and the unique relationship of the fraternity system to the institution, the staff may become involved in policies related to rush, transferring, social activities, chaperonage, and a host of other record-keeping and administrative functions. These functions must be periodically reviewed to assess if the requirements are a burden for the students or are taking a disproportionate amount of staff time. Those administrative areas that facilitate the organization's realization of its objectives are of value and can be useful tools to increase staff interaction with students.

The program development thrust of student activities occurs at several levels. It certainly must be an ingredient of work with the governing group or groups that coordinate Greek activities. The facilitation of this group planning process is of great importance. The staff member may serve a crucial role in working with the students in recognizing the potential of their governing body. Since the membership of the governing body is made up of representatives of each fraternity and sorority, the development of cooperation and goals for the governing group is a major thrust for the staff, and frequently is difficult.

An area that will require examination is the program orientation of many fraternities and sororities. The emphasis of the activities in many Greek houses is geared to the underclassman. This orientation can result in a lessening of interest in the activities of the chapter by the time the students reach their junior and senior years. When this situation occurs, there may be a noticeable attrition of upperclassmen from the affairs of the house and leadership is turned over to freshmen and sophomores. The lowerclassmen in this position may be very able, but lack the experience needed to keep the chapter operating at its highest level. Another area that must be examined is how the Greek system can be responsive to a wider variety of individuals and interests. Many houses have opened up their doors to minority students, but additional work must be done to get the system to relate to the needs of nontraditional students.

Fraternities and sororities have traditionally placed heavy emphasis upon the social aspects of programming. Although the social component of Greek living will probably always play an important role, it must be supplemented by other types of programming that will attract and retain members. This poses an exciting challenge to staff in program development within the Greek system and individual houses.

The staff member working with the fraternity system works on several levels. They work with the student governing group in developing programs and policies for the entire system. In this capacity, the staff serves in a consultative manner, providing information, strengthening the group's ability to work together, and working with the students to organize training programs for its members. At the chapter level, there are a variety of functions undertaken by the staff members. The staff is involved in administrative activities related to the operations of the houses and the chapter activities. The staff may work in a consultative manner on areas of concern ranging from the health inspection of cooks to planning a chapter dance. The staff is also involved with individudal members through individual work with the officers and with the membership.

Training is an integral aspect of work with the Greek system, and goes on at all levels of interaction. Training can be formalized and involve the governing group, or can be planned with the individual chapter houses. There is also a less formal aspect of training that goes on through the staff interaction with individual members. This training function is very important in houses confronted with the loss of upperclass leadership, and the need for freshmen and sophomores to assume the chapter leadership.

The major thrust of student activity work with the fraternities and sororities is directed toward governing groups, the campus chapters, and members, but there are other appropriate points at which interventions occur. The staff will have contacts with national offices, alumni (ae), and resident supervisors and housemothers. These groups are part of the entire system, yet they represent very different concerns and their influence varies from campus to campus.

As a part of the student activities area, the inclusion of Greek activities is very recent. It is evident that by including fraternity and sorority advisement in student activities, there are several changes that could result. One change will certainly be the placing of greater emphasis upon program development as a thrust for the Greek system. Another change that will eventually occur will be the breaking down of the tradition of having a male staff member working with fraternities and a woman with sororities. The notion that the sex of the staff member is a criterion for successful interaction with students does not take into account the skills of the staff. It is more important to have the Greek system able to utilize a wide variety of staff expertise than to assign staff on the basis of sex. This change will be slow to be accepted by the groups, but will eventually have the effect of being of greater benefit to all the groups.

## ASSESSMENT AND EVALUATION

The advent of student development as a model for student personnel services has provided a new and exciting perspective for student activities. A posture of reaction and enforcement has been replaced by a proactive model in which true student–staff partnership can exist. Essential components in the concept of student development are the understanding of the influence of the campus environment on the students and the opportunity for the students to reshape their learning and cocurricular environments. Traditional approaches to advisement need not be completely discarded, but can be modified to avoid vestiges of paternalism and move into modes of consultation and training.

One of the primary functions necessary to provide for a comprehensive program is that of investigation. The student activities professional must be able to support comprehensive and specific research projects aimed at determining what the critical components of student life on the campus are and how the total campus environment and the student characteristics mesh to maximize the total development of the students.

In order for student activities to effectively work with students, there must be a continuous appraisal made of the campus environment as well as assessments of the entire student population and campus subgroups.

The process of assessment is a vital element of student development in that it provides information on the students which can be used to determine the direction and type of interventions that will be most appropriate. Information gathered from assessments should be utilized in the consultation process with student groups. It is necessary to have a variety of data about students, in order to determine the programs that will best serve the students' needs. The gathering and the sharing of this information is a basis upon which a vital program of student activities can be developed and maintained.

Another basic element of student activities is evaluation of programs and personnel. The demands for accountability stress the utilization of evaluation techniques, yet servicing a system of accountability should not be the sole reason for evaluation. It should be a tool that can be utilized to strengthen programs and people. The student activities professional works with individuals and groups in the development of program goals and then employs evaluation techniques to determine how well the goals were met, the strengths and weaknesses of the program, and methods by which the program can be improved. Evaluation of individuals, both students and staff, can be used as guides for personal growth.

It may not be necessary for each staff person in student activities to have all the skills needed for assessment and evaluation, but each should have an awareness of the uses of the data once gathered. The student activities staff members should have access to the staff with assessment and evaluation skills and should use them as resources.

The student activities professional must understand the nature of assessment and evaluation in order to interpret this area to other administrators and the students. These are two very vital tools in examining a program's strengths or weaknesses and can point out ways that will enhance the student activities program now and in the future.

## CONCLUSION

The staff member in student activities plays a unique role in student affairs. The staff member must be responsive to the needs of students, while not losing sight of the professional obligations of the job. The staff member must be able to interpret the institutional position on various issues to the students and may be asked to present the "student view" to the administration. He or she must be administrator, teacher, and program developer. The staff member must be aware of the different values of the students while serving as a role model for them. In many areas, the staff member must serve as a generalist, although having sufficient skills in other areas to be seen as a specialist.

The role of the staff member in student activities is varied but requires some specific skills and knowledge. Probably the most critical skill in student activities is the ability to communicate effectively with college-age persons. This communication must be open and honest and involve active listening skills. The students must feel free to express their ideas and opinions. The staff member must be committed to the concept of student involvement in all aspects of student activities and the concept that students can and should have an impact on their environment.

The staff member must have knowledge of administration and management. Regardless of the nature of the student activities program, all programs have budgetary requirements and the staff member must understand the budget process and financial management. The administration component of student activities can be an avenue by which continued student contact is maintained and through which beneficial learnings for students take place.

In the program development aspect of student activities, the staff will have greatest involvement. The thrust of program development is to encourage the students to utilize their creative potential in planning activities that meet the needs and interests of students. A constant caution for the staff member in student activities is that programs should be student initiated and the continued involvement of students in all aspects of the program is essential.

The model of consultation used in student activities work may vary according to the nature of the group and the skills of the staff member (Blake and Mouton, 1976). The staff member must utilize different consultative techniques that will facilitate the students' achieving their own objectives. Each group of students is going to have expectations of the approach used by the staff member and these expectations may not coincide with the staff member's style or the approach that is believed to be the most productive. In these instances, the staff member has the responsibility of making the students aware of the role that will be played.

In program planning and consultation, there is an additional issue to be considered, that is, concern for successful outcomes. The measures of success for a specific program may be attendance, participation, or some quantifiable measure, yet for the student activities staff member, the quality of the student planning process may be as vital a measure of success. Thus when evaluation takes place it must include recognition and measurement of both quantity and quality if an accurate picture of the activity is to be achieved.

Training is an aspect of the work of student activities that takes place through formal and informal interaction. Without an understanding and appreciation of the potential for training of students, the work of student activities is only half done. There are innumerable opportunities for training in student activities: the use of workshops and seminars to aid students in doing their jobs more effectively, instruction in areas like arts and crafts, and close individual contacts on projects of interest to the student.

Student activities is an area in which there is a tremendous opportunity to provide experiences that encourage the development of students. The history of higher education demonstrates the desire of the students to have an impact on their own lives and this desire should be a primary concern for student activities. The opportunity to work with students in their efforts to have a meaningful impact upon their environments and develop their own skills at the same time makes the work of student activities challenging and exciting.

## REFERENCES

Blake, R. R. and J. S. Mouton *Consultation*. Reading, Mass.: Addison-Wesley Publishing Company, 1976.

Carlson, J. and T. M. Keys A structured program for student government. Unpublished work on the pattern for a workshop for student government leaders. May, 1978.

Hurst, J. C. The emergence of student/environment development as the conceptual foundation for student affairs. *Current Issues in Student Development*. American College Personnel Association Monograph, 1980.

Morrill, W. H., E. R. Oetting, and J. C. Hurst Dimensions of counselor functioning. *Personnel and Guidance Journal*, 1974, **52** (6), 354–359.

Stroup, H. *Toward a Philosophy of Organized Student Activities*. Minneapolis: University of Minnesota Press, 1965.

Williamson, E. G. *Student Personnel Services in Colleges and Universities*. New York: McGraw-Hill Book Company, 1961.

Wise, W. M. Conversations about organized student activities in colleges. *The NASPA Journal*, 1978, **15** (3), 2–10.

# 16

# Reading and Study Skills Programs

A. GARR CRANNEY AND TED PACKARD

Many adults are poor readers. A Texas study (Northcut et al., 1975) found that 23 million adult Americans, one-fifth of the adult population of the United States, have difficulty coping with reading tasks associated with shopping, getting a driver's license, or reading an insurance policy. Another 39 million are estimated to have reading skills that allow them to "just get by" as workers, consumers, citizens, and parents. Although evolving criteria for functional literacy do not permit accurate estimates, there are also large numbers of poor readers currently enrolled in post-secondary schools.

A national survey (Roueche and Snow, 1977) of public higher education indicated that 86 percent of the institutions are providing special services for the academically disadvantaged. Even highly selective institutions such as Berkeley, Stanford, and Harvard provide reading and study skills services to thousands of students each year. Although 2-year community colleges have generally developed the most comprehensive programs, virtually all campuses now provide reading and study skills services of some type.

Administratively such services take many forms. Most commonly, particularly in community colleges, they are aligned with departments of English. Substantial numbers are included with counseling services or colleges of education. A few such programs are associated with libraries. More recently with the growing acceptance of granting credit for skills instruction, separately budgeted divisions or departments of developmental studies have begun to appear.

Staffing patterns and training programs for reading and study skills specialists are less clear-cut. As a group, teachers of reading and study skills have diverse backgrounds including English, education, psychology, and counseling. Until the mid-1970s specific teacher training programs for adult reading and study skills were almost nonexistent. According to a recent survey (Cranney, 1976), however, adult reading teacher training courses are appearing in greater number in college catalogs. A significant current challenge to the field is to develop quality university-level training programs for reading and study skills educators who can then work with the wide range of college students requiring or requesting such services.

## PURPOSES OF READING AND STUDY SKILLS SERVICE

Because of the mixed backgrounds of reading and study skills specialists and the varied administrative settings in which they work, there is general lack of agreement concerning "missions" for such services. Further, there is not unanimous agreement among authorities on what is meant by "reading" or "study skills." In a classic presentation, Spache (1969) presented many definitions of reading that varied from a simple decoding process to reading as an extension of personality, self-concept, and related sociological implications. Similarly, study skills training to some is a prescriptive, mechanical "how-to-do-it" activity. To others, often from counseling backgrounds, study styles and practices are a delicate interweaving of personal and value factors that are highly individualistic.

From the counseling psychologist's viewpoint the development of coping behaviors is paramount. How can skills of reading rate, comprehension, time use, and exam preparation, for example, be developed so the student can better respond to the demands of the environment and the curriculum? The development of the student's self-concept is a related special concern given that a number of evaluation studies indicate this to be a characteristic of effective reading and study skills programs (Roueche and Snow, 1977; Fairbanks, 1974).

Other criteria must also receive attention given the current widespread emphasis in our society on accountability. For example, can it be specifically demonstrated that reading and study skills training is transferable to performance in various other areas of the educational curricula? Do such programs have positive effects on academic grades, retention in school, or progress towards a degree? Do students from educationally disadvantaged backgrounds enrolled in these programs more frequently complete degree or certificate programs than those who are not? Although implementers of reading and study skills programs may question the value of such global criteria, program effectiveness must be regularly evaluated using multiple criteria including those noted above. A balance must be continually sought between the admirable philosophical idealism of program developers and the ultra-pragmatic definitions of program mission formulated by policy makers and those controlling budgetary purse strings.

Some appropriate specific areas for investigation are as follows:

1 **Surveys of Reading Skills of Entering College Students:** Diagnostic and placement tests are widely required in admissions and preregistration procedures. These offer many opportunities for useful research concerning the variety and level of student skills in reading and study skills areas.
2 **Studies of Skills within Various Academic Curricula:** Establishment of specific local norms is useful within subject specialities. Engineering, education, law, and medical students have different learning demands and often different reading and study skills profiles.
3 **Studies of Skills within Specialized Trade–Technical Program Curricula:** Related to this are studies of specific skill needs of special occupational groups. Occupational task analyses can identify needs for skills such as skimming and scanning, comprehension for details, or specialized vocabulary development within a given trade–technical area.
4 **Evaluation Data of Various Types:** Student self-report reaction to instruction, pre–post-test data in reading, G.P.A. follow-up studies, and retention progress in school are examples of outcome studies.
5 **Other Descriptive and Specific Studies:** Additional potentially useful research questions include: Who uses the services? How did they find out about the services? How long did they come? Why did they stop coming? How do skill scores relate to other measures such as achievement, ability, or personality variables?
6 **Evaluation of Instructional Method:** Group counseling, individual teaching or laboratory versus classroom approaches are examples of instructional methods used. A substantial body of literature already exists in the field of adult reading and study skills describing each of these varying approaches. Much less is known about the relative effectiveness under differing conditions of the various learning modalities. For example, some learners seem to learn better by listening than by reading.
7 **Studies of the "Readability" of Textbooks and Other Instructional**

**Materials:** As many studies have shown, teachers sometimes select textbooks too difficult for the reading skills of their students. Data-based evidence can influence instructors' selection of reading materials.

8 **Evaluative Studies of Reading and Study Skills Psychometric Instruments:** Reliability and validity issues continue to be associated with many instruments and present opportunities for additional standardization research. In addition, new approaches to the teaching of reading and study skills may be most effectively evaluated through development of new instruments.

The reading and study skills specialist should be thoroughly familiar with the curriculum and the specific demands and goals of the learner. When the skills improvement services are available only on a noncredit voluntary basis, student motivation becomes a more important concern. In such situations it is imperative that the reading and study skills specialist act to identify specific skill areas in need of development and then quickly begin intervention efforts at opportune times.

When significant numbers of students are identified as having skill deficits, it is often appropriate to attempt intervening at the curriculum level. For example, when it is apparent that a group of students is reading below the tenth percentile rank on university norms, there are implications for the pace of instruction, examination time limits, the reading level of exams themselves, and textbook selection. Team teaching involving regular instructors and reading specialists can be a particularly effective approach in such situations.

The timing of interventions is important. Early in the fall term of the freshman year students are often receptive to invitations from reading and study skills services. Short workshop-type sessions focusing on preparation for examinations that occur toward the end of the academic term are often well attended. Students in academic difficulty often respond to invitations extended at the beginning of the second term after one set of grades has been received. Upper-division students preparing for graduate school examinations respond to specific exam preparation workshops as testing dates approach.

An understanding of the student environment beyond the curriculum has relevance to the reading and study skills specialist. Students are more likely to complete academic programs if they attend colleges with cohesive peer environments characterized by close relationships among students (Astin and Panos, 1969). A summary of many studies concerning these more general environmental variables suggests that student achievement and aspiration are enhanced in an atmosphere supportive of relationship and personal development dimensions (Roueche and Snow, 1977). Environmental assessment thus has excellent potential in assisting reading and study skills specialists in their work.

## INTERVENTIONS

Intervention to facilitate adult reading and study skills development can occur on many levels. At the individual level most colleges and universities provide walk-in voluntary services as part of their offerings for students. These can be scheduled at the convenience of students, and entry and termination can be at any time. Coordinated diagnostic testing, and counseling resources are also generally available on a demand basis.

Structured small groups with a study skills emphasis are often offered as time-limited workshops (e.g., two or three sessions each of 2 hours duration). Popular topics include exam prepartion (near examination time) or broader subjects such as test anxiety. Practice and research suggests that study skills groups work best when they are focused on specific topics and are clearly structured (Bednar and Weinberg, 1970).

Large group meetings in which college entrance test profiles are interpreted, using trained aides and slide–tape presentations, are often useful. These can acquaint students with their learning and reading skills potential, alert them to problems, and orient them to the availability of reading and study skills services.

A variety of involvements with associational groups are also possible. The reputation of the reading and study skills program spread from student to student is a powerful influence on overall student usage. Invitations to make presentations at fraternities and sororities, dormitory groups, preprofessional clubs such as law or medicine, or other associational groups often result in additional numbers of students receiving learning skills assistance. Small groups of student athletes who receive tutorial assistance in specific subject matter areas are also representative of interventions with associational groups. Learning skills specialists can also play a role in athletic recruiting by evaluating potential athletic scholarship recipients in skill areas and making recommendations for their academic programs.

Beyond the campus, widespread opportunities for involvement with adult programs are available. Various adult education offerings, church-related literacy programs, and English instruction for the foreign born are examples. The Laubach system (Laubach and Laubach,

1960) and its materials are credited with teaching more than 40 million people how to read by the "each one teach one" procedures. Community YMCA's and business and industrial firms offer various self-improvement courses to employees and interested participants. Some libraries provide learning skills services, as do labor unions and specially funded vocational programs such as Job Corps or CETA. Commercial speed reading courses are widespread and frequently have study skills components. Spache's definitive evaluation (Spache, 1962) indicates, however, that these courses primarily teach skimming and scanning and that many of their claims have little validity.

Purposes of intervention are well described in Chapters 5 and 7 of this text. There is no question that remedial concerns have provided the major impetus to growth of reading and learning skills services in the last decade. This has been particularly so in 4 year and graduate institutions as pressures to provide educational opportunities to previously inadmissible students have brought outside funding and significant program growth. Students needing remedial assistance are sometimes identified, pretested, and provided special services the summer before the fall term of their freshman year. Though carefully designed studies indicating substantial gains over a single academic term are not available, evidence is mounting that longer-term comprehensive remedial programs are effective in helping students with initially marginal skills to remain in school and make progress toward a degree (Roueche and Snow, 1977). Roueche and Snow also report that trained counselor participation as teachers of remedial services is a recent trend and is characteristic of such successful programs.

The prevention role for such services is evidenced by widespread student interest in examination preparation workshops focusing on specific test batteries. Many campuses offer workshops in preparing for exams such as General Educational Development tests, Graduate Record Examination, or various aptitude tests for professional training programs such as law or medicine. Students with such interest will sometimes appear several terms in advance of the anticipated testing date requesting assistance in preparing for such exams.

Significant numbers of students can be attracted to preventive work on reading and study skills through use of diagnostic screening batteries. Being made aware of their skill levels through classroom or other testing, they often voluntarily enroll in services to upgrade reading skills and enhance study techniques.

Most pre-freshmen year surveys indicate that the desire for reading and study skills help is second only to concerns about financial aid. Reading and study skills specialists can use such information in preventive programming that takes place during the weeks of initial registration.

Developmental concerns in this service area are widespread, particularly when voluntary programs exist. There are large numbers of students on every campus who have strong motivation for self-improvement. These are frequently higher achieving students with already developed reading and study skills. Such students often respond to advertising through the campus newspaper, orientation presentations, special invitations, notices on bulletin boards, or descriptive brochures. One enterprising staff prepared free bookmarks humorously advertising their service and left them with the cash register clerks at the campus bookstore. Every student who bought a book received one.

The widespread appeal of commercial speed reading courses relates to the development of potential among many who are already skilled readers. Such courses do indeed benefit many but are often suspect in their claims, guarantees, and teaching techniques. They are generally inappropriate for individuals who have severely crippled reading skills (Spache, 1962).

Methods of intervention in the reading and study skills area are also varied. Direct service in one-to-one counseling, classroom, and laboratory teaching are the familiar patterns. Particularly with remedial disadvantaged groups, it is essential that staff (1) have expressed desire to work with students requiring remediation, (2) have received specific training for their role, and (3) are themselves educated to a level congruent with the general expectations of the institution (i.e., usually the doctorate). Unfortunately, one or more of these basic qualifications are sometimes lacking in those assigned to work with such students. Working with students with significant reading and learning disabilities also requires intense dedication and strong social service orientation.

Working in consulting relationships is an increasingly evident pattern by counselors and other reading and study skills specialists. There is substantial use of supervised paraprofessionals, part-time faculty, graduate student, and student clerical help. Particularly in the operation of learning centers and reading laboratories, such staff can be trained to competently work with many students on an individualized basis. Learning skills specialists are then freed to develop new programs, conduct evaluation research, and provide in-service training to others such as dormitory residence counselors. Limited budgets for such programs often provide additional impetus for the development of such consulting functions. If staff with degrees lower than the doctorate are carefully selected, trained, and supervised they can perform well in many aspects of reading and study skills services.

Media use is widespread as a delivery system for such services. Elaborate computer-assisted instructional programs are available. Stanford, Brigham Young, and the University of Texas have utilized various programs of this type. Santa Fe Community College is one of the many 2 year institutions that provide computer-printed learning skills diagnostic information and course selection guidance to students. Most reading and learning skills centers also regularly provide a variety of modules, pacers, and filmstrip devices as practice materials. Phonics and vocabulary programs are available on filmstrips and cassettes, and entire courses are available on video tape through instructionsl television. The Kentucky State Department of Education is currently preparing an adult reading course to be offered via public television. Similar programs exist elsewhere and are in frequent use. Programmed materials, particularly vocabularly development, are available in many reading and learning skills areas. Evaluations of such delivery methods since the 1950s indicate that much of the hardware found in learning centers is not totally necessary to positive instructional outcomes (Kennedy, 1971). But most experts find them useful for *some* instructional objectives and for motivational purposes. Care should be taken, however, that media materials are not inappropriately used. A balanced treatment approach integrating use of such devices has been outlined by Kennedy (1971).

Program assessment and evaluation concerns are of paramount importance. Because of accountability demands and scarcity of funds, it is imperative that the reading and study skills professional constantly attend to program evaluation needs. Programs can be easily challenged, and without data to defend and justify such services, adverse decisions can be precipitously made. Reading and study skills programs must provide evidence to justify their existence or risk termination during times of funding cutbacks.

Results of surveys are worthy of mention since they provide much of the rationale for the field. As previously stated, short-term single criteria studies showing positive results with students with severe reading handicaps are almost nonexistent. However, when broader educational criteria such as long-term persistence in school are used rather than simple pre–post-testing, current service programs seem to be increasingly effective (Rouche and Snow, 1977).

In major surveys of reading and study skills programs Entwistle (1960), Fairbanks (1974), and Roueche and Snow (1977) have isolated characteristics typical of successful programs. The following list of basic recommendations are representative of their conclusions:

1 Combining of reading and study skills offerings.
2 Provision for voluntary services as at least part of the total available programming.
3 Emphasis on reading comprehension skills.
4 Involvement of students in diagnosis and evaluation of their programs.
5 In-class practice time for skills work.
6 Programs of longer than 40 hours duration.
7 Provision for counseling-oriented teachers.
8 Supportive services such as learning centers and peer helpers.
9 Continuing staff development through in-service training.
10 Comprehensive, explicit, written, and personalized objectives that are given to each student and that include both affective and cognitive goals.
11 Systematic instruction and evaluation.

Readers are invited to examine the Fairbanks (1974) and Roueche and Snow (1977) analyses, which provide primary basis for this listing. The Roueche and Snow study in particular provides an optimistic note on working with the reading and study skills of the learning-disabled remedial adult. It should be noted again, however, that short-term controlled studies based on pre–post-reading test data with such students are very scarce. With students functioning at average and higher skill levels, however, research justification for reading and study skills services has accepted and well-documented validity (Fairbanks, 1974). Also see annual research reviews in *Yearbooks of the National Reading Conference).* With the disabled adult learner, however, we are evidently doing better than a decade ago, judging by studies using criteria including progress toward degree and decreased student attrition rates. Happily, with these students we are getting better at what we do.

## REFERENCES

Astin, A. W. and R. Panos *The Educational and Vocational Development of College Students.* Washington, D.C.: American Council on Education, 1969.

Bednar, R. L. and S. L. Weinberg Ingredients of successful treatment programs for underachievers. *Journal of Counseling Psychology,* 1970, **17**, 1–7.

Cranney, A. G. The training of adult reading and study skills specialists. Paper presented at the National Reading Conference, St. Petersburg, Florida, 1976.

Entwistle, D. R. Evaluation of study-skills causes: a review. *Journal of Educational Research,* 1960, **53**, 243–251.

Fairbanks, M. The effect of college reading improvement programs on academic achievement. In P. Nacke (Ed.), *Interaction: Research and practice in college-adult reading.* 23rd Yearbook of the National Reading Conference, Clemson, S. C., 1974.

Kennedy, E. C. *Classroom Approaches to Remedial Reading.* Itasca, Ill.: Peacock Publishing Company, 1971.

Laubach, F. C. and R. S. Laubach *Toward world literacy: The each one teach one way.* Syracuse, N.Y.: Syracuse University Press, 1960.

Northcutt, N. et al. *Adult Functional Competency: A summary.* Austin, Tex.: University of Texas, Extension Division, 1975.

Roueche, J. E. and J. J. Snow *Overcoming Learning Problems.* San Francisco: Jossey-Bass, 1977.

Spache, G. D. Is this a breakthrough in reading? *Reading Teacher,* 1962, **15**, 258–268.

Spache, G. D. Ways of defining the reading process. In *Reading in the elementary school* (2nd ed.). Boston: Allyn and Bacon, 1969.

# 17
# Unique Student Populations

MELBA J. VASQUEZ AND
ERNEST L. CHAVEZ

Students from diverse backgrounds have been historically excluded from higher education. Various factors, including affirmative action and equal opportunity programs, have increased the numbers of these special and unique populations on campuses. Many of these students encounter special problems which often deter from a potentially successful university experience. Identification of the unique needs and concerns of special groups and implementation of appropriate interventions are crucial if student affairs professionals are to be impactful interveners in the university setting. This chapter discusses various issues that are relevant to the understanding of the special concerns of these groups and suggests intervention strategies that could enhance the success of students from diverse backgrounds.

Education is seen as a positive attainment in this country. There is, additionally, a strong ethos that education is a means to socioeconomic mobility. Education is consequently seen as a means of improving the social and economic situation of special, oppressed groups. The United States has thus made a commitment to provide equal education opportunities for all its citizens, which is reflected by a report by the Carnegie commission on higher education (1970, p. 3). It stated:

> The transcendent goal is that inequality in one generation should not, inevitably, be a legacy of succeeding generations. Each young person should have a full chance to demonstrate his intellectual ability and respond to his motivations to excel in constructive endeavor. From a national point of view, we cannot afford

the domestic brain drain of able young persons who, through no fault of their own, are handicapped in making valuable contributions to the life of society.

The commitment of our institutions of higher education to open doors to unique populations is a relatively new one and is partly an outgrowth of the activist movements of the 1960s, and of various judicial and legislative decisions. *Brown v. the Board of Education* is a landmark case which first promoted the desegregation of schools. Title VI of the Elementary and Secondary Education Act, resulting from the Carey committee hearings of 1966, and Section 504 of the Rehabilitation Act of 1973 set the stage for a national commitment to the rights of the handicapped individual (Martin, 1976; Dailey, 1978). The passage of some form of an equal rights amendment in many states, and the women's rights movement in general, have had a profound effect on the role of women in our society.

Opening university doors for special groups has not been sufficient in the attempt to raise educational levels. Institutions are subsequently recognizing the humanitarian responsibility of responding to the special needs of these groups to help facilitate and enhance their success. A review and identification of some of the problems encountered by these unique populations will illustrate some of the special needs which, if responded to, could help ensure success.

## THE TARGET GROUPS

Unique student populations in colleges and universities may be identified by their special characteristics and needs. Various populations have been identified as having unique needs, including ethnic minorities, women, older returning students (including women, veterans, retired and/or career change men and women), the physically disabled, and international students. Other groups such as married students, transfer students, and commuters may be considered unique on some campuses.

### Ethnic Minorities

Ethnic minorities in universities and colleges generally continue to be underrepresented and have high attrition rates. The relatively low numbers of ethnic minorities continue to perpetuate the low educational attainment which is evident at all levels of education. Ninety percent of the white teenagers in the United States graduate from high school; the comparable figures for minorities are 65 percent for blacks, and only 27 percent and 25 percent for Chicanos and Puerto Ricans, respectively (Fact Sheets on Institutional Racism, 1975). The figures concerning the educational attainment of ethnic minorities in higher education are similar. More than one-third (35.8 percent) of the whites between the ages of eighteen and twenty-one were enrolled in college in 1971 compared to only one-fifth (20.9 percent) of the black population (U.S. Department of Commerce, 1972).

There is evidence that the minority freshman enrollment may have reached a plateau or is on the brink of a decrease. Sedlacek and Webster (1978) monitored trends for 8 years and reported that black freshmen enrollment at large major universities increased from 3 percent in 1969 to 6 percent in 1973, but was down to 5 percent in 1976. Nonblack minority enrollment remains at less than 2 percent for any group, with 1975 figures reflecting 1.3 percent for Hispanic Americans, 0.8 percent for Asian Americans, and 0.3 percent for American Indians.

Attrition rates for ethnic minorities in general in colleges and universities are higher than those for whites. A report in the *Chronicle of Higher Education* (1975), for example, revealed that only one in four chicanos who entered college graduated; this ratio can be compared to the one in two for anglos.

Minority underrepresentation and attrition rates thus continue to contribute to the relative social and economic powerlessness of these groups in this country. Additionally, those ethnic minority students who do persevere often experience alienation and isolation from the majority of the student population. This alienation can serve to increase the anxiety that any new student feels upon entering a new institution, thus increasing the probability that the unique student will feel socially ostracized. Newcombe (1961) and Kerchoff and Davis (1962) have shown that interpersonal attraction is significantly affected by the similarity of attitudes, values, and interests. The unique individual, because of differing values and attitudes, may find him/herself socially isolated.

Self-esteem has been related to success and in this society both subtle and overt negative messages are communicated about ethnic minorities. These negative messages are often internalized, leading to an individual's personal sense of devaluation. Because of these negative internalized messages of selfworth, many ethnic minority individuals must struggle with issues of competence and often question their ability to compete and survive in the academic environment.

Various studies have identified additional needs and problem areas for minorities. Baron, et al. (1978) used a specially developed Minority

Student Needs Survey to assess the degree to which academic, financial, social, personal and institutional problems existed for minority students. They reported that the area of greatest concern to minority students was that of finances. Furthermore, those students reporting inadequate income also reported significantly higher levels of concern on 58 of the 63 items on the survey. Those students with financial problems thus also experienced more academic and social problems and experienced more discrimination and isolation in the university setting than those with less financial concerns. Thus lack of financial support interacts to increase other academic and psychological problems in university settings.

Westbrook, Mujares, and Roberts (1978) showed that finances were also a major problem for black students. The authors administered the Student Problem Areas Survey to 237 black and white students at a predominantly white university and to 55 black students at a predominantly black university. Regardless of university, black students reported experiencing more problems in the areas of finances and study efficiency. Black students at the white university also reported problems with racial composition and interactions.

There is reason to expect that minorities encounter more problems than nonminority students in adjusting to a large, predominantly white university. Minority students, especially those who come from small ethnically homogeneous hometowns, often express feelings of isolation, fail to engage in social situations, seek information less frequently, and have less contact with fellow students (National Board on Graduate Education, 1976). The higher adjustive demands and the "cultural shock" phenomenon experienced by ethnic minorities who come from a different cultural and often lower socioeconomic background may result in higher stress levels.

Muñoz and Garcia-Bahne (1978) devised the College Environmental Stress Index (CESI) to gain a comprehensive view of the stresses experienced by Chicanos at four California universities. They found that these minority students experienced significantly higher stress levels compared to Anglos; Chicanas reported higher levels than Chicanos. Vasquez (1978) utilized the same instrument to assess stress levels with Texas University Chicanas. Although the author did not find the same elevated stress levels that Muñoz and Garcia-Bahne found, she did find that Chicanas experienced higher levels of stress in two financial aid items and six academic items.

It is not surprising that ethnic minority students tend to report academic and study efficiency concerns. Since a large proportion of these students have low socioeconomic backgrounds, many have had few of the educational advantages that prepare one for a college education. These students may also have relatively less experience with institutions and bureaucracy and therefore have not "learned the ropes" of survival in a large institution.

Ethnic minorities thus experience higher stress levels and struggle to adjust to and compete in the academic environment because of educational disadvantages and lack of previous experience with institutions. They have higher concerns and often feel isolated and alienated. Such factors contribute to the lower entrance and retention rates for ethnic minorities and the resultant loss of potential for the individual, the ethnic group, and the nation as a whole.

## The Physically Disabled

The physically disabled are the most recent group to appear on campus in large numbers (Dailey, 1978). This group has perhaps been one of the most neglected of human resources. The needs and problems vary from individual to individual; some individuals have hidden disabilities, such as cardiac problems or severe asthma, but the physically disabled must generally deal with some form of incapacitation and often pain.

Environmental barriers in the university environment, including residences and classes, often aggravate the difficulties these individuals experience. Mobility impaired students struggle with access for wheelchairs. Sensory handicapped students (blind or deaf) must find alternative ways of acquiring information delivered through lectures and/or films. Besides having to deal with architectural barriers, those disabled students who cannot drive experience difficulty in acquiring transportation, a concern few of us ever experience!

Attitudinal barriers, including those from peers and faculty as well as their own, often result in the limitation of disabled students to fully realize their potential. Faculty and peer fear, apathy, or even antagonism present problems, and are often the result of lack of information and communication. Hessler (1976) found, for example, that although blind and deaf students often encountered difficulties in mobility (acquiring appropriate housing and other physical barriers), negative attitudes constituted the major barrier on college campuses. Many negative stereotypes and myths contribute to these negative attitudes. Because of lack of verbal skills, for example, deaf students convey the impression of retardation to many professors. What is frequently not recognized is that deaf students often have low skill levels in English because it is a second language; sign language is the primary one.

Disabled students themselves have often internalized negative self-images and ways of thinking or feeling that further restrict their potential. Anger at oneself, at one's parents, and at society is very often present and can be manifest or latent (Dailey, 1978). Unfortunately, disabled individuals often internalize their hostility and hence develop a poor self-concept. Boone, Roessler, and Cooper (1978) point out the importance of the process of acceptance of one's disability. Boone et al. (1978) examined the motivational significance of key factors in the acceptance of the disability and found that hope and anxiety were key factors which contributed to successful adaptation for young adults. Moderate levels of hope (measured by the Self Anchoring Striving Scale and defined as expectancy of future goal success) and anxiety (measured by the Taylor Manifest Anxiety Scale and defined as index of emotional arousal) facilitated acceptance. Too little or too much of either hope or anxiety negatively affected the acceptance of the disability.

Physically disabled students thus struggle with physical debilitation and/or pain, architectural barriers, and attitudinal barriers. They also struggle with feelings of inadequacy and acceptance of disabilities. These external and internal barriers deter disabled students from fully realizing their potential.

## Women

Women have long struggled with the oppression resulting from restrictive sex roles and socialization. The traditional expectations that men should have the primary responsibility as breadwinner and that women have the responsibilities of childbearing and homemaking are changing. Ideally, these roles can be freely chosen or rejected by both men and women (Farmer, 1978). One implication of the contemporary changes of social roles of women is the increase in the numbers of women in historically nontraditional majors and careers. Special needs may arise as a result of the increase of women in these nontraditional areas. Ott (1978), for example, noted that women have begun to study engineering in large numbers and investigated differences between men and women engineering students. Ott found important differences in background, expectations, activities and attitudes, implying special needs. Women were very high achievers and participated in a wide variety of high school activities compared to men, but had lower expectations for performance in college than men. Women had broader cultural interests, implying that they may experience frustration if they restricted themselves to technical courses. Women preferred math to science in high school and had little practical experience with mechanical and electrical skill, and thus needed basic skills training in those areas. On a positive note, women also reported being more concerned with aiding society whereas men were concerned with income and financial security. Perhaps the entry of women into such fields as engineering will have a positive societal impact!

## Older, Returning Women

Another implication of these contemporary changes in the social roles of women is the increase in the numbers of women students beyond the traditional student age (eighteen to twenty-one). This group now forms a large growing minority on college campuses, and these women often have special needs and experience unique problems in returning to school. Owing to higher motivation, the prognosis for success of these mature students is good. These students are generally more successful than younger students and are more likely to make use of their training (Lewis, 1968). However, because of their long absence from the academic setting, they frequently feel inadequate and threatened when reentering the academic setting. Many are unfamiliar with college curricula and course work demands (Tryon and Michael, 1977). Math-related courses are particularly identified as problem areas for women. Differences in socialization about mathematics are thought to account for the sex differences in mathematical performance (Maccoby and Jacklin, 1974). Math anxiety, defined as "feelings of tension and anxiety that interfere with the manipulation of numbers and the solving of mathematical problems" (Richardson and Suinn, 1972, p. 551), is thought to be the result of such socialized attitudes, and a major contributing factor to poor math performance among women (Hendel and Davis, 1978).

Besides academic concerns, returning women have needs for financial assistance and for convenient day-care centers for preschool children. They often experience need for assistance in vocational choice, vocational preparation, and job search (Kelman and Staley, 1975).

Divorced and/or widowed women whose situations have forced them to return to school to seek skills to become self-supporting often experience additional difficulties. It is a time of identity crisis and loneliness, especially for the woman who has previously built her identity around her husband. Lifestyles are often severely changed and need for financial aid becomes crucial. Carey (1977) found that, compared to widowers, widows experienced more difficulty in making decisions and in handling financial matters alone, were more concerned about personal safety, and worried about dependent children. Widowers experienced difficulty in maintaining homes and handling the physical and emotional needs of children alone. All these problems could interfere with the potential of returning women in the academic setting.

## Veterans

Older men, particularly veterans, are also a minority group on college campuses. Veterans are flocking to colleges and universities in increasing numbers because of the extension of the G.I. Bill eligibility from 8 to 10 years, and the limited job opportunities resulting from the recession of the 1970s. As regular student populations decrease, older students in general will be more and more welcomed by college and university administrators. Because they are older, have more financial commitments, are not prepared for college adjustment, and have the remnants of a military identity, problems often develop for these men. Veterans often experience personal and social attitudes of rejection and alienation, significant vocational adjustment problems, and negative family attitudes toward the educational pursuit (Mills, 1978). For example, using the Money Problem Checklist, Berry (1977) identified problem areas for veterans, which included concern for success in school, need for financial support, family pressures, concern for self-improvement, and getting established in a new occupation. This group presents a particular challenge since there is a tendency for veterans who demonstrate the greatest relative need for counseling and guidance to reject the idea the most (Berry, 1977).

## International Students

Another significant subset of the university population in most United States colleges and universities is the international student population. Various authors have identified significant difficulties in the adjustment problems of these students (Perkins et al., 1977; Hendricks and Skinner, 1977; Sharma, 1973). Because of special legal and social statuses, foreign students must operate from a position over which they have little control. The legal classification "alien" is supportive of the notion among many Americans that international students belong elsewhere and are transients in the United States society. They must thus deal with the difficulty of establishing relationships and being accepted by Americans with such attitudes. International students are also concerned with American social customs (Perkins, et al., 1977). Coming into a different society, students cannot be aware of all the accepted norms, important information, and sources of meeting their needs in

United States society. The international student thus tends to operate within a limited social field, including mostly those people who play instrumental roles in his/her functioning in this society. The international student thus tends not to be integrated into our society.

Problem areas in academic adjustment for international students generally center around English language-related problems, such as difficulty in understanding lectures, participating in class discussions, and preparing oral and written reports. The most serious personal problems include finances, housing, homesickness, food, and companionship with the opposite sex.

It is important to note that international students have both common problems and problems peculiar to their own groups. Perkins et al., (1977) found, for example, that although English proficiency and finances were problems for all groups, English proficiency was the problem most frequently noted by the Chinese, whereas Indians reported finances to be the problem most frequently encountered.

## THE NEED FOR ASSESSMENT

Up to this point, the chapter has identified those characteristics and needs most generally associated with the respective unique student populations. Student development has taken the primary responsibility in attempting to respond in a humanistic way to those special needs which could help ensure that individuals from these special groups remain in school and complete their degree. It is perhaps important to note at this point that needs of unique populations may be specific to each institution and may change over periods of time, and that assessment should thus be an ongoing process.

There are a variety of approaches to assessment. One is the use of paper and pencil surveys or questionnaires. Typical questionnaires used in assessment include the College and University Environmental Scales (CUES), the College Survey Questionnaire (CSQ), described by Aulepp and Delworth (1976), and the Environmental Satisfaction Questionnaire (ESQ) by Corazzini, Wilson, and Huebner (1977). It is often necessary to develop separate items or develop one's own instrument, such as the Minority Student Needs Survey developed by the University of Texas Dean of Students Office (Baron et al. 1978) or the College Environmental Stress Index (Muñoz and Garcia-Bahne, 1978), both of which were cited earlier in this chapter. Corazzini (1979) has discussed other sources of data including structured or unstructured interviews and naturalistic observation of the ongoing process in addition to unobtrusive measures, for example, grade point averages and dropout rates.

Evaluation should help determine whether the goals, the projects, various programs, and other interventions are being effectively met.

## INTERVENTIONS

The remainder of this chapter attempts to identify practical measures and specific approaches that could help minimize the chances of the unique individual dropping out and to maximize his/her potential for having a successful experience in school. The suggested interventions are not intended to be all encompassing, but to raise issues and to provide suggestions and examples.

The models discussed in earlier chapters, which were first proposed by Morrill and Hurst (1971) and Morrill, Oetting and Hurst (1974), will be utilized to conceptualize alternative methods of meeting the special needs of the unique student. This model is particularly helpful since it provides for the categorization and description of a very broad range of possible interventions. The "CUBE" model includes three major dimensions that compose any intervention including the target, purpose, and method. The *target* defines to whom or what the intervention is being aimed. Possible targets include (1) the individual, (2) the individual's primary group, (3) the associational group, or (4) the institution or community. The purpose of the intervention may be (1) the remediation of an existing problem, (2) the prevention of a potential one, or (3) the development of skills. The method of intervention can include (1) direct service, (2) consultation or training of allied professionals or paraprofessionals, or (3) use of media.

The interventions described are presented according to the target of the intervention. Thus sections are organized according to whether the target is the individual, the primary or associational group, or the institution or community. Interventions are then categorized according to purpose (remediation, prevention, or development) and methods (direct service, consultation and training, or media). Not every cell within each target discussed will be utilized (thirty-six potential cells). Given the purpose of this chapter, that is, identification of needs, most of the interventions described are aimed toward the individual. It is hoped that this emphasis will not devalue those crucial interventions aimed toward groups, institutions, or community.

### The Individual

Special considerations are often necessary in the direct delivery of remedial services by the counselor or agency to the student with special needs. Ethnic minorities, for example, generally underutilize traditional mental health services and few seem to trust existing campus agencies (Sue, 1973; Perez, 1975; Padilla and Ruiz, 1973). These students often avoid services because of such factors as "discouraging institutional policies," for example, inflexible intake procedures and long waiting lists. Additionally, limited alternative language fluency of staff members often impedes delivery of traditional services to Spanish-speaking (Ruiz, Casas, and Padilla, 1977) and international students.

The development of nontraditional approaches may help improve the utilization by those individuals who have need of such services. For example, Philippus (1971) found that having a Spanish-speaking receptionist, and using nonhospital-like admissions procedures increased the number of contacts for Chicanos from 35 to 60 percent. The author also reported increase in client contacts through the initiation of a "drop-in room" procedure which allowed clients immediate access to a staff member. Other authors (Ruiz and Padilla, in press; Padilla and Padilla, 1977) have offered suggestions for transcultural approaches for the delivery of services to minority individuals.

The availability of ethnic minority counselors seems to be an important factor in the encouragement of students to utilize services. It has been noted that relationships, particularly psychotherapeutic relationships, are more difficult to establish and maintain when the staff and clientele are members of different socioeconomic status groups and/or possess different cultural values (Abad, Ramos and Boyce, 1974; Torrey, 1972; Yamamoto, James, and Palley, 1968). Various studies have indicated that ethnic identification is a significant variable in student preferences for different types of help sources (Webster and Fretz, 1978; Sue and Kirk, 1975). Smith (1974) pointed out that students in general prefer a counselor's age, socioeconomic background, religious belief, and sex to be similar to their own, and that minorities prefer counselors of the same race. Black students reported a preference for black counselors (Harrison, 1975) and a significantly greater likelihood of taking a problem to the center if the counselor to be seen was black rather than white (Thompson and Cimbolic, 1978).

Other unique students may also require nontraditional approaches to the delivery of direct services. For example, a hearing-impaired student may require alternative methods of communication such as the possible inclusion of an interpreter in the therapeutic process or the careful selection of a counselor whose speech can be lip-read.

Individual and group therapy services can help individuals from special populations deal with the difficult adjustment and stressful situations described earlier. Counselors could be aware, for example, of the special key variables in rehabilitation counseling of disabled students. Given that acceptance of disability is negatively affected by too low or too high levels of hope and anxiety, Boone et al., (1978) suggested ways counselors may help disabled clients obtain appropriate levels. To decrease excessively high hopes of clients, counselors may help them examine self-delusional constructs and develop realistic goals to supplant unrealistic ones. Techniques for increasing hope include helping the individual change the self-depreciating cognitions associated with depression and develop new goals that give meaning and direction to the future. Disabled students handicapped by excessive anxiety might profit from desensitization and relaxation training, intensive one-to-one personal counseling, or role playing and vicarious learning techniques. The authors pointed out that more conceptualization and research are needed regarding strategies to raise anxiety to helpful levels.

Various remedial services including counseling intervention strategies may be employed to help reduce specific anxieties for members of unique populations. Deffenbacher and Rivera (1976) successfully applied relaxation as a self-control program to debilitating test anxiety of two black women. The authors treated the subjects together in five hourly sessions over a 6 week period which provided them with active, self-management skills. Hendel and Davis (1978) used a combined curricular counseling intervention strategy for reducing math anxiety among 69 adult women returning to college. Maximum effectiveness was achieved when participants both enrolled in a math course and attended a multifaceted counseling support group. The counseling group, which met for 7 weeks for 1½ hours each time provided exercises to reduce the anxiety, provided participants with a forum for discussing previous math experiences, and promoted awareness of the role of socialization in the development of their attitudes about math to help understand the dynamics of their own avoidance of math as a prelude to behavioral change and self-management.

Many individuals from the unique populations described here could benefit from remedial programs aimed at increasing academic and study skills. Older students, including women and veterans, ethnic minorities, women in nontraditional majors, and international students have all shown evidence of need for such programming. Tryon and Michael (1977) demonstrated the effectiveness of a study skills program with older students returning to college. Sessions were 1 hour a week for 10 weeks and topics included note taking, library tour, scheduling, examination taking, mechanics of term papers, memorization, and career planning. The authors pointed out the value of a lecture/discussion format which encouraged peer contact. Older students often feel that college programs are for younger people and consequently decline to participate in programs that might otherwise be helpful. Students who participated in the program showed an improvement in study habits and a decrease in concerns about school. Such programs can also be implemented for other groups who may demonstrate academic deficiencies, such as ethnic minorities from lower socioeconomic status groups. Women in such nontraditional careers as engineering may, because of lack of experience with mechanical and electrical areas, have skill deficits in those areas (Ott, 1978) and may benefit from brief, basic courses. International students may benefit from intensive English courses.

Assertion training may be especially appropriate with many unique group members since lack of assertiveness may result in loss of opportunity or even in being taken advantage of. However, to have maximum benefit, the special needs and sensitivities regarding assertion training of special group members should be taken into consideration. Alberti (1977) included special sections relevant to the development of assertive behaviors in unique populations such as blacks, Spanish-speaking Mexican-American mothers, Asian Americans, Chicanos, various socioeconomic groups, and the divorced. Discussion of all the issues described by these authors in the delivery of assertion training to these special groups would be too lengthy to present here. It should suffice to point out the importance of consideration of those issues if assertion training is to be effective.

Consultation and training can be used to deliver remedial services to unique student populations. Trained paraprofessionals who are also peers of respective populations can, for example, facilitate support groups for women adjusting to divorce, help nontraditional majors to develop more self-confidence, and aid minority group members experiencing alienation and veterans dealing with residuals of military identity. The peer group approach seems to be helpful since group members are able to focus on commonalities (Mills, 1978).

Media can also be used to deliver remedial services to unique student populations. Telephone counseling tapes, such as those used by the University of Texas–Austin counseling center, help provide pertinent information and to address issues pertinent to unique populations on a 24 hour basis. Self-help materials, such as the self-help planning and guidance materials developed by Nieves (1978) for minority students can facilitate the increase of students' control over his/her environment. This manual, entitled *College Achievement Through Self-Help,* was developed by Nieves and sponsored by the Graduate Record Examinations Board and the Office for Minority Education of Educational Testing Service; it offers a method of learning and applying academic and personal life skills according to needs and priorities.

These are several examples of how remedial programs aimed at decreasing stress caused by the discrepancy between the skills of the individual and the environmental demands can be delivered directly, through consultation and training, or through media.

Preventive services are developed to provide or enhance skills that may be needed in the future. Anticipating problems and moving to prevent them by providing interventions for unique populations are not only a humanistic approach, but a responsibility that student development is acknowledging more and more. Special orientation programs to aid in the difficult entry of unique populations to the university setting are certainly one way of preventing potential difficulties and easing the transition.

Systematic and ongoing special counseling programs such as those at Wichita State University have been reported to be effective in preventing attrition and increasing student retention for "educationally ill-prepared students." These programs are direct preventive interventions in that they attempt to predict and prevent the attrition of "high risk" students. Students who participated in these particular programs generally came from urban settings, were first-generation college students, included a large percentage of men and women from racial minorities, were predicted as high risks on standard achievement tests, had not fared well academically in the past, and generally coped poorly in traditional education settings (Crawford, McFarland, and Rhatiger, 1978).

Four counseling programs were instigated for various purposes. *Early Alert* helped to identify problems in courses at the earliest possible time. Faculty reported excessive absences. Counselors called students, and met with them to help explore and resolve problems indicated. This helped lower the incidence of the "walk away" student.

*Midterm Counseling* was designed to help students who received notice of deficient work at midterm. Each student who did so received a personal call from the academic advisor, who not only offered assistance with problems related to the grade warning but also offered information about important academic policies (e.g., course withdrawal option, deadlines). This helped reinforce orientation information, which was then painfully relevant. The personal contact encouraged students to return for assistance.

The *Sophomore Counseling Program* helped students identify a major and develop an academic plan. It also helped those ineligible to enter or transfer to a major because of low grades by focusing on academic and personal circumstances inhibiting success and developing a plan for overcoming academic deficiencies. Those students who remained undecided participated in a special program to help systematically search for a major.

*Readmission Counseling* was designed to assess individual goals and skills of students who had failed and returned. Specific assignments were often made to help students further clarify their own skills and interests and to focus their resources on realistic objectives. If a student was not recommended for readmission, alternative plans were considered. Those who were readmitted were required to establish a regular (weekly) visit with the readmissions counselor to follow progress closely. The authors reported that careful attention to these high risk students helped 86 percent of them attain academic success.

The special training and sensitization of help-givers to the issues and needs of unique populations through consultation and training are certainly crucial in maximizing the effectiveness of services to prevent future problems.

The American Psychological Association Task Force on Sex Bias and Sex-Role Stereotyping (1975), for example, recommended that training programs be developed to educate potential counselors in sex-fair counseling. Gilbert and Waldroop (1978) developed training procedures to increase sex-fair counseling. Students in an upper division university course were assigned to a treatment or control section. Training in the treatment group involved role playing exercises in identified areas of perceived sex bias and sex role stereotyping that affect women as clients (as defined by the APA Task Force, 1975). The procedure was effective in changing students' attitudes toward women's roles and increasing their sensitivity to sex bias in video-taped counseling sessions. Such procedures can be utilized to train help-givers in student development.

In-service training to sensitize student government staffs in general can prevent problems and enhance services. The Student Affairs Division at Colorado State University, for example, organized and presented an in-service training to sensitize members to the day-to-day experiences of disabled students. A panel presentation of disabled students and a presentation by the Director of the Office of Resources for the Disabled was effective in accomplishing the goals of the in-service training.

The establishment of a special office to serve as advocate for the special needs of unique populations is an additional preventive measure. The Office of Resources for the Disabled at Colorado State University, for example, was established to survey the needs of disabled students, develop programs to meet those needs, and disseminate information concerning services available to students with disabilities. At the University of Florida, a Civilian Basic Training model has been developed to aid the educational adjustment and the vocational adjustment of veterans. It has social/personal counseling components as well as an information component aimed at helping veterans to use V.A. benefits.

Developmental interventions for individuals from unique populations include those designed to enhance their functioning and developmental potential. According to Morrill, Oetting, and Hurst (1974), development has the "primary focus of promoting positive growth for all, not only for those identified as having or about to have problems" (p. 357).

Consciousness-raising groups, for example, have been used as a resocialization, an important developmental process for women, and as a means for raising self-esteem and autonomy (Cherniss, 1972; Eastman, 1973; Follingstad, Robinson, and Pugh, 1977). Follingstad, Robinson, and Pugh et al. (1977) suggested that leaderless consciousness-raising groups may be more effective since the variable of autonomous functioning may be important for an increase in self-esteem. The special developmental tasks of individuals from oppressed groups include the redefinition and establishment of identity without the negative, internalized messages received from society; consciousness-raising and self-awareness groups are one example of important stimuli which can be used to promote these developmental processes.

Consultation with student development staff, especially residence hall staff, about the special developmental issues of special groups can enhance the probability that these tasks will be promoted.

Use of media, such as telephone tapes on developmental issues for the special populations, films, and special reading lists can further promote development.

## Primary Groups

According to Morrill, Oetting, and Hurst (1974), primary groups include the family, spouse, and close friends, and are defined as "intimate, continuing personal associations on a face-to-face basis determined by the degree of intimacy rather than by proximity" (p. 356). Since these groups strongly affect the individual, interventions to improve communication and relationships can, for example, ultimately enhance the effectiveness of the unique member in the university setting.

Working directly with veteran's families experiencing stress and conflict owing to negative attitudes toward the educational pursuit could improve mutuality and understanding and communication. Such attempts would help remediate in troubled situations. Consultation and training with such staff as residence hall assistants in conflict management regarding racial issues could help remediate those situations.

Suggesting ways of maintaining supportive contact to families either directly or through media could help those ethnic minority students whose primary support has come chiefly from families.

### Associational Groups

Associational groups are classes, clubs, or organizations that meet on a regular basis. Remediation could involve the resolution of conflict among the members of associational groups with which special population groups tend to conflict.

Preventive consciousness raising and sensitizing of faculty and students in the university setting to some of the special issues discussed here, for example, could be accomplished through consultation and training and/or use of the media. The university women's committee at the University of Texas, for example, sponsored a series of symposia which addressed various issues influencing the changing roles of women. Key people in academia and student affairs, as well as students, were involved as both participants and audiences.

Faculty may need to learn alternatives in teaching methodology to facilitate transmission of class material to sensory disabled students. Use of visual materials might be deemphasized, for example, if a visually impaired student is to be enrolled in one's class.

### Institution or Community

Interventions can also be accomplished with an institution or the community. Perhaps one of the least utilized but most impactful interventions for unique student populations could be accomplished at this level.

Institutions and communities must be educated and sensitized to celebrate differences and promote them as strengths. Uniqueness traditionally has not been valued in our society. Social psychologists such as Asch (1956), Crutchfield (1955), and Milgram (1974) have found that conformity to peer pressure or authoritarian demands are an important aspect of the psychological makeup of the individual in our culture. As evidence that strong societal pressures for acculturation and assimilation exist, Smith et al. (1978) cite a number of studies indicating that, when given a choice of playing with white or black dolls or viewing black or white individual pictures, black and white children chose white. Srole et al. (1975) cite evidence indicating that assimilation or sense of belongingness to the majority culture appears to decrease the risk and occurrence of disordered behavior. Other findings show, however, that cultural factors may not be damaging and some researchers question the notion that one must acculturate to be successful. In fact, there is growing evidence that identifying with one's culture may enhance self-image (Hernandez, 1973). The notion of cultural pluralism suggests that a person may live comfortably and successfully in two or more sociocultural systems, and that these experiences may provide the basis for a more flexible and sophisticated psychological adjustment and therefore increase academic success (Henderson and Merritt, 1968; Long and Padilla, 1971; Ramirez, 1971; Ramirez and Castenada, 1974). The promotion of different cultural activities and programs that enhance differentness could change norms and promote the value of a pluralistic and multicultural viewpoint.

Responding to the many varied and changing needs of unique populations is challenging and demanding. The utilization of the models described in this book to identify, plan, and implement effective approaches to meet these needs can help meet this challenge and help to ensure and enhance the successful experiences of unique populations at our institutions. It is incumbent upon these agencies responsible for the physical and psychological needs of students to be in the forefront of the development of humanistic approaches to education. Student services must assist universities in the development and implementation of techniques and interventions that facilitate the development for unique populations.

## REFERENCES

Abad, V., J. Ramos, and E. Boyce A model for delivery of mental health services to Spanish-speaking minorities. *American Journal of Orthapsychiatry*, 1974, **44**, 584–595.

Alberti, R. E. *Assertiveness: Innovations, Applications, Issues*. San Luis Obispo, Calif.: Impact Publishers, 1977.

APA Task Force on Sex Bias and Sex-Role Stereotyping in Psychotherapeutic Practice. Report of the task force on sex bias and sex-role stereotyping in psychotherapeutic practice. *American Psychologist*, 1975, **30**, 1169–1175.

Asch, S. E. Effects of group pressure on the modification and distortion of judgement. In H. Geutzkow (Ed.), *Groups, Leadership, and Men*. Pittsburgh: Carnegie, 1951.

Asch, S. E. Studies of independence and conformity: a minority of one against a unanimous majority. *Psychological Monographs,* 1956, **70**, 9 (Whole No. 416).

Aulepp, L. and U. Delworth *Training Manual for an Ecosystem Model.* Boulder, Colo.: Western Interstate Commission for Higher Education, 1976.

Baron, A., J. Valdez, M. J. Vasquez, and J. C. Hurst Assessing the concerns of minority students: process and outcome. Paper presented at the 60th annual National Association of Student Personnel Administrators, Kansas City, Mo., 1978.

Berry, G. L. Counseling needs of disadvantaged veterans. *Journal of College Student Personnel,* 1977, **18** (5), 406–412.

Berry, J. Counseling older women; a perspective. *Personnel and Guidance Journal,* 1976, **55** (3), 130–131.

Boone, S. E., R. T. Roessler, and P. G. Cooper Hope and manifest anxiety: motivational dynamics of acceptance of disability. *Journal of Counseling Psychology,* 1978, **25** (6), 551–556.

Carey, R. G. The Widowed: a year later. *Journal of Counseling Psychology,* 1977, **24** (2), 125–131.

Carnegie Commission on Higher Education. *A chance to learn: an action agenda for equal opportunity in higher education.* New York: McGraw-Hill, 1970, pp. 2–7.

Cheek, D. K. Assertive behavior and black lifestyles. In R. E. Alberti, *Assertiveness: Innovations, Applications, Issues.* San Luis Obispo, Calif.: Impact Publishers, 1977, 111–118.

Cherniss, C. Personality and ideology: a personological study of women's liberation. *Psychiatry,* 1972, **35**, 109–125.

*Chronicle of Higher Education* 1975, **11** (7).

Corazzini, J. Environmental assessment and redesign. In U. Delworth and G. Hanson (Eds.), *Handbook of Student Services.* San Francisco: Jossey-Bass, 1979.

Corazzini, J., S. Wilson, and L. Huebner The environmental satisfaction questionnaire: a guide to assessment and program development. *Journal of College Student Personnel,* 1977, **18** (3), 169–173.

Crawford, A. E., D. E. McFarland, and J. J. Rhatigan Special counseling programs for academic survival. *Journal of College Student Personnel,* 1978, **19** (4), 298–301.

Crutchfield, R. S. Conformity and character. *American Psychologist,* 1955, **10**, 191–198.

Dailey, A. L. Counseling and guidance approaches to deaf college students. *Journal of College Student Personnel,* 1978, **19** (5), 393–397.

Dailey, L. Blind college students-counseling and guidance approaches. *Journal of College Student Personnel,* 1977, **18** (2), 1.

Deffenbacher, J. L. and N. Rivera A behavioral self-control treatment of test anxiety in minority populations: some cases and issues. *Psychological Reports,* 1976, **39**, 1188–1190.

Eastman, P. C. Consciousness-raising as a resocialization process for women. *Smith College Studies in Social Work,* 1973, **43**, 153–183.

Fact Sheets on Institutional Racism (August 1975). Foundation for Change, Inc., 1841 Broadway New York, NY 10023.

Farmer, H. Career counseling implications for the lower social class and women. *The Personnel and Guidance Journal,* 1978, **56** (8), 467–471.

Follingstad, D. R., E. A. Robinson, and M. Pugh Effects of consciousness-raising groups on measures of feminism, self-esteem, and social desirability. *Journal of Counseling Psychology,* 1977, **24** (3), 223–230.

Gilbert, L. A. and J. Waldroop Evaluation of a procedure for increasing sex-fair counseling. *Journal of Counseling Psychology,* 1978, **25** (5), 410–418.

Grodner, B. S. Assertiveness and anxiety: across-cultural and socio-economic perspective. In R. E. Alberti, *Assertiveness: Innovations, Applications, Issues.* San Luis Obispo, Calif.: Impact Publishers, 1977, 135–147.

Harrison, D. K. Race as a counselor-client variable in counseling and psychotherapy: a review of the research. *The Counseling Psychologist,* 1975, **5**, 124–133.

Hendel, D. D. and S. O. Davis Effectiveness of an intervention strategy for reducing mathematics anxiety. *Journal of Counseling Psychology,* 1978, **25** (5), 429–434.

Henderson, R. W. and C. B. Merritt Environmental backgrounds of Mexican-American children with different potentials for school success. *The Journal of Social Psychology.* 1968, **75**, 101–106.

Hendricks, G. L. and K. A. Skinner Adaptive social patterns of foreign students. *Journal of College Student Personnel,* 1977, **18** (2), 124–127.

Hernandez, N. G. Variables affecting achievement of middle school Mexican-American students. *Review of Educational Research,* 1973, **43** (1), 1–41.

Hessler, J. College education for the severely disabled. *American Rehabilitation,* 1976, **1** (5), 29–33.

Hwang, P. O. Assertion training for Asian-Americans. In R. E. Alberti, *Assertiveness: Innovations, applications, issues.* San Luis Obispo, Calif.: Impact Publishers, Inc., 1977, 129–135.

Kelman, E. and B. Staley *The Returning Woman Student: Needs of an Important Minority Group on College Campuses.* Student Development Report XII, **2**, 1974–75.

Kerchoff, A. and K. A. Davis Value consensus and need complementary in mate selection: *American Sociological Review,* 1962, **27**, 295–303.

Landau, P. and T. Paulson Group assertion training for Spanish-Speaking Mexican-American mothers. In R. E. Alberti, *Assertiveness: Innovations, Applications, Issues.* San Luis Obispo, Calif.: Impact Publishers, 1977, 119–128.

Lewis, E. C. *Developing Woman's Potential.* Ames, Iowa: Iowa State University Press, 1968.

Long, K. K. and A. M. Padilla An assessment of successful and unsuccessful college students. Paper presented at the American Association for the Advancement of Science Regional Meeting, Colorado Springs, Colo., 1969. Also in Evidence for bilingual antecedents of academic success in the groups of Spanish-American college students. *Journal of Cross Cultural Psychiatry,* 1971.

Maccoby, E. E. and C. N. Jacklin *The Psychology of Sex Differences,* Stanford, Calif.: Stanford University Press, 1974.

Martin, E. W. A national commitment to the rights of the individual: 1776 to 1976. *Exceptional Children,* 1976, **43** (3), 132–135.

Milgram, S. *Obedience to Authority.* New York: Harper Row, 1974.

Mills, G. D. Perceptions of the veteran student minority. *Journal of College Student Personnel,* 1978, **19** (3), 208–211.

Moos, R. H. and V. D. Tsu The crisis of physical illness: an over-view. In R. H. Moos (Ed.), *Coping with Physical Illness.* New York: Plenum Medical Book Company, 1977, 3–22.

Morrill, W. H. and J. C. Hurst A preventative and developmental role for the college counselor, *The Counseling Psychologist,* 1971, **2** (4), 90–95.

Morrill, W. H., E. R. Oetting, and J. C. Hurst Dimensions of counselor functioning. *Personnel and Guidance Journal,* 1974, **52** (6), 354–359.

Muñoz, D. and B. Garcia-Bahne *A Study of the Chicano Experience in Higher Education.* A final report for the Center for Minority Group Mental Health Programs and the National Institute of Mental Health, Grant #NN24597–01, University of California, San Diego, 1978.

Muskat, H. S. Women reentering college: some basic ingredients for curriculum development. *Personnel and Guidance Journal,* 1978, **57** (3), 153–156.

National Board on Graduate Education. *Minority Group Participation in Graduate Education.* Washington, D.C.: National Academy of Sciences, 1976.

Newcombe, T. M. *The Acquaintance Process.* New York: Holt, Rinehart and Winston, 1961.

Newman, J. Faculty attitudes toward handicapped students. *Rehabilitation Literature,* 1976, **37** (7), 194–197.

Nieves, L. College achievement through self-help: a planning and guidance manual for minority students. Princeton, N.J.: Educational Testing Service, 1978.

Ott, M. D. Differences between male and female freshman engineers. *Journal of College Student Personnel,* 1978, **19** (6), 552–556.

Padilla, A. M. and R. A. Ruiz *Latino Mental Health: A Review of Literature.* Washington, D.C.: U.S. Superintendent of Documents, 1973.

Padilla, E. R. and A. Padilla (Eds.) *Transcultural Psychiatry: An Hispanic Perspective.* Monograph Number 4. Los Angeles, Calif.: Research Center, 1977.

Paulson, T. L. and P. Landau Divorce recovery: assertion training for the divorced. In R. E. Alberti, *Assertiveness: Innovations, Applications, Issues.* San Luis Obispo, Calif.: Impact Publishers, 1977, 239–248.

Perez, M. S. Counseling services at University of California, Santa Cruz: attitudes and perspectives of Chicano students. Unpublished manuscript. 1975, 38 pp.

Perkins, C. S., M. L. Perkins, L. M. Guglielmino, and R. F. Reiff A comparison of the adjustment problems of three international student groups. *Journal of College Student Personnel,* 1977, **18** (5), 382–388.

Philippus, M. J. Successful and unsuccessful approaches to mental health for an urban Hispano-American population. *American Journal of Public Health,* 1971, **61**, 1, 820–830.

Ramirez, M., III, The relationship of acculturation to educational achievement and psychological adjustment in Chicano children and adolescents: a review of the literature. *El Grito,* 1971, **4** (4), 21–28.

Ramirez, M., III, and A. Castaneda *Cultural Democracy, Bicognitive Development and Education,* New York: Academic Press, 1974.

Richardson, F., and R. M. Suinn The mathematics anxiety rating scale: psychometric data. *Journal of Counseling Psychology,* 1972, **19**, 551–554.

Ruiz, R. A., J. M. Casas, and A. M. Padilla *Culturally Relevant Behavioristic Counseling* (2nd ed.). Occasional Paper No. 5. Los Angeles, Calif.: Spanish-Speaking Mental Health Reserach Center, 1977.

Ruiz, R. A., and A. M. Padilla Counseling Latinos. *Personnel and Guidance Journal,* 1977, **55** (7), 401–408.

Sedlacek, W. E., and G. C. Brooks, Jr. Black freshman in large colleges: a survey. *The Personnel and Guidance Journal,* 1970, **49** (4), 307–312.

Sedlacek, W. E., and D. W. Webster Admission and retention of minority students in large universities. *Journal of College Student Personnel,* 1978, **19** (3), 242–248.

Sharma, S. A study to identify and analyze adjustment problems experienced by foreign non-European graduate students enrolled in selected universities in the state of North Carolina. *California Journal of Educational Research,* 1973, **24**, 135–146.

Smith, D. Preferences of university students for counselors and counseling settings. *Journal of College Student Personnel,* 1974, **15**, 53–57.

Smith, D. S., A. K. Burlow, M. H. Mosley, and W. M. Whitney *Minority Issues in Mental Health.* Reading, Mass.: Addison-Wesley Publishing Co., 1978.

Sparks, D. and B. Mullally Sexism and education: a workshop to increase awareness. *Personnel and Guidance Journal,* 1978, **57** (2), 124–125.

Srole, L., T. Langer, S. Michael, M. Opler, and T. Rennie Measurement and classification in sociopsychiatric epidemiology: Midtown Manhattan Study (1954) and Midtown Restudy II (1974). *Journal of Health and Social Behavior,* 1975, **16**, 347–364.

Sue, D. W. and B. Kirk Asian-Americans: use of counseling and psychiatric services on a college campus. *Journal of Counseling Psychology,* 1975, **22**, 84–86.

Sue, S. Training of "Third World" students to function as counselors. *Journal of Counseling Psychology,* 1973, **20**, 73–78.

Thompson, R. A. and P. Cimbolic Black student counselor preference and attitudes toward counseling center use. *Journal of Counseling Psychology,* 1978, **25** (6), 570–575.

Torrey, E. T. The mind game. *Witchdoctors and Psychiatrists.* New York: Emerson Hall, 1972.

Tryon, G. S. and J. S. Michael The effectiveness of study skills instruction with students in an adult degree program. *Journal of College Student Personnel,* 1977, **18** (6), 478–481.

U.S. Commission on Civil Rights. Mexican-American study, Report II. *The Unfinished Education: Outcomes for Minorities in the five Southwestern States.* Washington, D.C.: U.S. Government Printing Office, 1971.

U.S. Department of Commerce, Bureau of the Census (1972). *Current Population Reports.* Special Studies Series, p. 23, No. 40, Table 62. Washington, D.C.: U.S. Government Printing Office.

Vasquez, M. J. Chicano and anglo university women: factors related to their performance, persistence and attrition. Unpublished dissertation, University of Texas, Austin, 1978.

Webster, D. W. and B. R. Fretz Asian American, black and white college students' preferences for help-giving sources. *Journal of Counseling Psychology,* 1978, **25** (2), 124–130.

Westbrook, F. D., J. Mujares, and J. H. Roberts Perceived problem areas by black and white students and hints about comparative counseling needs, *Journal of Counseling Psychology,* 1978, **25** (2), 119–123.

Withey, S. B. *A Degree and What Else.* New York: McGraw-Hill, 1971.

Yamamoto, J., T. C. James, and N. Palley Cultural problems in psychiatric therapy. *Archives of General Psychiatry,* 1968, **19**, 45–49.

# 18
# Career Decision Making

KATHLEEN R. BOGGS

Critical development tasks of the college years are choosing a major field of study, acquiring the basic education and training for that field, and selecting a specific occupation upon graduation. The purpose of career education within a college or university setting is to facilitate the achievement of these goals. Ideally, this opportunity should be available to students throughout their educational experience. Beyond the provision of specific services, students should be taught the necessary skills for effective self-evaluation and work assessment so that after graduation they will not be as dependent on others for this information.

A variety of factors influence a person at each career decision point. These include information about self such as values, life-style preferences, interests, aptitudes, abilities and skills, and personal and behavioral characteristics as well as information about training programs, employment opportunity predictions, and other career-related environmental data.

Most people do not seek the help of career counselors or vocational psychologists in helping them to make career-related decisions. Nevertheless, they move through developmental stages, carry out self and environment assessments, make vocational decisions, test the reality of these decisions, and make career commitments. Students who seek counseling usually have run into obstacles to their career decision making.

## OBSTACLES TO CAREER DECISION MAKING

### Lack of Information About Self

Some students have only a vague awareness of their personal values and the satisfactions they would like to obtain within a work environment. They may have thought little about life-style preferences, aptitudes, and interests and how these relate to occupational choice.

Another area of self-knowledge has to do with an individual's habitual personal traits, characterological qualities, as well as means of coping with stress. Some types of work require, for example, particularly high levels of consistency or conscientiousness in performance. Others involve complex interpersonal relationships and unavoidable confrontation in which self-control and emotional stability are important for successful coping. Students must be able to identify how their personal and work characteristics might affect their functioning in a work setting and which occupational environments would be most conducive to feelings of well-being and productivity.

### Lack of Information About the Environment

Students should learn how to use sources of occupational information to discover educational programs and occupations consistent with their interests, abilities, and needs. Data on a specific occupation include entry level requirements, salary and fringe benefits, potential for promotion, physical and psychological demands, working conditions, and economic future in terms of supply and demand. Part of this information can best be obtained by training students to interview others working in a field that interests them. Much of the knowledge about a worker's typical day and life style as related to occupational choice can be obtained in no other way.

Becoming directly involved in an on-the-job experience may be particularly valuable. During college, this can be achieved through a part-time job, cooperative education, internships, practicums, volunteer work, or being able to shadow someone on a job for a period of time. Some individuals cannot carry out the self-assessment necessary to recognize a discrepancy between the information that they have and the information that they need. One cannot resolve this discrepancy unless one is aware of it.

## Lack of Decision-Making Skills

Many students have difficulty making career choices because of lack of experience with the decision-making process itself. Perhaps parents or others had always made decisions for them, or they felt that the decisions made never turned out well or someone always questioned the quality of judgment reflected in decisions that they had made. Others seek confirmation for tentative decisions already made. They want support through testing or discussion with others.

Some students lack skills in goal setting. They may have wishes and hopes about getting a college degree or about becoming a doctor, but have never taken the time to outline specific time-limited objectives to turn those wishes into realities. Timing is of particular importance in goal setting. Earning good grades late may not compensate for an individual's previous poor records. Students should be able to set appropriate short-range, medium-range, and long-range goals. It is to be hoped they will find success and gratification in the daily tasks directed toward those goals rather than in preoccupations with eventual monetary rewards that may lead them prematurely to drop out of the educational process.

## Lack of Other Skills

A majority of students lack effective communication skills and are without adequate background in grammar, punctuation, spelling, sentence, and paragraph construction. Many also lack the vocabulary, confidence, and experience to express themselves well in writing or even orally. Since there are few college-related occupations that do not require these basic skills, it is important that all college graduates achieve at least a minimal level of communication competence.

Lack of ability in mathematics or anxiety about potential capability in this area is a frequent concern of students and may become major detriments in choice of a scientific versus a nonscientific field (Goldman and Hewitt, 1976). Social and cultural factors as well as anxiety impact particularly upon women in deterring them from scientific pursuits (Boggs and Pappas, 1979).

Students often lack job-seeking skills. They do not know how to write an effective résumé, compose a cover letter, do a job search, or conduct themselves in a job interview. Even with good credentials, they may fail because of inability to present themselves effectively.

## Conflict with Self

Some students have unrealistic self-expectations and therefore often feel frustrated and self-deprecating because they fail to measure up to these standards. Fear of failure or even achieving an average grade keeps a number of students from attempting courses that they might find valuable and even enjoyable. Fear of success has also been postulated as an inhibiting factor for some people. Schuster (1955) observed that individuals may fail to enjoy good fortune or to attain success because of the fear that if they asserted themselves, they would be resented and opposed by others. The idea that anxiety inhibits behaviors expected to have negative consequences has been particularly emphasized in explaining career choice in women. Since the prevalent stereotype is that competition, independence, and academic achievements are generally inconsistent with femininity, Horner (1968, 1969, 1970) has argued that most women have a fear of success, particularly in nontraditional roles.

Sex-role stereotyping of occupations (Almquist, 1974) appears to be as pervasive and persistent as sex-role stereotyping in general (e.g., Bem, 1975; Spence, Helmreich, and Stapp, 1975). Occupations associated with intelligence, logical reasoning, competence, and assertion are perceived as masculine whereas those occupations associated with dependence, passivity, nurture, and interpersonal warmth are viewed as feminine (Shinar, 1975). These preconceptions have not so far been more than modestly changed by the social and political activism of women's liberation groups (Broverman et al, 1972; Penn, 1975; Schultz, 1973).

For college women, Peplau (1976) found that sex-role traditionalism was associated with significantly lower career aspirations, lower Scholastic Aptitude Test verbal scores, and lower self-ratings of intelligence. A review of the literature on sex-role conformity (Page, 1973) indicated that women who adhere to the traditional feminine role were characterized by low self-esteem, restriction of personal growth, and inhibition of achievement striving, and women who defied traditional sex-role expectations fell prey to anxiety. Changing moral, social, and political values pose bewilderment and frustration for today's college students. Few role models exist for either men or women in nontraditional careers or for dual career families, which have become very common.

Self-concept is also related to vocational choice. Persons try to implement their self-concepts by choosing occupations most likely to permit self-expression. Self-concepts and occupational concepts should be integrated in order to make realistic choices. Interestingly, Korman (1966) found that high self-esteem individuals are more likely to implement their self concepts through occupational choice than are low self-esteem individuals.

### Conflict with Others

Conflict with others can also interfere with career decision making. The expectations, real or imagined, of significant others (e.g., parents, spouse, friends) can have a profound impact. Some individuals do not do what they really want but do what others expect of them.

Identifications as well as conflicts with authority figures (e.g., employers, teachers) can also influence career choice for some students. They choose college majors because of supportive academic experiences with favorite professors in those fields. Likewise some students will reject an otherwise favorable field based on negative experiences with professors or employers. In either case, the decisions have not been made rationally, but they have been made.

Students also experience conflict with institutions in a variety of forms. One may not know how to get through the system in terms of meeting its requirements, experiencing rejection by an institution by not being accepted for financial aid or work study programs, or being placed on scholastic probation. Sometimes it may be a matter of teaching the student the academic system and how to manage it. In other cases it may be necessary for the counselor to intercede in the system on the part of the student. In either case, the counselor can be a facilitator in helping the student adapt to institutional stress.

## CAMPUS RESOURCES FOR CAREER DECISION MAKING

Campus resources for career decision making will be presented in terms of their specific functions. The reason for this is that the student personnel services on various campuses are organized differently. The specific organization is much less important than the services provided.

### Academic Advising

Academic advisers, whether they are trained particularly for this job or are simply faculty advisers, provide students with data on requirements regarding admissions procedures, general or liberal education requirements, class scheduling, and course planning. Once a student has chosen a major department, a faculty adviser usually takes over in terms of helping the student plan the best class schedule that will jointly meet the needs of the individual and the requirements of the academic department. Academic advisers may also work with students on scholastic probation to help improve grades and interpret the institution's policy on scholastic standards. They may also provide counseling to cushion the impact of withdrawal if the student does not perform up to required academic levels.

In terms of obtaining information about oneself, an academic adviser along with the registrar's office can help students to assess the status of their academic records. Such assessment might include evaluating transcripts from another college or university, scholastic standing, or the level of completion of the institutional and departmental requirements.

### Career Information and Job Placement

A placement specialist can provide students with information on the status of their credential files. For students having job interviews, the placement specialist can provide feedback from the recruiters on the student's presentation style, particularly its effectiveness and appeal to the interviewer.

The placement and/or career information specialist can also provide information about undergraduate programs at other colleges or universities, graduate or professional schools, technical schools, apprenticeship training programs, or cooperative education programs. Often they can, for specific careers, describe the nature of the work, working conditions, qualifications, preparation, entry, number and distribution of workers, lines of advancement or collateral job opportunities, economic benefits, and employment prospects.

Placement specialists can inform students about types of employers such as private business, nonprofit organizations, educational institutions, government agencies, self-employment, or the military services as well as sources of employment information. The latter would include the College Placement Annual, Standard and Poor's Register of Corporation Directors and Executives, Dunn and Bradstreet's Reference Book, publications of national professional societies, equal opportunity publications, Encyclopedia of Associations, newspaper ads, telephone directories, and international employment directories. Placement specialists may also teach students important job-seeking skills such as résumé writing, job interviewing, researching employers, conducting a job search, the ethics of a job search, completing job application forms, and writing cover letters. They might hold workshops for students in the liberal arts to help them assess how to best apply their skills in the job market.

## Career Counseling

The vocational counselor can assist students in clarification of values and life-style preferences, as well as assessment of interests, aptitudes, abilities and skills, and personal characteristics. The career counselor can also help students to improve skills in verbal communication and assertion so that they can more clearly express their needs and desires. Arranging exploratory interviews with workers can provide access to valuable information for students' career planning and an opportunity to check out the reality of what they have read, heard, and thought. Such interviews can also help them gain self-confidence and take comfortable, assertive control in job hunting and interview encounters.

One of the tasks of the counselor may be to help students reduce the conflict between the idealized self and the actual self. This is often a problem for students with high-success parents. They strive for unrealistically high goals and continuously fall short with resultant negative self-concept and lowered self-esteem. A corollary can be found in students who have inflated self-perceptions. They typically believe that if they work hard enough, they can be successful at anything. External data to the contrary may be denied. Another group of students perceive themselves to be less capable than they actually are. Experiences in reality testing are often helpful for these students to begin to perceive themselves differently. In each of these cases, students are likely to make unrealistic career choices if they do so before these inaccurate self-perceptions are modified. For some it is necessary to make wrong choices and fail at them before they are ready to seek help in dealing with underlying problems. Counseling would hopefully reduce the frequency of inappropriate choices and consequent failures.

Irrational assumptions influence many decisions and may lead to self-defeating behaviors (Adler, 1970; Ellis, 1972). Some counselors have made examining and restructuring such misconceptions a central focus of their interventions (Raimy, 1975). Combining and extending Thompson's (1976) ideas of how irrational assumptions affect career planning with Tosi's (1973) model for changing irrational beliefs, Carney (1978) has designed a self-directed activity to help students identify, test, and change their irrational beliefs about career decision-making. Some of these irrational beliefs are as follows: (1) The choice of a major or occupation is irreversible; once you make it, you can't or shouldn't change your mind. (2) You have to decide on a major before you can enroll in college. (3) There is a test or expert who can tell you what major or career to choose. (4) Others already know in what they want to major. There must be something wrong with you that you don't know.

There are other myths that are specifically related to women. For example, a woman isn't safe doing a man's work with men. She is more vulnerable sexually than she would be in a traditional job. Another is that a traditional woman's job (e.g., secretary, social worker, nurse, or elementary teacher) will interfere less with her family life than a non-traditional job. Many young women do not prepare themselves to work for good wages because they don't expect to work for any length of time. Many expect marriage to end their need to earn money for the rest of their lives. Suffice it to say, these goals are often unrealistic.

Students sometimes need to resolve conflicts with others before they can make career choices. Students make assumptions about the expectations that they think others have for them, and it is important for them to be able to confront and test out these assumptions to see if they are based on reality. If the expectations of others are real, the students must decide whether they are congruent with their own self-images and whether an attempt will be made to meet them. It is often difficult for students to differentiate whether they are following their own desires or those of others. They don't realize that the two may coincide. When resolution of conflict involves dealing with others, counseling may revolve around communication skills to help the student gain the self-confidence in order to deal directly with the situation.

Group counseling can be effectively used for skills identification, value clarification, and interest or personality assessment. It can also be used for conflict resolution or the reality testing of an individual's career choices. Based on personal experience, I have found a course designed to incorporate individual and group work (e.g., Boggs and Phillips, 1979) to be particularly effective in accomplishing these goals. Such courses and workshops provide the opportunity to integrate psychometric assessment with other relevant career information.

A number of test methods are available for measuring interests (e.g., Career Assessment Inventory, Kuder Occupational Interest Survey, Strong-Campbell Interest Inventory), abilities (e.g., General Aptitude Test Battery, School and College Ability Test, Word and Number Assessment Inventory), personal characteristics (e.g., California Personality Inventory, Personality Research Form, Self-Description Inventory, Sixteen Personality Factors), and values (e.g., Minnesota Importance Questionnaire, Study of Values, Temperament and Values Inventory). Information gained through test procedures can be reviewed in the course/workshop in the proper perspective of information achieved through self-evaluation in terms of discussions and group exercises.

A challenge in career counseling is helping students to integrate and sort out the extensive information they have obtained about themselves. The workshop called My Career, Myself (Schultz-Duarte, Johansson, and Boggs, 1980) has proved particularly effective for achieving a synthesis that can lead to career decisions.

Group meetings and workshops are also particularly helpful to teach students the skills they need to continue their own career development after the structured experience has ended. They are more efficient in terms of staff time than individual meetings or counseling sessions. Through the group meetings, students have experiences not available in individual counseling sessions. Students often have the feeling that they are unique in their experiences, self-concepts, fears, aspirations, and dreams. In the group sessions they learn that others have similar experiences, desires, and fears. This awareness provides the support they need to continue struggling with their own problems. They also realize that others can still accept them even when they know the "worst about them." It is often helpful, however, for students to have short-term individual counseling after the termination of a course or workshop to resolve personal issues that were not dealt with during those structured group experiences.

In developing a career course or workshop, it is important first to assess the needs of the population to be served. For some groups, modules on financial planning, communication skills, retirement, and résumé writing may be included whereas for other groups they may not be appropriate. Professionals in the field of career counseling should have a background in theories of career development and in tests and measurements and should have supervised experience in individual and group counseling with particular emphasis on the career area. Course and workshop manuals must be available for instructors, and formal staff training should be conducted on teaching the courses and workshops.

The importance of experiential learning in career education has become increasingly emphasized through federal support of cooperative education. There has been a substantial increase in the number of these programs particularly in community colleges. The marriage of career education and cooperative education is a positive step in helping students to make more informed and realistic career decisions.

## NEEDS OF SPECIAL POPULATIONS

In helping students with career decision making, the needs of special populations must be considered. An obvious one is career development of women which was introduced earlier in this chapter. Individual differences in the abilities of women are, of course, obviously important determinants of success in the vocational choices they may make. However, attitudes toward women of faculty members and even of those professionals involved in student services can have an important influence on career choices of students. Schwartz (1974) asked 206 men and 200 women professional guidance counselors from six eastern states to make occupational recommendations for intellectually superior female and male students described to them in short case summaries. The guidance counselors recommended both traditional female role and low ability occupations significantly more often for females of superior intelligence than for identically described male students. Male guidance counselors recommended lower ability occupations for the females significantly more often than did female counselors. There was no difference between male and female counselors in the recommendation of female role occupations for female students of superior intelligence. Efforts in the correction of such biases should be directed at all levels of staff providing career relevant student services.

Although most men continue to follow traditional paths of career development, changing cultural and social values permit a wider range of options to them. The "house husband" providing homemaker and child care services for a working wife does exist. Husband and wife may also share one position and its remuneration. However, a variety of personal, financial, and social conflicts have to be resolved before such unconventional options are realistic. Counselors may be of much assistance in achieving that goal.

Colleges now have increasing numbers of nontraditional students, those 25 years of age or older who have experienced a gap of about 5 years or more in their formal education. They may be homemakers or mid-career changers returning to or starting college, retired persons, or often divorced or widowed women. They have a number of special needs and concerns. They question their ability to compete academically with other students. Some have low self-esteem. They may require more assistance than traditional students in applying for admissions, selecting classes, and registering. They need help in finding classes congruent with present skills yet extending them. Central concerns may be financial aid, child care, time management, support systems, or reassessment of established priorities. They are concerned about whether they are too old to be in school and criticisms they expect from their families and friends of doing something that is different from most of the people their age. Some have less comfort and familiarity with "mechanics of survival" than do the younger undergraduates. Others, of course, may be highly adaptive individuals who are changing direction from previous successful careers. Even more than their younger counterparts, they are concerned about making "correct" career choices for they know that the sooner that they can get into the job market the better, because of employers' preferences for younger people. Classes must be scheduled around jobs and families. They fear failure and are anxious about tests and that past grade point averages do not reflect their present ability.

Ethnic minorities, foreign students, and handicapped students have obvious special needs in their academic and career pursuits. Rather than asserting that they have the same opportunities for education as any other students and demanding that they cope with the system in the same way, they may need to be given additional assistance and emotional support. Most universities provide such services, now widely federally subsidized.

## INTEGRATION OF SERVICES

In many colleges and universities, the previously described services are scattered in various agencies across the campus. Organizing these services within a single agency has distinct advantages. Such an agency would include the components of academic advising, career and personal counseling, occupational information, cooperative education, and job placement. Students could select the service most appropriate to their needs or have an intake interview as an aid in making that assessment. Figure 1 (Boggs, 1979) represents such an organization. Exchange of information among professionals involved permits more effective delivery of services as well as follow-up of individual students to assess the outcome of the institution's programs.

## REFERENCES

Adler, A. Fundamentals of individual psychology. *Journal of Individual Psychology*, 1970, **26**, 36–49.

Almquist, E. M. Sex stereotypes in occupational choice: the case for college women. *Journal of Vocational Behavior*, 1974, **5**, 13–21.

Bem, S. L. Sex role adaptability: one consequence of psychological androgyny. *Journal of Personality and Social Psychology*, 1975, **31**, 634–643.

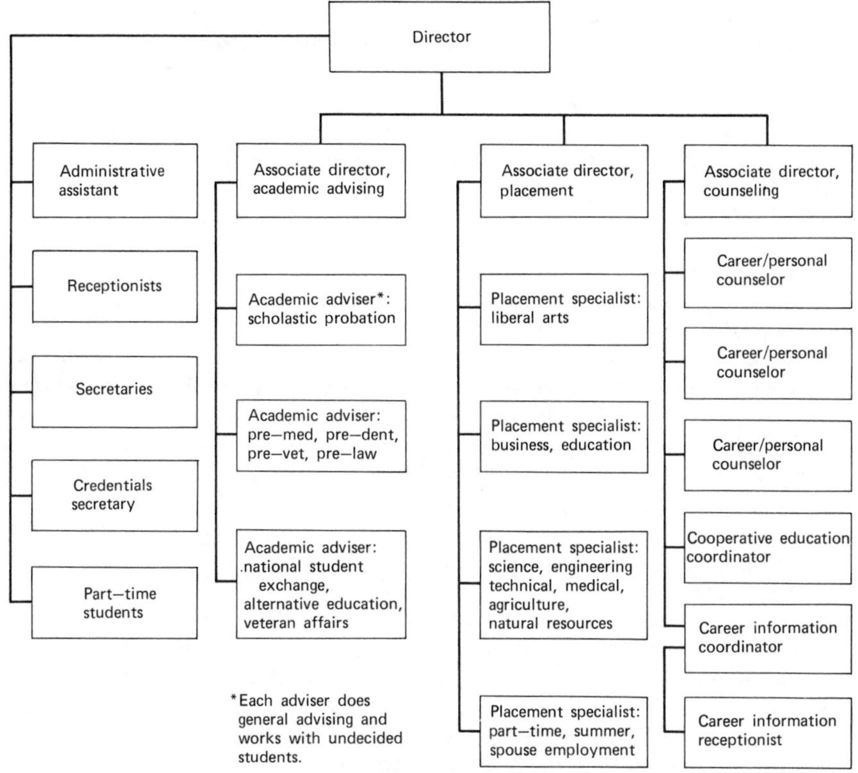


**Figure 1** Counseling and career planning center.

Boggs, K. R. Developing a model for merging career education, placement, and cooperative education. Paper presented at the meeting of the Midwest Cooperative Education Association, LaCross, Wis., 1979.

Boggs, K. R. and J. P. Pappas Psychosocial variables influencing women's choices of traditional versus nontraditional careers. Paper presented at the meeting of the American Psychological Association, New York, 1979.

Boggs, K. R. and S. Phillips Career and life planning course manual. Unpublished manuscript, University of Utah, 1979.

Broverman, I. K., S. R. Vogel, E. M. Broverman, F. E. Clarkson, and P. S. Rosenkrantz Sex-role stereotypes: a current appraisal. *Journal of Social Issues,* 1972, **28**, 59–78.

Carney, C. G. Removing attitudinal blocks to career decision making: a self-directed module. *Counseling and Human Development*, 1978, *11*(4). 1–12.

Ellis, A. *Reason and Emotion in Psychotherapy.* New York: Lyle Stuart, 1972.

Goldman, R. D. and B. M. Hewitt The scholastic aptitude test "explains" why college men major in science more often than college women. *Journal of Counseling Psychology,* 1976, **23**, 50–54.

Horner, M. S. Sex differences in achievement motivation and performance in competitive and non-competitive situations [Doctoral dissertation, The University of Michigan, 1968]. *Dissertation Abstracts International,* 1969, **30**, 407B.

Horner, M. S. Fail: bright woman. *Psychology Today,* November 1969, **3**, 36–38, 62.

Horner, M. S. Femininity and successful achievement: a basic inconsistency. In J. M. Bardwick, E. Douvan, M. S. Horner, and D. Gutmann, *Feminine Personality and Conflict.* Belmont, Calif.: Brooks/Cole, 1970.

Korman, A. K. Self-esteem variable in vocational choice. *Journal of Applied Psychology,* 1966, **50**, 479–486.

Page, J. P. Relationship between sex role conformity and self-esteem, anxiety, and motive to avoid success [Doctoral dissertation, The University of New York, 1973]. *Dissertation Abstracts International,* 1973, **34**, 1281B.

Penn, L. S. Current sex role identification, sex role stereotypes, and role conflict in university women [Doctoral dissertation, Adelphi University, 1975]. *Dissertation Abstracts International,* 1975, **36**, 425B–426B.

Peplau, L. A. Impact of fear of success and sex-role attitudes on women's competitive achievement. *Journal of Personality and Social Psychology,* 1976, **34**, 561–568.

Raimy, V. *Misunderstandings of the Self.* London: Jossey-Bass, 1975.

Schultz, G. E. Changing conceptions of masculinity and femininity [Doctoral dissertation, Arizona State University, 1973]. *Dissertation Abstracts International,* 1974, **34**, 3508B–3509B.

Schultz-Duarte, S., C. B. Johansson, and K. R. Boggs *My Career, Myself: a Career Decision-making Workshop.* Minneapolis: National Computer Systems, 1980.

Schuster, D. B. On the fear of success. *Psychiatric Quarterly,* 1955, **29**, 412–420.

Schwartz, J. L. A study of guidance counselor sex biases in the occupational recommendations made for female students of superior intelligence [Doctoral dissertation, New York University, 1974]. *Dissertation Abstracts International,* 1975, **35**, 7069A.

Shinar, E. H. Sexual stereotypes of occupations. *Journal of Vocational Behavior,* 1975, **7**, 99–111.

Spence, J. T., R. Helmreich, and J. Stapp Ratings of self and peers on sex role attributes and their function to self-esteem and conceptions of masculinity and femininity. *Journal of Personality and Social Psychology,* 1975, **32**, 29–39.

Thompson, A. P. Client misconceptions in vocational counseling. *Personnel and Guidance Journal,* September 1976, 30–33.

Tosi, D. J. Self-directed behavior change in the cognitive, affective, and behavioral motoric domains: a rational-emotive approach. *Focus on Guidance*, 1973, *6*(4), 6–10.

# IV

# The Student Development Professional—Training and Prospects

A model for evaluating the scope of training programs in student affairs is presented in Chapter 19. Chapter 20 presents some concluding observations about the challenges and prospects for student affairs in the future.

# 19
# Training Student Affairs Professionals

WESTON H. MORRILL

The purpose of this chapter is to present a scheme for evaluating the scope of training programs for student affairs professionals. The evolution from in loco parentis, the oft-referred to crisis of student affairs as a profession, and the changing nature of higher education have all influenced a reevaluation of the role of student affairs and with that a needed reevaluation of training programs for student affairs professionals.

Rentz (1976) presented a triadic model student development program focusing on the roles of administrator, instructor, and consultant. Newton and Richardson (1976) surveyed practitioners in Georgia using the Delphi technique to reach consensus on the expected entry-level competencies of student personnel workers. The skills ranked highest by the final sample were those of developing interpersonal relationships, being aware of the scope of student personnel, and skills in organization and administration, self-awareness, and counseling.

Pruitt (1979) surveyed leaders in the American College Personnel Association to determine their views on the preparation of student development specialists during the 1980s. They expressed affirmative views on the need for competencies in group processes, organization and administration, statistics, measurement and evaluation, and counseling theory.

Brown (1972) suggested a number of roles for student development specialists including those of diagnostician, consultant, programmer, technologist, professor, behavioral scientist, and administrator.

Sedlacek and Horowitz (1974) suggested that an overemphasis on interventions with individuals might be inappropriate and backward. They recommended an about-face, with emphasis on the environment, suggesting that student personnel workers need to work to "change the environment so that ultimately it may serve individuals better" (p. 39).

Although the above review is not exhaustive, it does indicate the range of skills and roles that are considered important for student affairs professionals. Figure 2 in chapter 1 suggests that the foundation of knowledge and skills for student affairs must include the three areas of (1) investigation, (2) theory, and (3) intervention. The investigation foundation would include data generation, program evaluation, and theory building and testing. The theoretical foundation should include knowledge and theory about human and student development, about environmental development, and about organizational development and management. The intervention foundation would include skills in a variety of intervention strategies including the use of media, consultation, administration, counseling, and training.

Without some means of organizing these concepts in a manageable way, the above lists may seem confusing and contradictory. Figure 1 presents a parsimonious way to visualize the scope of training for student affairs professionals. This is based on the models presented in Chapters 1 and 5 and encompasses a variety of professional roles and intervention targets. The professional roles dimension encompasses both the investigative and intervention categories suggested as part of the foundation of skills and knowledge by Hurst. The necessity of knowledge and theory about the development of individuals and environments is encompassed within the target dimension. The concern of Sedlacek and Horowitz (1974) about environmental intervention is also addressed within the target dimension. As they indicated, a majority of training programs focus only on the individual with little or no emphasis on understanding environmental interventions. Similarly, many programs ignore some of the professional roles.

One area of confusion in reviewing articles about training student affairs professionals is that professional roles, targets, and the competencies needed to carry out these roles are not distinguished in any way. Thus the lists that are presented contain different classes of items and are difficult to translate into a training program. Within the cells of the model presented in Figure 1 are listed some of the competencies needed to carry out the roles with the targets. This is not intended to be exhaustive, but only suggestive of the types of competencies that might be considered. The competencies are additive in that competencies to work with individuals are a necessary foundation for working with couples,

| PROFESSIONAL ROLES | TARGETS | | | |
|---|---|---|---|---|
| | Individual | Environment | | |
| | | Primary Group | Associational Group | Institution/ Community |
| Assessment/ Diagnosis | Testing: ability, interest, personality<br>Interviewing<br>Needs assess ment | Marital assessment<br>Family analysis | Ecomapping<br>Organizational analysis | Ecomapping<br>Community analysis |
| Counseling/ Consultation | Test interpretation<br>Counseling therapy<br>Self-awareness<br>Group counseling | Couples counseling<br>Family therapy<br>Group process | Consultation skills<br>Aware of personal impact with group<br>Conflict resolution | Change agent |
| Administration | Interpersonal relationship<br>Leadership<br>Organizational skills | | Organizational development<br>Group consensus and decision skills<br>Milieu management | Political skills |
| Program Development | Ability to work cooperatively<br>Goal setting<br>Behavioral analysis | Communication skills | | |
| Teaching/ Training | Didactic teaching skills<br>Paraprofessional training<br>Curriculum development | | | |
| Evaluation/ Research | Statistics<br>Research design<br>Single subject design<br>Measurement<br>Test development | | | |

**Figure 1** Training student affairs professionals for a variety of roles with diverse targets.

After a similar model by Morrill and Banning (1973).

groups, and institutions. Similarly, the skills of assessment and counseling provide an important basis for and are additive to the skills lower on the model.

The cells created by considering the professional roles and targets provide a means for assessing the scope of training experiences offered by a training program. Within each cell the competencies required for that cell can be determined and the availability of experiences and courses in the training program to provide those competencies can be evaluated.

Actually, we recognize that this model, even simplified as it is, is too complex for any one program. A training program that could provide adequate training in all of the cells of the model would have to have huge resources; similarly, a student or professional able to intervene effectively in every cell would be more than human.

The model, then, is only a guide to indicate the kind of skills that might be taught, not those that have to be taught. An individual training program should establish its own goals and determine the kind of professional person they want to prepare. Faculty and students can then use the model to consider what skills are required and whether skills in a particular cell are available in the training program. Students can then broaden their training through the selection of practicum, internship, or elective courses to cover skills and competencies not covered in their training programs. The model does provide a useful means of organizing and categorizing the competencies needed by student affairs professionals for carrying out a variety of professional roles with a variety of targets.

## REFERENCES

Brown, R. D. *Student Development in Tomorrow's Higher Education—a Return to the Academy*. Student Personnel Series No. 16, American College Personnel Association, 1972.

Morrill, W. H. and J. H. Banning *Dimensions of Training Campus Mental Health Professionals*. Mimeographed report. Boulder, Colo.: WICHE Task Force on Training, 1973.

Newton, F. B. and R. L. Richardson Expected entry-level competencies of student personnel workers. *Journal of College Student Personnel*, 1976, **17**(5), 426–429.

Pruitt, A. S. Preparation of student development specialists during the 1980s. *Counselor Education and Supervision*, 1979, **18**(3), 190–198.

Rentz, A. L. A triadic model master's program in student development. *Journal of College Student Personnel*, 1976, **17**(6), 453–458.

Sedlacek, W. E. and J. L. Horowitz Changing perceptions: An individual or environmental approach. *NASPA Journal*, 1974, **11**(4), 48–51.

# 20
# Challenges for the Future

JAMES C. HURST

Student affairs work in higher education is uniquely American. Its foundation is as stable as the commitment of the founding fathers of the Constitution to an educated electorate, as deep as the Judeo-Christian belief in the potential and worth of the individual. Whereas other Western and Eastern cultures were emphasizing the selection of the intellectual elite for continuing education, the United States was working to provide for higher education for all who were capable through the Morrill Act of 1865, open door admissions to state institutions, and the development of a junior and community college system. The commitment to the success of individual students was first expressed through in loco parentis and the attendant administrative structure designed to implement that goal. More recently the commitment is being expressed through student resource and environmental resource development.

The in loco parentis era of student affairs work was marked by an emphasis on administrators functioning within an administrative structure designed to provide services and supports ordinarily provided by parents. With the emergence of student and environmental resource development, the emphasis is changing toward educators operating within the administrative and academic structure to teach and provide students with the skills, attitudes, and resources necessary for them to maximally utilize the educational environment and fully develop their individual potential. With the in loco parentis emphasis on administration, student affairs work was destined to be perceived as ancillary and secondary by an academic system that primarily values the educational process. With the student/environmental development emphasis on education for student development and environmental modification, student affairs work is on the threshhold of being accepted and incorporated into the academic mainstream. Several tasks must be completed before a full colleagueship can occur.

The first challenge is the continuing development and evolution of the student/environmental development model as a prototype conceptualization of the what, how, and why of student affairs work. This work must incorporate an increased understanding of student development theory. It must also attend to increasing the richness of ecomapping and environmental development theory, and finally, must continue to explore the interaction between students and their environment. Part I of this text contains chapters that expand our horizons of understanding of students and their development, the environment as a resource for the educational process, and their interaction which may be for better or worse.

The second challenge confronting student affairs professionals is the translation of the knowledge of students, their environment, and their interaction into intervention programs and activities. Just as student affairs professionals should be the on-campus experts on student needs and environmental characteristics, they should also be the experts on intervention strategies. Part II of this text presents the three-dimensional "cube" model of interventions developed by Morrill, Oetting, and Hurst in the early 1970s. Each of the three dimensions of target, purpose, and method defines an area of potential expertise for the student affairs professional. Although it is unrealistic to expect the expertise in each of the three dimensions to reside in one person, it is highly desirable that a student affairs division contain a cross section of professionals with a combined expertise along each of the dimensions. Part III contains descriptions of student affairs components and their efforts toward building adequate programs of intervention. A careful reading of this part reveals that some of the programs described have been carefully developed according to a comprehensive model whereas others are more traditional in a less intentional and systematic approach.

A third challenge needing attention if student affairs professionals are to become full colleagues in the academic community is the sustained and thorough investigation of student needs, environmental characteristics, and intervention program effectiveness. The emphasis here is on descriptive, evaluative, and empirical research. The administrators of the in loco parentis period were not inclined toward investigation by either interest or skill. The new professional of the student/environmental development era is inclined toward investigation by interest, skill, and training. Student affairs will come of age as a profession only with the identification of a cohesive body of literature and a substantial data base generated within each institution. Only in this way will the cohesion of the profession be matched with relevant uniqueness of each institution.

A fourth challenge for the future of the profession is the need to discriminate between the different roles of the generalist and the specialist. For too many years student affairs professionals have been generalists with specialist orientation. This was appropriate and to be expected under the auspices of in loco parentis. The new professionals, however, must be specialists with generalist orientations. A major weakness of the past has been the expectation that generalists could perform specialists' functions. The result is an historically weaker body of literature with the more substantial contributions coming from academicians in related disciplines. Specialists in research design, statistical procedures, theoretical foundation, program development, consultation, management, media, training models, and learning must be raised up through training programs that are either rare or nonexistent. This is not to say that generalists no longer have a place in the profession. Indeed they do. It is to say that the day is past when we can expect to be full colleagues as generalists in a system of specialists. The expertise referred to in the third challenge mentioned above will not be achieved by generalists. The expertise referred to there is the expertise of specialists. If not, the specialists of the psychology, sociology, social work, management, and education departments will continue to be the experts of the student affairs arena.

Finally, the fifth and perhaps most important challenge to the profession is the creation of training programs substantial enough to attract and train some of the brightest and most talented young people on the educational scene today. These training programs must provide a foundation of theory in human and environmental development, management, and the learning process. They must also thoroughly teach research design, statistical analysis, evaluative research, and basic research within the investigative skills realm. They must provide skills and experience in intervention activities on all dimensions of the cube referred to so extensively in this text. An internship must be developed as well as a method of accreditation so that programs that adequately prepare new professionals can be distinguished from those that do not. The training programs are the birth and nurturing process of the profession. It is essential that they be developed and modified to reflect the changes that are occurring in the profession.

Never before has the student affairs profession stood on the threshold of such great opportunity. The concepts presented in this text, along with others being presented by newly enlightened professionals, provide the guidelines and parameters for future movement. Opportunities for leadership are there for those who adequately prepare themselves for that task.

Recently a dean of students received a telephone call from one of the academic departments on his campus. The caller explained that he had been referred to the office of the dean of students by his department chairman and academic dean. He explained that he had recently been denied tenure and therefore would need to leave his department at the conclusion of the academic year. He had been referred to the dean of students office because he was perceived as having "good rapport" with students and it was therefore assumed that he had the skills and expertise necessary to become a student affairs professional. As the conversation progressed, it became obvious that he knew little or nothing about the theoretical knowledge, investigative skills, or intervention strategies necessary to fill a professional role in student affairs. Subsequent reflection on the incident revealed how absurd it would be for someone being terminated from a student affairs position to be referred to the philosophy department because he or she seemed to philosophize well. It is equally as absurd to think that someone who simply has a good rapport with students is prepared to serve as a full professional in a division of student affairs. Yet the above incident has probably been repeated many times across the country. How many former coaches, attorneys, and business managers have become deans of students and vice-presidents for student affairs!

A conceptual foundation for student affairs and a full commitment to it by the profession in both practice and training is imperative to the survival of student affairs as a profession. If in the year 2001 deans of students are still receiving calls from academicians with good rapport with students seeking employment, we will know we failed.

# Author Index

# Subject Index